The Lake Michigan
Cottage Cookbook

The LAKE MICHIGAN COTTAGE *Cookbook*

DOOR COUNTY *Cherry Pie*, SHEBOYGAN *Bratwurst*, TRAVERSE CITY *Trout*, AND 115 MORE *Regional Favorites*

AMELIA LEVIN

Storey Publishing

The mission of Storey Publishing is to serve our customers by
publishing practical information that encourages
personal independence in harmony with the environment.

Edited by Margaret Sutherland and Sarah Guare
Art direction and book design by Michaela Jebb
Text production by Jennifer Jepson Smith
Indexed by Samantha Miller

Cover photography by © **Johnny Autry**, front (bottom), back (row 3 left); © **Teri Genovese**, front (top), spine, back (row 1 left, row 2, row 4), inside (front & back); © **David Nevala**, back (left, row 1 right, row 3 right)

Interior photography by © David Nevala, ii, iii, vii (top right & bottom left), viii (top right & bottom right), 3 (with food styling by Laurel Z Food Stylist), 6 (top), 10, 13, 23, 29, 31, 35 (top), 38, 41, 48, 49, 51, 55, 68, 74, 75, 110, 113, 114, 121, 122, 132–137, 140, 143, 146, 147; © Johnny Autry, with food styling by Charlotte Autry, v, 20, 36, 45, 52, 76, 83, 90, 101, 107, 124, 153, 164, 173, 195, 201, 202, 220, 237, 244, 251; © Teri Genovese, i, iv, vi, vii (top left & bottom right), viii (top left, middle, bottom left) 1, 2, 4, 5, 6 (bottom), 25, 35 (except top), 60, 80, 104, 118, 156, 158, 162, 163, 175, 178, 179, 181, 183, 187, 188, 196, 206, 208, 212, 213, 215, 216, 223, 226, 227, 228 (background), 231, 232, 243, 257, 258, 260, 261, 264

Additional photography by © Bruce Block/Getty Images, 247 (bottom); © Michael Burrell/iStock.com, 11 (and throughout); © Photos Lamontagne/Getty Images, 247 (top); © Ralf-Finn Hestoft/Getty Images, 94 & 95

Maps courtesy of NOAA's Office of Coast Survey

Illustrations pages 62, 63, and back cover by Ilona Sherratt

© 2018 by Amelia Levin

Storey Publishing
210 MASS MoCA Way
North Adams, MA 01247

storey.com
Printed in China by Toppan Leefung Printing Ltd.
10 9 8 7 6 5 4 3 2 1

LIBRARY OF CONGRESS CATALOGING-IN-PUBLICATION DATA
Names: Levin, Amelia, author.
Title: The Lake Michigan cottage cookbook :
    door county cherry pie, sheboygan bratwurst, traverse city
    trout, and 115 more regional favorites / Amelia Levin.
Description: North Adams, MA : Storey Publishing, [2018]
    | Includes bibliographical references and index.
Identifiers: LCCN 2017046691 (print)
    | LCCN 2017050485 (ebook)
    | ISBN 9781612127330 (ebook)
    | ISBN 9781612127323 (pbk. : alk. paper)
Subjects: LCSH: Cooking, American—Midwestern style.
    | Cooking—Illinois—Chicago—Michigan, Lake, Region.
    | LCGFT: Cookbooks.
Classification: LCC TX715.2.M53 (ebook)
    | LCC TX715.2.M53 L48 2018 (print)
    | DDC 641.9774—dc23
LC record available at https://lccn.loc.gov/2017046691

dedication

To my mom, Karen Levin, who is an amazing and talented recipe developer, tester, and cookbook author. She is my partner in all things food and in this book, and my greatest mentor.

Contents

Introduction 1

How to Use This Book 4

Wisconsin 8

CHAPTER 1: Door County 11

CHAPTER 2: Sheboygan and Kohler 81

CHAPTER 3: Milwaukee 105

Illinois and Indiana 116

CHAPTER 4: Chicago and Northwest Indiana 119

Michigan 154

CHAPTER 5: Harbor Country 157

CHAPTER 6: Southwest Michigan 189

CHAPTER 7: Saugatuck, Douglas, and Fennville 207

CHAPTER 8: Traverse City and the Peninsulas 229

Recipes by Type 262

Acknowledgments 264

Resources 265

Metric Conversion Charts 266

Index 267

Introduction

LAKE MICHIGAN IS A QUIET, SUBTLE FORCE in the American landscape. It's a source for recreation and fishing and food, affecting what we grow, the water we drink, and the air we breathe. On clear days, we stare into the sunset, thinking we can catch a glimpse of our neighbors on the other side of the lake, but let us not fool ourselves; we never do.

This is the vast and clear *mishigami* ("great water"), as the Ojibwa call it — the place in and around where Native American tribes go for fish and wild rice, and indigenous berries, nuts, and more. This is the lake where for centuries, fishermen have cracked the dawn with their boats and tugs and trap nets of whitefish. It's the place where the rocks can either hurt your feet or the sand will tickle your toes; where cool winds blow at night, tempering the air and earth for vineyards and fruit orchards nearby and tenderizing asparagus and sweet onions after the first snow's thaw. This is the lake where tourists flock from Memorial Day to Labor Day in hopes of a relaxing retreat or, come winter, where sheets of ice coat the surface and powerful winds make for oceanic sailing. This is the nearly 23,000-square-foot body of water that can give life as easily as it can take it. This is the spirit, power, and beauty of the Upper Midwest.

The Lake Effect is truly a phenomenon. And I'm not just talking about the weather.

If you're a city dweller heading toward America's Third Coast, something happens when you venture into these lakeside towns. Your blood pressure starts to drop as you take a big breath of fresh, clean air, sighing as a wave of calm washes over you. The quiet and stillness quickly become restfulness.

As a child, my family took vacations to Lake Michigan from our home in the Chicago area. One of my earliest food memories comes from the crunch of crispy fried perch, its steaming-hot tender flesh falling apart with every bite and every dip into my jar of tangy tartar sauce. Another memory stems from cherry pie — that craveable contrast of sweet and tart cherries encased in a buttery crust, flaking with every stab of my fork.

As an adult, I enjoy visiting farms and farmers' markets throughout the Upper Midwest, grabbing hold of just-picked peaches, blueberries, and crisp, tart apples in Michigan; supersweet carrots and asparagus in Wisconsin; and big, bright tomatoes from Illinois, taking the loot back to the vacation cottage to create delicious meals for family and friends. The tradition of vacationing, cooking, and eating along Lake Michigan spans generations.

It's my intent — and hope — that this book might stir up some nostalgia among those who live or vacation on Lake Michigan, and perhaps create new traditions and memories of family, friends, barbecues, beaches, cooking, and cottages. But it's also my hope that this book inspires those who are new to the area to join in what is for so many of us a special community of return vacationers, long-time residents, and artisan food purveyors, bonded by the lakefront on all sides.

When it comes to the food of the region, things are starting to change. We're going back to our roots, getting to know our farmers and ranchers and fisheries. We may make the same recipes our grandparents did, but they're made with the cleanest, most sustainable local ingredients that have helped those recipes stand the test of time. There's nothing quite like a homemade pie with just a few ingredients, grown with the most care and attention, or lake perch that came straight from the waters

next door. A growing force of food artisans in different communities, buoyed by the enthusiasm we the consumers have shown for them, has also helped propel this heritage movement forward. We're going back to old traditions, slowing down and enjoying life. We're cooking from scratch and spending more time with friends and families. What better place to do this than in our homes, cottages, and cabins near the lake?

You may be lucky enough to live year-round in Door County or Traverse City or elsewhere along the lakefront, letting friends, family, and visitors in on your secrets (from time to time) for the best fish fry and brandy old-fashioned, the best farmers' market and fresh-baked fruit pie. You may have a second home you visit often, whenever you can find the time to escape. Or, you may be more like me, a city dweller who only dreams about this second home but finds solace in different borrowed homes along the way.

Many people who live on the East or West Coasts or in the South like to lump us into one category as the vast, mysterious "Midwest." But those of us who live in the Upper Midwest know we share traits, foods, and cultures unique to our region and far different from those in states like Kansas and Ohio. We may have our unique preferences and playful rivalries — between Michiganders and Wisconsinites, and with "Illinois people" like me — but the closer to Lake Michigan you go, the more similar we become, bonded by this source of drinking water, food, happy memories, and peace. Even visitors who have fallen in love with the likes of Door County and Traverse City are welcomed with open arms into the club I like to call Lake Michiganites: a little rough around the edges, perhaps, but warm and welcoming at the core.

Whatever your story, it's my hope that our shared love of this region's delicious food and great people — and, of course, the lake — unites us all.

How to Use This Book

FIRST, THIS IS A COOKBOOK FOR LAKE MICHIGAN DWELLERS who also happen to be food enthusiasts. It's for those who grew up in the Midwest or those who have since left and crave that feeling of home and vacation. It's for those who spend their summers — or winters, in some cases — at different spots along the Lake Michigan coast, from Door County to Chicago, Saugatuck, and Traverse City and who are looking to re-create or reinvent their favorite comfort dishes on the road or at home.

This book is for the hobby cook, the advanced cook, or the cook who wants to take a little extra time to explore in the kitchen. Some recipes are super-simple, while others might require a little extra time, patience, and TLC. Many combine old traditions with local ingredients and progressive chef-inspired ideas.

Second, this is not just a cookbook. This is a book you can curl up with in bed to remember the ways you spent your childhood or adulthood vacations. It's a book to help you remember the way it was when your family rented that cottage on the beach, or that bed-and-breakfast or supper club you went to once that you'll never forget. This is a storybook, one about our lives, past and present, of vacationing and visiting and living all up and down the wonderful lake we think of as an ocean, even if our East Coast friends don't quite understand.

Use this book, also, as you travel; you can read about and remember those favorite places that have stood the test of time while discovering newfound treasures. You'll discover old and new restaurants and inns, cozy cafés and pubs, coffee shops, supper clubs, food shops, cheese shops, wineries, breweries, cideries, distilleries, and more.

That said, it is impossible to squeeze the cuisine from the entire coastline of Lake Michigan into one reasonably sized book. I didn't get to all of the best restaurants, inns, shops, and farms in the region, but that's a testament to the breadth

of great food and people in our area. You might wonder where the recipes from Petoskey, or Charlevoix, or Michigan's upper peninsula or Mackinac Island are — or the recipes from places and towns farther inland in Wisconsin. That just might be the motivator for a second edition down the line.

For this book, my focus was set on the most popular tourist destinations along the lake, with the intent that the local foods and flavors from this region transcend village borders. Wisconsin, Illinois, Indiana, and Michigan share similar crops and growing conditions, and people living in these states will have no problem finding the local fresh ingredients I mention. Those living outside the area can make substitutions, using ingredients local to them to create dishes that remind them of their time spent on the lake.

Think of this book, also, as a bit of a seasonal cookbook; some recipes work best when cooked in the summer using the peak of the season's produce, while other recipes run richer and heartier, perfect for a colder fall or winter day. The seasons, after all, have always governed how we Midwesterners both live and cook.

A NOTE ABOUT THE RECIPES: You might notice many recipes have very little or even no salt. My husband and I have made an effort in recent years to reduce our salt (and sugar) intake, and the improvements to our health have been remarkable. We weigh a little less, have a lot more energy, and have much more discerning palates as a result. You'll see that I like to use more flavor-balancing ingredients, like acid in the form of bright lemons, good-quality vinegars, or juicy tomatoes; fresh herbs; and heat in the form of peppers and spices.

Still, these recipes are not set in stone. If you feel something needs a little more salt or sugar or herbs or spice, go for it. If you don't have a particular spice on hand and want to substitute another, it'll probably work out just fine. And feel free to take shortcuts — sometimes we just don't have the time to make our own mayonnaise or barbecue sauce or fresh pasta or ice cream. Luckily, there are so many more good-quality artisan-style products on store shelves these days that it's becoming easier and easier to cook with "cleaner" ingredients that don't contain unnecessary chemicals or additives.

THE LAKE MICHIGAN CIRCLE TOUR

One of the most scenic routes in the United States is the Lake Michigan Circle Tour. As the name implies, it follows state highways around Lake Michigan, through Illinois, Indiana, Wisconsin, and Michigan. It would take 14½ hours with no stops to cover the roughly 900 miles. A special "spur route" runs between Ludington, Michigan, and Manitowoc, Wisconsin, and follows the *S.S. Badger* car ferry across Lake Michigan. In the summer, you'll pass by sun-drenched beach towns. In the fall, watch as the leaves change to their brilliant reds, oranges, and yellows, and in the spring, catch the first green grasses and crops emerging from the previously snow-covered ground.

The Lake Michigan Circle Tour is just one of about a dozen designated scenic road systems around the Great Lakes and Upper Midwest. Presented in 1985 by Jack Morgan, who worked for the Michigan Department of Transportation, the route was finalized in 1988 by the governors of Michigan and Indiana. Today, you'll find signs guiding you along the various highways, freeways, and scenic roads. Lake Michigan is the only one of the Great Lakes that lies entirely within the United States, and among all five Great Lakes, it is the second largest in volume and third largest in surface area.

LAKE MICHIGAN
CIRCLE TOUR

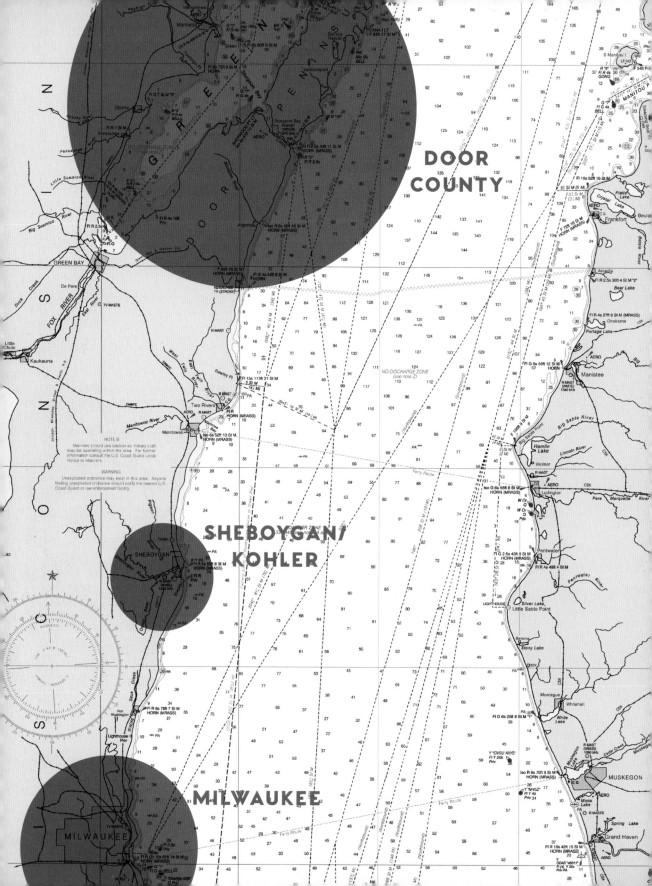

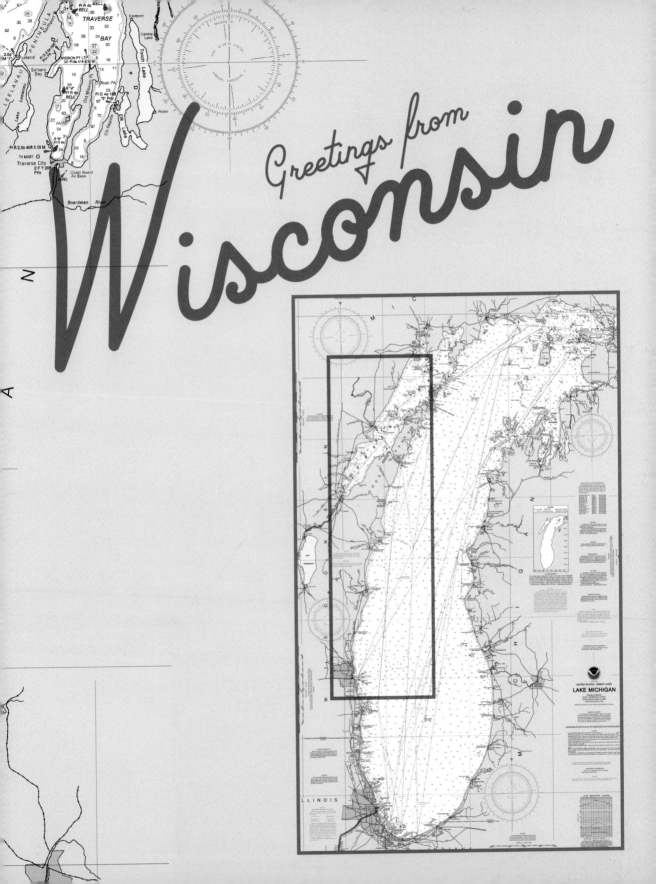

Greetings from Wisconsin

5210—Lovers' Leap, near Cabot's Point, Sturgeon Bay, Door Co

Chapter 1

DOOR COUNTY

I **F CIVILIZATION ENDED AND NATURE TOOK BACK ITS DOMAIN,** I imagine it would look a lot like Door County. Not necessarily like Fish Creek, with its throngs of tourists in the summer, but like the birch trees and rolling hills flanked by miles of beautiful sandy beaches with their orange- and purple-hued bayside sunsets.

Nicknamed Cape Cod of the Midwest and a central spot in the Upper Midwest for vacationers, Door County includes the communities of Sturgeon Bay (the only city on the peninsula), Egg Harbor, Carlsville, Fish Creek, Jacksonport, Ephraim, Sister Bay, Ellison Bay, Rowleys Bay, and Gills Rock at the far north. A year-round vehicle and passenger ferry connects the northern tip of the peninsula with Washington Island, the largest of Door County's islands with a population of 700 residents. A smaller seasonal ferry connects Rock Island State Park to Washington Island.

Home to many of those with Belgian, Icelandic, Scandinavian, and Eastern European roots, Door County has not only sustained many food-friendly customs like Friday night fish fries and fish boils, but it also has brought together traditional and modern water activities from various cultures to become a popular destination for fishing, sailing, kayaking, boating and water skiing, paddleboarding, parasailing, and even scuba diving. Land activities include biking and hiking in Peninsula State Park, golfing, and horseback riding, as well as shopping, art and pottery gallery visiting, and wine tasting.

HOME-STYLE FISH BOIL

HERE'S A RECIPE FOR THOSE LONGING FOR A TRADITIONAL FISH BOIL. *The amount of salt used at a fish boil might seem alarming, but the oils of the fish act as a protective barrier, allowing in just enough salt to add the right amount of flavor. Serve with Bavarian Dark Rye Bread (page 14) and butter and Creamy Coleslaw (page 15), along with your favorite local craft beer. For dessert, try a slice of Door County Cherry Pie (page 21), just like you'd finish off any traditional boil.*

INGREDIENTS

- 2 cups water
- 1½ pounds red potatoes, cut into 1-inch chunks
- 1 cup coarsely chopped sweet onion or yellow onion
- ¾ teaspoon salt
- 2 teaspoons black peppercorns
- 4 Lake Michigan trout or whitefish steaks, cut ½ inch thick (about 1¼ pounds)
- 2 tablespoons butter, melted
- ¼ cup sour cream
- 1 teaspoon prepared horseradish

1. Combine the water, potatoes, onion, ½ teaspoon of the salt, and the peppercorns in a 10-inch, deep skillet. Bring to a boil over high heat. Reduce the heat, cover, and simmer for 10 minutes.

2. Place the fish over the potatoes and sprinkle the remaining ¼ teaspoon salt over the fish. Cover and continue to simmer until the fish is opaque, 5 to 7 minutes.

3. Using a slotted spatula, transfer the fish to warm serving plates, then transfer the potatoes and onions alongside the fish. Drizzle the butter over the fish. Combine the sour cream and horseradish in a small bowl and serve on the side for the potatoes.

PREP TIME: 15 minutes

COOKING TIME: 20 minutes

Serves 4

A TRADITIONAL DOOR COUNTY FISH BOIL

A skilled boil master — or in some cases, a local firefighter — throws kerosene onto a roaring fire that's serving as the heat source for a large cauldron of salted water, fish, onions, and potatoes. A large group of local residents, vacationers, and other visitors — who planned ahead and reserved their spots — look on, plates and forks in hand, in eager anticipation of the hot meal to come. The foaming water violently bubbles up, hissing and spilling over the sides and bringing the fleshy chunks of whitefish to the top so they can be scooped off and served. Fish boils like this are held at supper clubs, inns, restaurants, and other spots up and down the lakefront on Friday nights, and occasionally on other nights of the week come summer. These boils — in addition to feeding the masses — also make for a good excuse to soak up the day's last few moments and enjoy a gorgeous bayside sunset over the lake.

Bavarian Dark RYE BREAD

IN AN HOMAGE TO THE GERMAN ANCESTRY IN THE AREA, *you'll often find dark rye bread on the menu at local supper clubs and Friday night fish boils in Door County, along with other traditional sides like boiled red potatoes and fresh-made coleslaw (page 15). Pair this recipe — inspired by the same ubiquitous supper club bread — with Homemade Dill-Cured Salmon (page 59) and/or Compound Butter (page 19), or toast it and top with Blackberry-Blueberry Jam (page 198).*

INGREDIENTS

- 3 cups unbleached all-purpose flour
- ¼ cup unsweetened cocoa powder
- 2 packets (¼ ounce each) active dry yeast (not rapid rising)
- 1 tablespoon salt
- 1 tablespoon caraway seeds
- 2 cups water
- ⅓ cup molasses
- 4 tablespoons unsalted butter
- 3½ cups rye flour
- Vegetable oil, for brushing

1. Combine the all-purpose flour, cocoa powder, yeast, salt, and caraway seeds in the large bowl of an electric mixer. Combine the water, molasses, and butter in a small saucepan. Mix well and heat until the temperature reaches 115°F (46°C). Add to the dry ingredients in the bowl. Mix on low speed for 1 minute. Scrape down the sides of the bowl and beat on high speed for 3 minutes. Scrape down the sides of the bowl again and add the rye flour. Mix on low speed until blended to a soft dough.

2. Transfer the dough to a work surface dusted with all-purpose flour and knead by hand for 5 minutes, dusting with additional flour if needed. When the dough is light and elastic, cover and let rest for 20 minutes.

3. Grease a large baking sheet. Divide the dough in half, shape to form two round or oval loaves, and place on the baking sheet. Brush the tops of the loaves lightly with vegetable oil. Use a sharp knife to slash the tops of the loaves in several places. Cover with waxed paper and let stand in a warm place for about 50 minutes or until the loaves have doubled in size.

4. Preheat the oven to 400°F (200°C). Uncover and bake the loaves for 28 minutes or until browned and slightly crispy on the outside and soft in the middle. A toothpick inserted into the bread should come out clean. Transfer to a wire rack and cool completely.

PREP TIME: 55 minutes (including resting time)

RISING TIME: 50 minutes

BAKING TIME: 28 minutes

Makes 2 loaves

CREAMY COLESLAW

THIS CLASSIC RECIPE IS MORE TANGY THAN SWEET. *It goes great with New Buffalo Bill's Wood-Smoked BBQ Ribs (page 159) for a barbecue, and it packs well for a beach picnic. And it's easily doubled to serve a bigger crowd.*

1. Cut the cabbage into chunks. Process in batches in a food processor using on-off pulses just until finely chopped. You should have about 6 cups cabbage. (Do not wash the food processor). Transfer the cabbage to a large bowl.

2. Add the mayonnaise, sour cream, sugar, horseradish, lemon juice, salt, dry mustard, cayenne, and celery salt, if desired, to the food processor; process until well blended. Pour over the cabbage and toss well. Cover and refrigerate for at least 8 hours before serving.

INGREDIENTS

- 1 small or ½ large head cabbage (1½–1¾ pounds)
- ¾ cup good-quality mayonnaise or Homemade Mayonnaise (page 87)
- ½ cup sour cream
- 3 tablespoons sugar
- 3 tablespoons prepared horseradish
- 2 teaspoons fresh lemon juice
- ½ teaspoon salt
- ¼ teaspoon dry mustard or 2 teaspoons Dijon mustard
- ⅛ teaspoon cayenne pepper
- ⅛ teaspoon celery salt (optional)

PREP TIME: 20 minutes

CHILLING TIME: 8 hours

Serves 8

PANFRIED PERCH

with Tartar Sauce

I REMEMBER EATING MY FIRST OF MANY BASKETS OF PANFRIED PERCH *when I was just 5 years old. My family and I often dined at Schartner's, down the street from Bay Shore Inn, where we stayed while in town. Later, I enjoyed perch at Donny's at Glidden Lodge, and farther north in Fish Creek at Greenwood Supper Club. The Mill in Sturgeon Bay and Sister Bay Bowl are also favorite stops in Door County for fish fries.*

This recipe is for panfried perch, but you could just as easily deep-fry them for a heartier, more indulgent meal. Heat oil to 350°F (180°C), follow with the dredging process as outlined in step 2, and fry for just 30 seconds to 1 minute, until golden brown. If lake perch are out of season, you may substitute smelts or thin fresh whitefish fillets with the skin on, cut into smaller pieces.

Have some leftover perch? Make it into a sandwich — bake to reheat and stuff into brioche buns spread with tartar sauce and topped with arugula or other fresh lettuce and perhaps some Pickled Red Onions (page 44).

FOR THE TARTAR SAUCE

- ¼ cup finely chopped dill pickles
- 1 tablespoon chopped fresh parsley
- 1 teaspoon drained, chopped capers (optional)
- ½ teaspoon dried tarragon or 1 tablespoon chopped fresh (optional)
- 2 teaspoons fresh lemon juice
- ¼ teaspoon lemon zest
- ¼ teaspoon Old Bay seasoning
- 1 cup mayonnaise

FOR THE FISH

- ¼ cup unbleached all-purpose flour
- 1 teaspoon paprika or smoked paprika
- ½ teaspoon salt
- ½ teaspoon freshly ground black pepper
- 2 tablespoons canola or vegetable oil, plus more if needed
- 2 tablespoons unsalted butter
- 1¼–1½ pounds small fresh lake perch fish fillets, with skin

  Lemon wedges, for garnish

1. For the tartar sauce, mix the pickles, parsley, capers, tarragon, lemon juice, lemon zest, and Old Bay in a small bowl. Fold in the mayonnaise to combine, and chill until serving time. The sauce will keep for up to 3 days in the refrigerator.

PREP TIME: 15 minutes

COOKING TIME: 9 minutes

Serves 4

2. For the fish, place the flour, paprika, salt, and pepper in a plastic or paper bag. Heat the oil and butter in a large nonstick skillet over medium-high heat until the butter is melted and very hot. Shake several perch fillets at a time in the flour mixture and add to the skillet. When all the fish is in the skillet, turn the heat to medium and cook until golden brown on the bottom, about 5 minutes. Turn and continue to cook until golden brown on the bottom and the fish is cooked through, about 4 minutes.

3. Serve immediately with the tartar sauce and lemon wedges.

THE FRIDAY NIGHT FISH FRY

Like the Home-Style Fish Boil (page 12), the Friday night fish fry remains a tradition in Door County at any classic Wisconsin supper club. For decades, residents and visitors alike have come together as a community to catch up and share in a feast of fried perch, walleye, and whitefish, usually served with buttery rolls (page 18), rye bread (page 14), coleslaw (page 15), and, since the end of Prohibition, brandy old-fashioned cocktails (page 112). The tradition began when early Irish, German, and Norwegian Catholics in Wisconsin would forgo meat on Friday nights in observation of Lent. Local church chefs would fry up fish in big batches to feed their patrons, but supper clubs and inns later took over the job.

BUTTERY DINNER ROLLS

A STAPLE AT MANY SUPPER CLUBS, *these rich, pull-apart rolls come out in a basket before the meal. If you're like me, you spread that warm, pull-apart treat with a little whipped butter and let it soak up your brandy old-fashioned while you wait hungrily for your fried perch or prime rib.*

INGREDIENTS

- 1½ cups whole milk
- ½ cup (1 stick) unsalted butter, cut into pieces, plus 2 tablespoons, melted
- ¼ cup sugar
- 1 package active dry yeast (not rapid rising)
- ½ cup warm water
- 3 eggs, lightly beaten
- 1¼ teaspoons salt
- 7 cups unbleached all-purpose flour, plus more if needed

  Coarse sea salt or kosher salt, for sprinkling (optional)

1. Place the milk in a small saucepan and bring to a simmer. Remove from the heat, stir in the butter pieces and sugar, and let cool. Dissolve the yeast in the warm water and let sit until foamy. Combine the milk mixture, eggs, yeast mixture, salt, and 4 cups of the flour in the large bowl of an electric mixer fitted with the dough attachment. Mix on medium-low speed until smooth. Add the remaining 3 cups flour, ½ cup at a time, and mix until a smooth ball forms. If the dough is sticky, add additional flour ¼ cup at a time.

2. Knead the dough on medium speed until the dough is smooth and elastic, about 5 minutes. Butter a large bowl, place the dough in the bowl, cover with waxed paper, and let rise in a warm place until doubled in bulk, about 1 hour.

3. Butter a 9- by 13-inch baking dish. Punch the dough down and transfer to a floured surface. Roll into a ball and cut the ball into quarters with a large sharp knife. Pull each quarter of dough into 6 pieces (2 ounces each). Shape each into a ball and place close together in the baking dish. Cover again and let rise until doubled, 30 to 40 minutes.

4. Preheat the oven to 350°F (180°C). Brush the melted butter over the rolls and, if desired, sprinkle with coarse salt. Bake the rolls for 25 to 30 minutes or until deep golden brown. Serve warm or at room temperature. Any leftover rolls may be frozen for up to 1 month.

PREP TIME: 30 minutes

RISING TIME: 1 hour 40 minutes

BAKING TIME: 30 minutes

Makes 24 rolls

COMPOUND BUTTERS

THESE BUTTERS TASTE DELICIOUS WHEN SPREAD ON BREAD AND TOAST, *of course, but they also add a silky, elegant touch as a topping for steaks and fish. They're a great way to use extra herbs from the farmers' market, grocery store, or garden. In addition to the ones below, I've made butters with roasted garlic, garlic scapes, maple syrup, shallots, red pepper, mustard, and more. The options really are endless.*

For the blue cheese butter, I like using Hook's Little Boy Blue cheese from Mineral Point, Wisconsin, where I've seen them take extra care with their work. For butter, I'm a huge fan of Nordic Creamery's naturally grass-fed butter because of its sweet, tangy taste. You can find this butter, made in Westby, Wisconsin, and other artisan butters like it at many farmers' markets and gourmet food stores throughout the state, as well as at Schoolhouse Artisan Cheese in Door County (see page 31).

For each butter, purée all of the ingredients in a food processor until smooth. Spread the butter out in a long strip along one of the long ends of an 8- by 12-inch rectangular piece of parchment paper, leaving an inch along the outer edge. Starting with the butter side, roll the butter tightly, like a sushi roll, tucking the butter under to shape it into a cylinder about 1½ inches thick. Tie off the ends by twisting them like candy wrappers. Store in a resealable plastic bag in the refrigerator for up to 1 week or in the freezer for longer-term storage. Slice off rounds as needed.

FOR THE HERB BUTTER

- 1 cup (2 sticks) unsalted butter, softened
- 1 tablespoon chopped fresh rosemary
- 1 tablespoon chopped fresh thyme
- 1 tablespoon chopped fresh sage
  Pinch of sea salt (optional)
- ⅛ teaspoon freshly ground black pepper

FOR THE BLUE CHEESE AND CHIVE BUTTER

- 1 cup (2 sticks) unsalted butter, softened
- ¼ cup crumbled blue cheese
- 2 tablespoons chopped fresh chives

FOR THE ROASTED SHALLOT, HONEY, AND BLACK PEPPER BUTTER

- 1 cup (2 sticks) unsalted butter, softened
- 2 shallots, peeled, coated with olive oil, roasted in a 400°F (200°C) oven until tender and cooled
- ¼ teaspoon freshly ground black pepper
- 1–2 tablespoons honey

PREP TIME: 7 minutes

Each butter recipe makes 1 cup

Door County CHERRY PIE

A STAPLE IN THIS PART OF THE COUNTRY *(and in Traverse City, Michigan), cherry pie makes for a delicious dessert, afternoon pick-me-up, and even comforting breakfast treat. Traverse City folks will tell you their cherry pie is the best. Door County residents might beg to differ. I've found joy in both versions. Some are more crumbly, some are sweeter, others are more tart. Everyone seems to have his or her own nuanced variation. I modeled this recipe after the one from Sweetie Pies in Fish Creek, Door County (see page 23), but I use an all-butter crust instead of shortening for an even richer, flakier consistency. To learn more about the cherries that go into this all-Midwestern pie, see page 247.*

FOR THE PASTRY

- 1¼ cups unbleached all-purpose flour
- ½ teaspoon salt
- ½ cup (1 stick) unsalted butter, cut into pieces, cold
- 3–5 tablespoons ice water

FOR THE FILLING

- ½ cup sugar
- ¼ cup unbleached all-purpose flour
- 4 cups well-drained bottled tart Montmorency cherries in unsweetened cherry juice (see Note)
- 1 tablespoon unsalted butter, cut into small pieces

FOR THE TOPPING

- 1 tablespoon whole milk
- 1 tablespoon sugar

NOTE: *Save the juice from the bottled tart cherries for poaching pears (see page 28).*

1. For the pastry, combine the flour and salt in a medium bowl. Add the butter and use a pastry blender or two knives to cut in the butter until it is the size of coarse crumbs. Drizzle 3 tablespoons of the ice water over the top and stir with a fork. Gently knead the mixture with your hands until the dough holds together. If it is dry, add more ice water, 1 tablespoon at a time, and knead until the dough holds together. Shape into two oval disks, wrap each in plastic wrap, and refrigerate for at least 40 minutes.

Recipe continues on next page

PREP TIME: 20 minutes

CHILLING TIME: 40 minutes

BAKING TIME: 1 hour 30 minutes

Serves 6–8

2. Roll one of the chilled dough disks on a lightly floured surface to ⅛-inch thickness and about 11 inches in diameter. Gently roll the pastry around the rolling pin and transfer it to a 9-inch pie pan or dish. Without stretching the dough, fit it into the bottom and up the sides of the pan.

3. Preheat the oven to 325°F (160°C).

4. For the filling, combine the sugar and flour in a large bowl. Add the cherries and mix well. Spoon the mixture into the pie shell and top with the butter.

5. Roll out the remaining dough disk to ⅛ inch thick and about 11 inches in diameter. Drape the dough over the cherry filling. Fold the edges under the bottom crust and flute attractively or use a fork to press down the crust. Cut several slits in the center of the pie to allow steam to escape during baking.

6. For the topping, brush the milk over the top and sprinkle the sugar evenly over the pie.

7. Place the pie on a rimmed baking sheet and bake for 1 hour 30 minutes or until golden brown. Let stand on a wire rack for at least 1 hour before serving.

Sweetie Pies

FISH CREEK, WISCONSIN

SUSAN CROISSANT, WITH A FITTING NAME FOR A BAKER, founded Sweetie Pies in Fish Creek in 1995, baking pies using her grandmother's recipes. Eight years later, she married and moved away, selling the shop to Corinne Lea, who ramped up the baking to 200 pies a day, from her signature cherry to apple-cranberry-walnut, apple-blackberry, caramel-walnut, lemon meringue, chocolate-pecan, pumpkin, strawberry-rhubarb, peach, peach-raspberry, peach-blueberry, and a number of other flavors. Since then, Lea's parents, Dave and Renny Lea, and another couple, Cathy and Larry Mazurek, have taken over the shop.

When I'm there, I always make sure to grab a bag of crust cookies — little pieces of leftover pie dough coated with cinnamon sugar and baked. For their cherry pie, Sweetie Pies uses Montmorency cherries (sometimes referred to as "red," "sour," or "pie" cherries) locally grown in Door County as well as in the Traverse City, Michigan, area. Twice a year, Sweetie Pies teams up with Savory Spoon Cooking School (see page 31) to host pie-baking classes you don't want to miss.

APPLE CAKE

EVERY SUMMER, WE WAIT ANXIOUSLY FOR THE END OF AUGUST TO COME, *when we escape to Door County for a week of rest, relaxation, swimming, cooking, eating, and exploring. As an adult, I was lucky enough to stumble upon the Suchy family's historic log cabin on a tree-lined road that sits on the serene and gorgeous Whitefish Bay, with its powdery white sand and walkable shores.*

The Suchy family's history on Whitefish Bay dates back to when Fred and Helen Suchy built their dream cottage, which would later become their retirement home. They built this cottage in the summers of 1948, '49, and '50, using local wood and their own sweat and hard work. After the couple's passing, their children took over and maintained the home as a rental cabin for city dwellers like my husband and me to find real peace. It's a fitting memorial to their parents. This apple cake is a Suchy family favorite. Look for locally grown apples at Seaquist Orchards (see page 38).

FOR THE CAKE

- 2 cups unbleached all-purpose flour
- ½ cup granulated sugar
- 1 tablespoon baking powder
- ¼ teaspoon kosher or sea salt
- 4 tablespoons butter, cold
- ¾ cup whole milk
- 1 egg, lightly beaten
- 1 teaspoon vanilla extract
- 2 pounds apples (about 5 medium), such as Cortland or McIntosh

FOR THE TOPPING

- ¾ cup firmly packed brown sugar
- ¼ cup unbleached all-purpose flour
- 2 teaspoons ground cinnamon
- 4 tablespoons butter, cold

FOR SERVING

Whipped cream or vanilla ice cream (optional)

PREP TIME: 30 minutes

BAKING TIME: 45 minutes

Serves 10

1. For the cake, preheat the oven to 350°F (180°C). Butter a 9- by 13-inch baking dish. Combine the flour, granulated sugar, baking powder, and salt in a large bowl. Using a pastry cutter or two knives, cut the butter into the dry ingredients until the size of small peas.

2. Combine the milk, egg, and vanilla in a medium bowl, mixing well. Add to the flour mixture and mix just until the dry ingredients are moistened. Spread the batter into the baking dish.

3. Peel and core the apples and cut into thin slices. Arrange the slices evenly over the batter in the baking dish.

4. For the topping, combine the brown sugar, flour, and cinnamon in a medium bowl. Using a pastry cutter or two knives, cut the butter into the dry ingredients until the size of small peas. Sprinkle the topping evenly over the apples.

5. Bake for 45 minutes, until lightly browned. Let cool on a wire rack for at least 15 minutes. Serve warm or at room temperature, with whipped cream or ice cream, if desired.

MAKING THE MOST OF FARMERS' MARKETS

Farmers' markets supply many ingredients for the recipes in this book. If you have one nearby, don't be afraid to buy veggies that look a little lumpy or even slightly bruised — they'll taste just as delicious when prepared, and you can often get a discount on the "ugly" stuff if you show up late. Otherwise, try to get to the market early for the freshest pick of the loot. As a former farmers' market employee and author of a farmers' market cookbook, I have had the pleasure of being able to enjoy local farm produce and learn these shopping tricks. If you can't get to a farmers' market, many area farms sell their produce right off their land or at roadside stands. And, more groceries now carry locally produced seasonal farm food.

CHICKEN AND RIB BOOYAH

"BOOYAH" IS A CHICKEN AND BEEF STEW MADE POPULAR IN NORTHERN WISCONSIN *by Walloon Belgian settlers. Legend has it that the name came about sometime in the early 1900s from a misspelling of the French word* bouillir *or the Walloon* bouyon, *which both mean "to boil." Since then, booyah has been a fixture of community fundraisers in northern Wisconsin (particularly the Fox River Valley region of Green Bay), where residents sometimes even cook the stew in huge pots over an open fire stirred with a canoe paddle. Using short ribs naturally thickens the stew because of the collagen in the bones.*

INGREDIENTS

- 3 pounds bone-in beef chuck short ribs
- 2 pounds bone-in chicken thighs
- 2¼ teaspoons salt
- 2¼ teaspoons freshly ground black pepper
- 2 tablespoons vegetable oil
- 4 celery stalks, sliced
- 2 small yellow onions, chopped
- 7 cups reduced-sodium chicken broth

- 2 bay leaves
- 1½ pounds russet potatoes, peeled and cut into ½-inch pieces
- 4 cups shredded green cabbage
- 3–4 large carrots, thickly sliced
- 1 (28-ounce) can diced tomatoes, undrained
- 2 cups frozen peas (see Note)

NOTE: *Or stir 2 cups dried split peas into the broth at the beginning of step 3.*

1. Cut the short ribs into pieces, slicing along every other bone so each piece has a bone with meat attached. Pat the beef and chicken dry with paper towels and season both sides of the beef and the meaty sides of the chicken with the salt and pepper. Heat the oil in a large Dutch oven or stockpot over medium-high heat. Brown the beef on all sides, about 10 minutes, and transfer to a plate. Cook the chicken until browned on both sides, about 10 minutes. Transfer to a plate. When the chicken is cool enough to handle, remove and discard the skin.

2. Pour off all but 2 tablespoons fat from the pan. Add the celery and onions and cook over medium heat until softened, about 5 minutes. Stir in the broth and bay leaves, scraping up any browned bits. Add the beef and chicken, and bring to a boil. Reduce the heat to low, cover, and simmer until the chicken is cooked through, about 30 minutes. Transfer the chicken to a bowl. When cool enough to handle, cut the meat into bite-size pieces, discarding the bones. Set aside.

PREP TIME: 1 hour

COOKING TIME: 1 hour 30 minutes

Serves 10–12

3. Continue to simmer the stew until the beef is tender, about 30 minutes longer. Transfer the beef to a plate. When cool enough to handle, cut into bite-size pieces, discarding the bones and any extra fat. Remove and discard the bay leaves.

4. Add the potatoes, cabbage, carrots, and tomatoes to the pot and bring to a boil. Reduce the heat to medium-low and cook uncovered until the vegetables are tender, about 20 minutes. Add the reserved beef and chicken and the peas, and simmer until heated through, about 10 minutes. Remove from the heat and season to taste with additional salt and pepper, if desired.

CHERRY-POACHED PEARS

with Mascarpone Cream

IT'S NOT HARD TO FIND BEAUTIFUL PEARS IN DOOR COUNTY *during the late summer and fall, and cherries can be found year-round preserved in jars with their juices. Janice Thomas developed this recipe as a way to use those juices from a jar of unsweetened cherries without having to waste a drop. For more cherry flavor, throw in some of the cherries during the last few minutes of poaching the pears.*

INGREDIENTS

- 6 large ripe but firm pears, such as Bartlett, Anjou, or Bosc
- 4 cups unsweetened cherry juice
- 2 cups Riesling, Vouvray, or other sweet white wine
- 1 cinnamon stick or 1 teaspoon ground cinnamon

- 1 cup heavy cream, cold
- ½ teaspoon vanilla extract or vanilla bean paste
- ⅓ cup mascarpone cheese
- 1 tablespoon sugar
- Fresh mint sprigs, for garnish (optional)
- Ground or freshly grated nutmeg, for garnish (optional)

1. Peel and core the pears, leaving the stems intact. (If you have an apple corer, core the pears from the bottom up to the start of the narrow top.) Pour the cherry juice, wine, and cinnamon stick into a large saucepan or Dutch oven that is large enough to hold the pears in a single layer. Add the pears and bring the mixture to a boil over high heat. Reduce the heat to maintain a gentle simmer. Simmer for 15 minutes, rolling the pears over every 5 minutes. Check the pears for tenderness by inserting a paring knife into the thickest part of the pear. If there is resistance, continue simmering the pears, checking every 5 minutes. When tender, transfer each pear with a slotted spoon to a large shallow bowl. Add enough of the poaching liquid to the bowl to come up 1 inch around the pears. (Reserve any remaining poaching liquid to use in Champagne cocktails!) The pears may be served at room temperature or covered with plastic wrap and refrigerated for up to 24 hours.

2. Meanwhile, combine the cream and vanilla in a medium bowl and beat on medium-high speed with an electric mixer to firm peaks. Add the mascarpone cheese and sugar and continue beating on medium speed until well combined. Refrigerate the mixture until serving time.

3. Place each pear in a serving bowl and spoon some of the poaching liquid over the top. Use a large soup spoon to scoop an oval of the mascarpone cream and place it alongside the pear. Garnish with mint sprigs and nutmeg, if desired.

PREP TIME: 20 minutes

COOKING TIME: 25 minutes

Serves 6

WHITEFISH *with* BASIL PESTO *and* ARUGULA SALAD

THIS RECIPE COMES FROM ONE OF JANICE THOMAS'S CLASSES *at Savory Spoon Cooking School. I amended it somewhat, but the theme of using fresh herbs from the garden or farmers' market remains, and making pesto is a great way to use extras. With such a simple recipe as this, buying fresh local fish makes a huge difference.*

FOR THE BASIL PESTO

- 1 garlic clove, peeled
- 1 cup packed fresh basil leaves
- ¼ cup chopped walnuts, toasted
- ¼ cup extra-virgin olive oil
- ⅓ cup finely grated Parmesan cheese
  - Sea salt or kosher salt

FOR THE FISH

- 4 (6-ounce) whitefish fillets, with or without skin, pin bones removed
- ⅓ cup panko, preferably whole wheat (or fresh breadcrumbs)
- 2 teaspoons olive oil or melted butter

FOR THE ARUGULA SALAD

- 2 teaspoons extra-virgin olive oil
- 2 teaspoons fresh lemon juice
- 4 cups packed baby arugula
- 4 lemon wedges

1. For the basil pesto, drop the garlic clove through the feed tube of a food processor with the motor running. Process until minced. Add the basil and walnuts and process until fairly smooth, scraping down the sides once. With the motor running, add the oil in a thin stream and process until smooth. Add the Parmesan and pulse just until the cheese is incorporated. Taste and add salt, if needed.

2. For the fish, preheat the oven to 400°F (200°C). Line a rimmed baking sheet with parchment paper. Arrange the fish fillets on the baking sheet. Spread the pesto evenly over the fish. Reserve and refrigerate any extra pesto for another use. Toss the panko with the oil and sprinkle evenly over the fish. Bake for 8 to 10 minutes, until the fish is opaque and the crumbs are golden brown. Check the fish after 5 minutes to make sure the crumb topping is not browning too fast. If so, turn down the oven to 350°F (180°C).

3. For the arugula salad, whisk together the oil and lemon juice in a medium bowl. Add the arugula and toss well. Transfer to serving plates and top each with a fish fillet. Garnish with the lemon wedges.

PREP TIME: 5 minutes

BAKING TIME: 8–10 minutes

Serves 4

Savory Spoon
Cooking School
ELLISON BAY, WISCONSIN

JANICE THOMAS HAS A SOFT BUT STRAIGHTFORWARD VOICE when leading cooking classes at her charming Savory Spoon Cooking School in Ellison Bay. Classes take place in a converted late-1800s schoolhouse, which she and her husband, Michael, bought in 2004.

Old photos from the building's days as a school greet you as you walk into the charming space and kitchen, outfitted in clean whites, blond wood, antique kitchen tools, and colorful ceramic plates. The serene space, warmed by sunlight spilling through the windows and skylight, has a calming effect.

A former ER nurse, Thomas switched careers when her husband bought a restaurant — which eventually grew into four restaurants and a catering business with 300-plus employees. "You grow what you eat, you eat what you grow," she says of her mission. Case in point: At Savory Spoon, Thomas maintains a salad

lettuce, herb, and edible flower garden in a wheel-barrow set just outside the front door, and she manages two honeybee hives for fresh honey. While many of her classes revolve around local food, she's also taught many globally themed sessions inspired by her public tours to China, Italy, and elsewhere.

Adjacent to the school, Thomas's husband, Michael, manages Schoolhouse Artisan Cheese with its selection of artisan Wisconsin cheeses and butters. The school/shop also supplies artisan Wisconsin cheeses to a variety of restaurants and other food service outlets in the state.

CHEDDAR CHEESE SCONES

YEARS AGO I WENT ON AN AMAZING CHEESE TOUR *through the Racine/Kenosha area and farther west, near the Wisconsin Dells and Madison. At one point I tried a scone very similar to this one, spread with honey butter, at a small bed-and-breakfast. This recipe is adapted from the Wisconsin Milk Marketing Board, which sponsored the trip.*

My favorite aged cheddars to use are from Hook's, Bleu Mont Dairy, and Carr Valley Cheese.

INGREDIENTS

- 2 cups unbleached all-purpose flour
- 2 tablespoons sugar
- 1 tablespoon baking powder
- ½ teaspoon salt
- ¼ teaspoon baking soda
- 1¼ cups shredded sharp cheddar cheese
- ½ cup sour cream (not light)
- 5 tablespoons plus 1 teaspoon butter, melted and cooled
- 3 tablespoons whole milk
- 1 egg, beaten

  Milk or melted butter, for brushing (optional)

NOTE: *As I suggest elsewhere in this book, avoid using packaged shredded cheese, since it can be laced with potato starch, which mars the taste and impedes melting. Instead, use a grater or even a food processor to shred a block of cheese yourself for best results.*

1. Preheat the oven to 425°F (220°C). Grease a baking sheet. Combine the flour, sugar, baking powder, salt, and baking soda in a large bowl. Mix well. Stir in the cheese.

2. Combine the sour cream, butter, milk, and egg in a small bowl. Mix well. Add to the flour mixture and stir just until the dry ingredients are moistened. Knead the dough in the bowl 4 or 5 times and transfer the dough to a floured work surface. Divide the dough in half and roll each half into a ball. Roll out one ball into a 7-inch circle. Cut the circle into four wedges. Transfer the wedges to the baking sheet. Repeat with the remaining dough half.

3. Brush milk or butter over the tops of the scones, if desired. Bake for 10 to 12 minutes, until lightly browned. Serve warm or at room temperature. Leftover scones may be frozen for up to 3 months.

PREP TIME: 35 minutes

BAKING TIME: 12 minutes

Makes 8 scones

Bleu Mont Dairy

BLUE MOUNDS, WISCONSIN

ONE OF MY FAVORITE ARTISAN CHEESE MAKERS is Willi Lehner of Bleu Mont Dairy. From the name of his business, it may sound like he makes blue cheese, but Lehner's specialty is actually his unique "bandaged cheddar."

Lehner first wraps the cheese in cloth "bandages" to introduce flavor-enhancing bacteria, yeast, and mold; then he ages it for at least a year in a cave he built himself on his hilly farm just west of Madison. French and Swiss cheese makers have used the same techniques of bandaging and cave aging for centuries, even eschewing electrical methods to maintain humidity the natural way and to protect the cheese from cracking and developing bad-tasting mold. Lehner learned this method from his Swiss-born father, a cheese maker himself, and from other cheese makers in Switzerland when he lived there in his twenties. "When I was a kid, we made cheeses that weren't packed in plastic," he says. "I wanted to get back to that."

To build the cave, Lehner dug a huge hole out of the side of a hill and stabilized the interior with concrete rebar. He maintains the temperature at a consistent 55°F (13°C) with humidity at 85 to 95 percent — perfect for aging his 10- and 40-pound cheddar wheels on shelves.

To introduce more flavor into the cheese, Lehner sources milk only from nearby farms that keep their cows on pasture, so he takes a break during the rough Midwestern winters, when the cows have less grass to eat. For this reason, one can compare his cheese to fine wine — its taste is influenced by terroir, or the soil and climate of the area. In this region, happy cows feast on hearty grass, which imparts a sweet, tangy flavor to the cheese.

WEDGE SALAD

with Blue Cheese Dressing, Bacon, and Cherry Tomatoes

WHEN IT COMES TO ARTISAN BLUE CHEESE MADE IN WISCONSIN, *I'm a big fan of Hook's Original Blue, Roth Cheese's Buttermilk Blue (made from raw milk and great for salad dressings such as this one), and Carr Valley's Billy Blue (made from goat's milk for an extra-tangy taste and crumbly texture that works best as a topping). You can find these cheeses at Schoolhouse Artisan Cheese (see page 31) in Door County or at specialty grocers and gourmet food retailers throughout the state. If you like, top this salad with Pickled Red Onions (page 44), like Boathouse Restaurant in Traverse City does, and enjoy with Grilled Waseda Farms Rib Steak (page 53), New Buffalo Bill's Wood-Smoked BBQ Ribs (page 159), or simply on its own.*

INGREDIENTS

- ⅓ cup mayonnaise
- ⅓ cup sour cream
- 3 tablespoons milk
- 2 tablespoons white wine vinegar or sherry vinegar
- ½ teaspoon salt
- ¼ teaspoon freshly ground black pepper, plus more for serving
- 1 cup crumbled blue cheese
- 1 small head iceberg lettuce, cut into 4 wedges
- 1 cup halved heirloom cherry tomatoes
- 2 thick smoked bacon strips, crisply cooked and crumbled (I like Neuske's Applewood)

  Chopped fresh chives, for garnish (optional)

1. Combine the mayonnaise, sour cream, milk, vinegar, salt, and pepper in a medium bowl; mix well. Stir in ½ cup of the blue cheese. Chill for at least 1 hour.

2. Arrange the lettuce wedges on chilled salad plates. Spoon the dressing over the wedges; top with the tomatoes, bacon, and remaining ½ cup blue cheese. Garnish with chives, if desired. Serve with more pepper.

PREP TIME: 20 minutes

CHILLING TIME: 1 hour

Serves 4

WISCONSIN CHEESE

Wisconsin supplies nearly 15 percent of the nation's milk, 23 percent of its butter, and nearly 30 percent of its cheese, according to the Wisconsin Milk Marketing Board (WMMB). In 2015, the state achieved record-breaking cheese production at 3.1 billion pounds, along with 722 million pounds of specialty cheese. In fact, based on available U.S. Department of Agriculture data, WMMB estimates that Wisconsin produces about 45 percent of the nation's specialty cheese — more than any other state.

CHERRY STREUSEL MUFFINS

NATALIE NEDDERSON AND HER HUSBAND, NEDD, *are some of the warmest and most hospitable innkeepers I have ever met. Their "hidden treasure" in Door County, a collection of charming and quaint bright white cottages, sits tucked in a little cul de sac across from the gorgeous Ephraim Yacht Harbor, which is packed in the summertime with boats, parasailors, water skiers, and jet skiers. While I'm a fan of all their baked goods, these muffins in particular have become a family addiction and a regular request from my son. It's pretty easy to find jarred fresh cherries throughout Door County at groceries, gourmet stores, and orchard stands. Seaquist Orchards in Sister Bay (see page 38) always has a regular supply.*

1. For the muffin batter, preheat the oven to 350°F (180°C). Line 12 standard muffin cups with paper liners or butter the cups. Combine the flour, granulated and brown sugars, baking powder, cinnamon, and salt in a large bowl. Make a well in the center and add the egg, butter, and milk. Mix just until the dry ingredients are moistened. Stir in the cherries and lemon zest. Spoon a level ¼ cup of the batter into each muffin cup.

2. For the streusel, combine the pecans, brown sugar, flour, cinnamon, and lemon zest in a medium bowl, mixing well. Add the butter and mix until crumbly. Spoon about 1 tablespoon of the streusel over each muffin.

3. Bake for 22 to 25 minutes, until a wooden pick inserted in the center comes out clean and the topping is golden brown. Transfer the pan with the muffins to a wire rack and let cool for 10 minutes. Remove the muffins from the pan and serve warm or at room temperature. Any extra muffins may be frozen for up to 3 months.

FOR THE MUFFIN BATTER

- 1½ cups unbleached all-purpose flour
- ⅓ cup granulated sugar
- ¼ cup firmly packed dark or light brown sugar
- 2 teaspoons baking powder
- 1 teaspoon ground cinnamon
- ½ teaspoon salt
- 1 egg, slightly beaten
- ½ cup (1 stick) unsalted butter, melted
- ½ cup whole or 2% milk
- 1 cup pitted tart fresh cherries or well-drained bottled cherries, coarsely chopped
- 1 teaspoon grated lemon zest

FOR THE STREUSEL TOPPING

- ½ cup coarsely chopped pecans or walnuts
- ½ cup firmly packed dark or light brown sugar
- ¼ cup unbleached all-purpose flour
- 1 teaspoon ground cinnamon
- 1 teaspoon grated lemon zest
- 2 tablespoons unsalted butter, melted

PREP TIME: 40 minutes

BAKING TIME: 25 minutes

Makes 12 muffins

Seaquist Orchards

SISTER BAY, WISCONSIN

SEAQUIST ORCHARDS, WITH ITS LARGE EXPANSE OF APPLE AND CHERRY TREES and its busy orchard market in the heart of Sister Bay, has drawn hungry Door County locals and visitors alike for years. Most recently, the orchard earned praise for its SweeTango apples, a cross between juicy, sweet Honeycrisp (another Door County native) and tart Vestar apples. SweeTango apples taste great on their own, but they also work well in pies and other dishes.

In the mid to late summer, visit Seaquist for fresh, just-picked cherries. Throughout the year, Seaquist also stocks its shelves with jars of preserved cherries, bags of dried cherries, cherry topping, cherry jam, and other cherry-infused products. Seaquist Orchards has the largest acreage of cherries in Wisconsin and processes about two-thirds of the state's cherries.

DOOR COUNTY
CHERRY FRENCH TOAST

THE WHITE GULL INN IN FISH CREEK HAS EARNED AWARDS AND ACCOLADES *for its amazing breakfasts, some of which come laden with Door County cherries. This is my own rendition of the inn's famous cherry-stuffed French toast. For more mouthwatering recipes from the inn, check out* The White Gull Inn Door County: Favorite Recipes from Our Kitchen *(Amherst Press, 1990) or* The White Gull Inn Centennial Cookbook: More Favorite Recipes from Our Kitchen *(Amherst Press, 1998).*

1. Spread 1 tablespoon of the cream cheese over each slice of bread. Arrange 1 cup of the cherries over 4 slices of the bread. Close the sandwiches with the remaining 4 slices of bread. Cut each sandwich on the diagonal.

2. Combine the remaining 1 cup of cherries and the maple syrup in a small saucepan and place over low heat to start warming.

3. Combine the eggs, milk, and nutmeg in a shallow pie plate, mixing well. Melt 2 tablespoons of the butter on a large griddle over medium heat, spreading evenly. Or, melt 1 tablespoon of the butter in each of 2 large skillets over medium heat. Dip the sandwich halves into the milk mixture for a few seconds on each side and place in the hot butter. Cook until golden brown, 2 to 3 minutes per side. Transfer to warm serving plates and serve with the warmed cherry-maple syrup. Place the confectioners' sugar in a strainer and shake over the French toast, if desired.

INGREDIENTS

- ½ cup cream cheese, softened
- 8 slices egg bread, such as brioche
- 2 cups pitted tart cherries, well drained if bottled
- 1 cup maple syrup
- 2 eggs, beaten
- ½ cup whole milk
- ½ teaspoon ground nutmeg
- 2–3 tablespoons unsalted butter, plus more if needed
- 1 tablespoon confectioners' sugar (optional)

PREP TIME: 20 minutes

COOKING TIME: 6 minutes

Serves 4

STORING SYRUP

Store maple syrup in the refrigerator after opening the bottle, and it will keep for a year or more. Should you see any mold appear on the top of the syrup, simply skim it off and heat the syrup to the boiling point. This will help restore the original flavor.

WILSON'S VANILLA SUNDAES

with Seaquist Orchards Cherry Topping

THAT CRAVEABLE, NOSTALGIC FRENCH VANILLA ICE CREAM *from Wilson's that many of us grew up eating — the creamy, extra vanilla-y kind that dripped over our waffle cones and down the sides of our faces as we watched the boats go by in Ephraim Harbor across the way — forms the basis of this sundae. Wilson's ice creams are prepared fresh weekly by Wisconsin-based Cedar Crest and they wouldn't divulge their recipe, so you'll have to pick up a pint at Wilson's or substitute with your favorite brand. Sarah Martin of Wilson's did, however, divulge the cherry topping recipe they use for their famous sundae using Seaquist Orchards cherries. Here's a quick tip: Save the jar the cherries came in to store the cherry topping in the refrigerator.*

FOR THE TOPPING

- 1 (32-ounce) jar Door County pitted red cherries in unsweetened cherry juice
- 1 cup granulated sugar
- ¼ cup cornstarch
- 1 tablespoon fresh lemon juice

FOR THE WHIPPED CREAM

- 1 cup heavy cream
- 2 tablespoons confectioners' sugar
- 4 scoops Wilson's vanilla or French vanilla ice cream or other favorite flavor

1. For the topping, drain the juice from the cherries into a medium saucepan, reserving 2 cherries for the garnish. Whisk in the granulated sugar, cornstarch, and lemon juice. Cook over medium heat, stirring occasionally, until it comes to a boil, about 5 minutes. Cook, stirring constantly, until thickened, about 1 minute longer. Remove from the heat and stir in the cherries. Set aside, or refrigerate for up to 1 week.

2. For the whipped cream, process the cream and confectioners' sugar in a blender or food processor until thickened. Scoop into a container and refrigerate until serving.

3. To serve, layer 2 chilled parfait glasses each with a scoop of ice cream and 2 tablespoons of the cherry topping. Add another scoop of ice cream, more cherry topping, a dollop of the whipped cream, and a cherry for garnish.

PREP TIME: 10 minutes

COOKING TIME: 6 minutes

Serves 2 (Makes 10–12 servings of cherry topping)

Wilson's Ice Cream

EPHRAIM, WISCONSIN

SINCE 1906, WILSON'S HAS DELIGHTED EPHRAIM RESIDENTS and Door County visitors alike with its ice cream. The Wilson family, who moved to the area from Milwaukee, sold the popular soda fountain and ice cream parlor to another family in 1961.

Since then, it has evolved into a full-scale restaurant, with an iconic red and white awning and Southern-style front porch, serving American comfort food like burgers, hot dogs, and fries, along with a wider variety of ice cream flavors. Very few can pass up one of Wilson's elaborate, indulgent sundaes or homemade root beer floats. Now, Sarah Martin and her husband own the institution. Martin, a native of Ephraim, took over the store from her parents, who were the eighth set of owners since the 1960s.

"We look at our job as keepers of the Wilson's tradition," Martin says. "Going to Wilson's is like taking a trip down memory lane or a step back in time for so many people. It's a happy place with a lot of people making new memories here."

To this day, the Wilson's traditions continue; staff at the shop still draft homemade root beer from soda taps, place a few jelly beans at the bottom of your sundae, and serve the sweets with a smile. In the back, the old jukebox continues to play its vintage tunes. Some things never change, and in this case, that's a great thing.

Door County
Coffee & Tea
STURGEON BAY, WISCONSIN

VICKI WILSON'S VOICE RISES WITH EXCITEMENT when talking about coffee. And why shouldn't it? Since 1993, the owner of Door County Coffee & Tea in Sturgeon Bay, Wisconsin, has put her passion into roasting a variety of beans — from single-origin beans from Colombia to house-made light, medium, and dark blends, along with a wide variety of flavored beans like hazelnut and chocolate-cherry.

Walking into the shop, you're immediately hit with the pleasantly competing smells of different roasts, from the nutty to the earthy and slightly sweet. In the back, employees manage roasting drums filled with different beans, monitoring them in small batches as they turn from green to caramelized and fragrant.

Wilson compares the nuanced techniques of coffee roasters to those of winemakers. Just as winemakers coax different flavors out of their grapes through different growing and aging methods, coffee roasters bring out the natural flavors of the beans by roasting them at different temperatures and for varying lengths of time. Afterward, the beans are vacuum-packed to lock in freshness. We always pick up a few bags when in town, and they make great host gifts, too.

COLD-BREWED COFFEE

THIS COFFEE HAS ENJOYED A BOOM IN POPULARITY, *and for good reason. The technique of using cold or room temperature water and steeping slowly brings out the beans' natural sweetness, creating a smooth, refreshing beverage perfect for summer mornings or an afternoon pick-me-up year-round. It's also super easy to make at home; all you need is a large container, a strainer, filtered water, and time. I try to use freshly ground beans from a local coffee roaster wherever I am, and fortunately, thanks to a craft coffee renaissance of late, they are much easier to find all over the country. This recipe makes a pretty strong concentrate, which can be enjoyed as is or smoothed out with some milk, cream, or extra filtered water.*

1. Place the coffee in a glass pitcher. Slowly pour in the water in circular motions. Mix well, cover loosely with aluminum foil, and let stand at room temperature for at least 12 hours and up to 24 hours.

2. Line a fine sieve with a coffee filter and place it over another glass container. Slowly strain the coffee through the sieve, letting it drip into the glass container. When the coffee filter gets full, stop adding the coffee and let it drip before adding more. Refrigerate the coffee for up to 3 days.

3. For each glass of iced coffee, fill a tall glass with ice cubes. Add ⅓ cup of the coffee, or more as desired. Add milk, if desired, to taste.

INGREDIENTS

½ cup finely ground coffee beans

3 cups cool, filtered water

Milk of choice, for serving

PREP TIME: 5 minutes

STANDING TIME: 12–24 hours

Serves 4 to 8 (makes 2½ cups coffee concentrate)

WHITEFISH TACOS

with Pickled Red Onions, Red-Hot Aioli, and Guacamole

MOST MIDWESTERNERS ARE USED TO EATING FLAKY WHITEFISH *served simply with boiled potatoes, incorporated into chowders, or fried up with tartar sauce. But in taco form (akin to the beachside delicacy from Baja), we're reminded of its freshness and mild, clean flavor, amped up here by some spicy aioli and tangy onions.*

FOR THE PICKLED RED ONIONS

- 1 large red onion, very thinly sliced
- ¼ cup apple cider vinegar
- 2 teaspoons honey or agave syrup
- 1 teaspoon kosher or coarse sea salt

FOR THE RED-HOT AIOLI

- ⅓ cup mayonnaise
- 1–1½ tablespoons sriracha sauce, as desired

FOR THE GUACAMOLE

- 2 Hass avocados, pitted, peeled, and diced
- 1 jalapeño, seeded and minced
- ¼ cup chopped fresh cilantro
- 2 teaspoons fresh lime juice
- 1 garlic clove or roasted garlic clove, minced (optional)
- ¼ teaspoon salt

FOR THE FISH TACOS

- 1 tablespoon vegetable oil
- 1 pound skinless, boneless whitefish fillets, cut into 1½-inch pieces
- 1 egg, beaten
- ¾ cup panko
- 8 corn or small flour tortillas, warmed
  Chopped fresh cilantro, for sprinkling
  Lime wedges, for serving

1. For the pickled onions, bring 4 cups water to a boil. Separate the onion slices into rings and place in a colander in the sink. Slowly pour the boiling water over the onions and allow to drain. Whisk together the vinegar, honey, and salt in a medium bowl. Add the drained onions and mix well. Let stand at room temperature for at least 1 hour, tossing occasionally. Mix well and place in a glass jar or container. Cover and refrigerate until serving time.

Recipe continues on page 46

PREP TIME: 20 minutes

STANDING TIME: 1 hour

COOKING TIME: 6 minutes

Serves 4

2. For the red-hot aioli, combine the mayonnaise and sriracha sauce in a small bowl. Cover and refrigerate until serving time.

3. For the guacamole, mash together the avocados, jalapeño, cilantro, lime juice, garlic, and salt to the desired consistency. Taste and add additional salt if desired. Chill for 15 minutes to blend the flavors. The guacamole may be prepared up to 2 hours before serving, but if waiting longer than 15 minutes to serve, drizzle the lime juice over the guacamole at the end and place a piece of plastic wrap directly on the surface to prevent browning. Stir well before serving.

4. For the fish, heat the oil in a large nonstick skillet over medium heat. Toss the fish pieces with the beaten egg to coat well. Place the breadcrumbs in a shallow bowl and add the fish, stirring to coat. Add the fish to the hot oil in one layer and cook for 3 minutes. Turn the fish over and continue cooking until the fish is opaque, about 3 minutes.

5. Spoon the fish into the warmed tortillas and spoon the aioli over the fish. Place some pickled red onions and cilantro in the tacos and serve immediately with the lime wedges and guacamole.

Belgian-Style HAND-CUT FRIES

PARTIALLY FRYING THE FRIES FIRST HELPS COOK THE INTERIOR *so that when you fry them a second time, they crisp up on the outside. Make sure you use a deep-frying thermometer fitted to the side of the pot and maintain a constant oil temperature. I prefer to use a ceramic Dutch oven because it will hold an even temperature when frying, but cast iron also works. In a pinch, you can use a heavy pot that is at least 5 inches deep. You will also need a long-handled wire skimmer or a long-handled very large slotted spoon.*

Make sure to pat dry the potatoes before you fry them. Keep the bottle the oil came in for discarding the oil afterward. To discard oil safely, cover the frying pot with a lid once done frying, then allow the oil to cool completely before transferring it to the container. Oil can be strained and used again or discarded in the trash.

1. Pour enough oil in a large heavy saucepan at least 5 inches deep to reach 3 inches up the sides of the pan. Hook a deep-frying thermometer onto the side of the pan almost down to the bottom of the pan. Place over medium heat and heat until the temperature of the oil reaches 325°F (160°C).

2. Meanwhile, slice the potatoes lengthwise into ½-inch-thick slabs, then cut the slabs lengthwise again into ½-inch strips. Cut any longer strips in half. Dry the potatoes thoroughly with paper towels.

3. Working in batches so as to not overcrowd the pot, cook the fries until lightly colored but not brown, 4 to 5 minutes. Using a slotted spoon or long-handled skimmer, transfer the fries to paper towels to drain. Make sure to bring the oil temperature back up to 325°F (160°C) before frying another batch.

Recipe continues on next page

INGREDIENTS

Corn or canola oil, for frying

4   medium russet potatoes

Sea salt, for sprinkling

PREP TIME: 20 minutes

COOKING TIME: 20 minutes for first frying;
   20 minutes for second frying

STANDING TIME: up to 2 hours
   (between fryings)

Serves 4–6

4. Allow the fries to cool to room temperature. The fries can be cooked to this point hours ahead and then fried again (in the same oil) just before serving.

5. When the fries have cooled, bring the oil up to 350°F (180°C). Working in batches again, cook the fries until browned and crispy, 1 to 2 minutes. Transfer to paper towels to drain. Pat any excess oil with more paper towels as needed. Sprinkle salt over the hot fries and serve immediately. Do not cover the potatoes to keep warm, as they will become soggy.

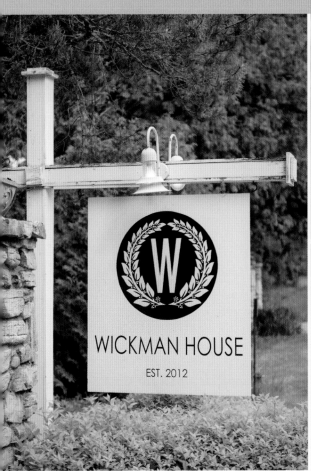

Wickman House

ELLISON BAY, WISCONSIN

IT'S NO SURPRISE THAT WICKMAN HOUSE HAS EARNED MULTIPLE STARS and media attention as one of those progressive chef-driven sleepers of a restaurant. Executive Chef Matt Chambas, with a background in fine dining and modern cuisine, leads his team of talented young chefs in an exploration not only of seasonal local cuisine, but also of Door County food from farmers truly making a difference in sustainable farming. One of those farms is Waseda Farms in Baileys Harbor, which provides the restaurant with beef from pastured cows raised on the farm from birth. Chambas also sources his whitefish from local sustainable fisheries, such as Charlie's Smokehouse, which has a long history of fishing in Lake Michigan off Gills Rock.

Grilled Grass-Fed Waseda Farm
BACON CHEESEBURGERS

THIS RECIPE WAS INSPIRED BY THE POPULAR BURGERS *from executive chef Matt Chambas of Wickman House. In addition to beef from Waseda Farms (see page 55), Chambas showcases Sky Brook Cheese, made by Master Cheesemaker Chris Roelli exclusively for Schoolhouse Artisan Cheese (see page 31). The cheese is a semisoft, Jack-style cheese with a rich, buttery taste and a slightly sweet finish. If you can't find it, substitute another buttery cheese, like Havarti or butterkase. Serve with Belgian-Style Hand-Cut Fries (page 47).*

INGREDIENTS

- 4 good-quality bacon strips (I like Waseda Farms or Neuske's)
- 1 pound ground beef, preferably grass-fed
- ½ teaspoon salt
- ½ teaspoon freshly ground black pepper
- Butter, melted, for the buns
- 4 sesame seed buns, split
- 4 slices Sky Brook or Havarti cheese
- 1½ cups packed arugula
- 2 teaspoons extra-virgin olive oil
- 1 teaspoon red wine vinegar
- Pickled Red Onions (page 44), for serving
- Red-Hot Aioli (page 44), stone-ground mustard, or Homemade Mayonnaise (page 87), for serving

1. To cook the bacon, preheat the oven to 400°F (200°C). Line a small baking sheet with aluminum foil. Lay the bacon on the baking sheet and bake for 15 to 20 minutes or until the desired crispiness. Transfer the bacon to paper towels to drain.

2. Prepare a gas or charcoal grill for medium-heat grilling.

3. Gently shape the meat into patties. Do not over-pat, press, or slap the meat into patties, because this can result in toughness. Season the outsides of the patties with salt and pepper. Brush the butter evenly over the burger bun halves.

4. Grill the burgers over medium heat, covered, flipping once, until the internal temperature reaches 140°F (60°C), about 5 minutes per side (the burgers will rise 5 more degrees to 145°F [63°C], or medium-rare, while resting). In the last minute of cooking, place the cheese over the burgers to melt and place the buns, cut side down, around the burgers to toast lightly.

5. Toss the arugula with the olive oil and vinegar in a bowl to coat lightly. To assemble, place the arugula and burgers on the bottoms of the buns. Top with the bacon and pickled red onions. Spread the top buns with 1 to 2 teaspoons of the aioli or other desired condiment.

PREP TIME: 20 minutes

COOKING TIME: 10 minutes

Serves 4

GRILLED WASEDA FARMS RIB-EYE STEAK *with Roasted Tomato, Jalapeño, and Cilantro Salsa and Grilled Asparagus*

HEIRLOOM TOMATOES AT THE HEIGHT OF THEIR SEASON *make amazing salsa. You can buy tomatoes, peppers, and steak at Waseda's store in Baileys Harbor (see page 55). The most important thing when working with grass-fed steak like that from Waseda Farms, Matt Lutsey notes, is to not overcook the meat. Instead of relying on time, check steaks with a thermometer and cook to a certain temperature. Grass-fed steak takes only several minutes to cook on the grill; the meat will continue to cook as it rests. If you buy frozen steaks, make sure they come to room temperature before seasoning and grilling.*

FOR THE SALSA

- 2 medium tomatoes, preferably heirloom
- 1 large or 2 small jalapeños
- 4 garlic cloves, unpeeled
- 1 tablespoon olive oil
- ¼ cup chopped fresh cilantro

FOR THE ASPARAGUS

- 3 tablespoons extra-virgin olive oil
- 1½ tablespoons apple cider vinegar
- ½ teaspoon smoked paprika
- ½ teaspoon red pepper flakes (optional)

- ½ teaspoon coarse sea salt
- ¼ teaspoon freshly ground black pepper
- 1 bunch (about 1 pound) fresh asparagus, preferably thin stalks

FOR THE STEAK

- 2 bone-in Waseda Farms rib-eye steaks or other grass-fed steaks, cut 1 inch thick, at room temperature
- 1 teaspoon smoked salt
- 1 teaspoon freshly ground black pepper
  Extra-virgin olive oil, for drizzling
- ¼ cup crumbled blue cheese (optional)

1. For the salsa, preheat the oven to broil. Place the tomatoes, jalapeño(s), and garlic cloves on a rimmed baking sheet. Broil until the vegetables are charred in spots, 7 to 8 minutes, using tongs to carefully turn the vegetables over once or twice. Remove from the oven and transfer the vegetables to a cutting board. Let cool to room temperature. Peel and mince the garlic. Transfer to a small bowl. Discard the stems from the jalapeños and cut open and discard the seeds. (For a spicier salsa, leave the seeds in.) Finely chop the chiles and add to the bowl. Peel off and discard the skin from the tomatoes. Cut the tomatoes in half and remove the seeds with your fingers. Cut the tomatoes into ½-inch pieces and add to the bowl. Add the oil to the bowl and mix gently. Stir in the cilantro, and set aside.

Recipe continues on next page

PREP TIME: 20 minutes

COOKING TIME: 6–7 minutes

Serves 2–4 depending on size of steaks

2. For the asparagus. combine the oil, vinegar, paprika, pepper flakes (if desired), salt, and pepper in a shallow 1½-quart casserole dish. Whisk well. Break or cut off the tough stems from the asparagus stalks. Add the stalks to the marinade and turn over with tongs so that all the asparagus is coated. Allow to marinate at room temperature for 30 minutes to 1 hour.

3. For the steak, prepare a gas or charcoal grill for high-heat grilling. Sprinkle the steaks evenly with the salt and pepper. Drizzle lightly with olive oil. Place the steaks on the grill and sear for about 1 minute per side, uncovered, over direct high heat. Move the steaks to indirect heat and grill until a meat thermometer reads 130°F (54°C) (the temperature will rise to 140°F to 145°F [60–63°C] for medium-rare doneness while resting). Transfer the steaks to warm serving plates and tent with aluminum foil. Let stand while grilling the asparagus.

4. Remove the asparagus with tongs from the marinade, reserving the marinade. Place the spears on the grill grid over high heat. Sear for 1 to 2 minutes, turning often, until lightly charred and crisp-tender. Return to the marinade to briefly coat, and add to warm serving plates alongside the steaks. Sprinkle the blue cheese over the asparagus, if desired. Serve with the salsa.

Waseda Farms

BAILEYS HARBOR, WISCONSIN

A GRAVEL DRIVEWAY TAKES YOU RIGHT TO THE FRONT DOOR of the charming farm store at Waseda Farms, run by the Lutsey family. Follow the path behind the store and you'll pass by some rabbits bouncing around near a garden overgrown with ripening tomatoes, cucumbers, and other summer vegetables.

The path continues, closer to the groups of black steer happily roaming about while munching on the bright green grass beneath their feet, their tails swinging while others moo to say hello. There are pigs, too, happily burrowing in some dirt and oinking away. It's like a picture of a farm in a child's book come to life.

The Lutsey family started farming in the early 2000s when a doctor urgently suggested Tom Lutsey cut back on his red meat intake. He thought to himself, what if I simply ate better red meat? He bought a couple of steers from a nearby farmer, and the farm grew from there.

The Lutseys raise every animal from birth to harvest. The animals eat only high-quality, chemical-free grass.

The farm store, which opened in 2010, features wall-to-wall coolers holding fresh and flash-frozen Waseda Farms meat, while baskets lining the shelves overflow with some of the farm's own produce and other bounty from neighboring farms in Door County. A walk-in cooler holds artisan cheeses and grass-fed milk, cream, yogurt, eggs, and more fresh herbs and produce. When the Lutseys began to outgrow their Door County space in 2014, they opened a second, much larger location in De Pere with its own retail beef-cutting operation and more specialty products like fresh-made bratwurst and other sausages.

RED WINE–BRAISED BRISKET

with Autumn Root Vegetables and Fresh Horseradish

WE'VE BEEN KNOWN TO TAKE ICE-PACKED COOLERS FULL OF WASEDA FARMS MEAT *back home with us from summer vacation, for enjoying when the temperature starts to drop in the fall. Pair this hearty dish with a red wine from Door Peninsula Winery, or if in Michigan, perhaps with a local Zinfandel.*

FOR THE BRISKET

- 2 tablespoons coarse-grain or brown mustard
- 1 tablespoon dried thyme
- 1 tablespoon coarse sea salt or kosher salt
- 2 teaspoons freshly ground black pepper
- 1 beef brisket (about 5 pounds), trimmed, leaving ¼ inch of fat
- 2 tablespoons olive oil
- 2 cups chopped sweet onions
- 8 garlic cloves, minced
- 2 cups reduced-sodium beef broth
- 1½ cups dry red wine (such as Cabernet Sauvignon or Pinot Noir)

FOR THE GREMOLATA

- 1½–2 cups fresh parsley sprigs, coarsely chopped
- Zest of 1 small lemon
- 3½–4 tablespoons coarsely grated fresh horseradish

FOR THE VEGETABLES

- 1 pound assorted small potatoes, such as colorful fingerlings or small red potatoes
- 1 pound mixed colored carrots, cut crosswise into 2-inch pieces
- 1 pound parsnips, peeled and cut into 2-inch pieces

1. For the brisket, preheat the oven to 350°F (180°C). Combine the mustard, thyme, salt, and pepper in a small bowl and mix well. Spread the mixture over the top of the brisket and place in an oval roasting pan (about 12- by 17-inches) or a wide 8-quart Dutch oven. (If the brisket is too big for your pan, it may be cut into two pieces.)

2. Heat the oil in a large skillet over medium-high heat. Add the onions and garlic and sauté for 5 minutes. Add the broth and wine and bring to a boil. Reduce the heat and simmer for 5 minutes. Pour over the brisket and place in the oven. Cook for 3 hours, turning the meat halfway through.

PREP TIME: 20 minutes

COOKING TIME: 4 hours

Serves 10–12

3. Meanwhile for the gremolata, toss together the parsley, lemon zest, and horseradish in a bowl.

4. For the vegetables, turn the meat again and add the potatoes, carrots, and parsnips to the pan. Cover and return to the oven. Bake for 40 to 45 minutes, until the brisket is fork-tender and the vegetables are tender. Transfer the brisket to a carving board and cover with aluminum foil. Use a slotted spoon to transfer the vegetables to a serving bowl. Cover with foil to keep warm.

5. Boil the juices remaining in the pan over high heat for about 10 minutes to reduce slightly. (You may need to use two burners.) Season to taste with salt and pepper.

6. If desired, cut off and refrigerate 1 pound of the brisket for the Waseda Farms Leftover Brisket Chili recipe (page 58). To serve, carve the meat thinly across the grain. Transfer the meat to a large platter. Spoon the vegetables over the meat and spoon half of the juices over all. Top with the gremolata and serve with extra juices on the side.

LEFTOVER BRISKET CHILI

I TRY TO ROAST AND FREEZE AS MANY EXTRA TOMATOES FROM THE SUMMER AS POSSIBLE
so I'll have some on hand for the winter to make brisket chili like this. Just thaw and purée when ready to cook. When tomatoes fall out of season, you may substitute a 28-ounce can of crushed tomatoes (San Marzano tomatoes are sweetest) with their juices for the fresh tomatoes in this hearty chili. I prefer this chili recipe over many others for its beefier base and sweeter notes, thanks to those summertime tomatoes.

INGREDIENTS

6 or 7   medium tomatoes

1   pound leftover brisket (page 56)

2   tablespoons vegetable oil or butter

1   large sweet onion, chopped

1   jalapeño, seeded and chopped

8   garlic cloves, minced

2   bay leaves (optional)

2   tablespoons chili powder

2   teaspoons ground cumin

2   cups cooked black or other beans (optional)

2   bell peppers, preferably 1 red and 1 green

4   ears corn on the cob

Salt and freshly ground black pepper

OPTIONAL GARNISHES:
chopped fresh cilantro or scallions, sour cream, shredded pepper jack or cheddar cheese, and hot pepper sauce

1. Preheat the broiler to high. Line a rimmed baking sheet with aluminum foil. Place the tomatoes on the baking sheet. Broil 4 inches from the heat source for 5 minutes. Turn the tomatoes with tongs and continue to broil for 4 to 5 minutes, until the tomato skins split and are beginning to brown. Remove from the broiler and let stand until cool enough to handle. Remove and discard the skin. Holding on to the edges of the foil, transfer the tomatoes with their juices to a food processor or blender. Pulse several times or blend just until the mixture is puréed but still slightly chunky.

2. Meanwhile, cut the brisket into ½-inch chunks. Heat the oil or melt the butter in a large saucepan over medium heat. Add the onion and sauté for 5 minutes. Add the jalapeño, garlic, and bay leaves, if using, and sauté for 3 minutes. Add the brisket, chili powder, and cumin, and sauté for 4 minutes, stirring occasionally. Stir in the tomatoes and beans, if using. Simmer for 30 minutes, stirring occasionally.

3. Meanwhile, dice the bell peppers and cut the kernels from the corncobs. Once the chili has simmered for 30 minutes, stir in the bell peppers and corn kernels. Continue to simmer for 25 minutes longer, stirring occasionally. Taste and add salt and pepper if needed. Discard the bay leaves, if using. If the chili is too thick, thin with a little water to the desired consistency. Ladle into shallow bowls and garnish as desired. Leftover chili will keep for 5 days in the refrigerator or up to 3 months in the freezer.

PREP TIME: 20 minutes

COOKING TIME: 55 minutes

Serves 8

HOMEMADE DILL-CURED SALMON *with Lemon Crème Fraîche and Accoutrements*

GROWING UP IN A JEWISH COMMUNITY, I WAS RAISED ON LOX. *Later, when I learned how to make gravlax from scratch in culinary school, it was a revelation. This recipe comes from that experience and pays homage to Door County's Scandinavian heritage. Traditionally, one makes gravlax with a ton of dill and serves it with* hovmästarsås, *a mustard-dill sauce. For this simpler, "Americanized" version, I like to pair the cured salmon with* Bavarian Dark Rye Bread (page 14), *lemon crème fraîche (recipe below), really great farm butter or Compound Butter (page 19), Pickled Red Onions (page 44), capers, and/or chopped dill. If you get your hands on some juniper berries (perhaps from Death's Door Spirits [see page 78] juniper harvest on Washington Island in September or from Harbor Tea & Spice Company in Sister Bay), throw some of those into the cure and even crush some up and sprinkle them over the top of the salmon for another herbal flavor note. If you go that route, you might pair this with a little Death's Door gin — or vodka, of course.*

1. To prepare the salmon, remove all visible small bones with needle-nose pliers (you can also ask the fishmonger to help you with this).

2. Mix together the salt, sugar, pepper, and juniper berries, if using, in a small bowl. Sprinkle half of the spice mixture in the bottom of a 9- by 12-inch glass dish, and then layer half of the dill over the spices. Place the salmon fillet skin-side down in the pan. Sprinkle the remaining salt mixture and three-quarters of the remaining dill over the top and press lightly into the salmon. Cover the pan tightly with plastic wrap and refrigerate for 3 to 4 days, flipping the salmon every other day.

3. To make the lemon crème fraîche before serving the salmon, whisk together the crème fraîche, lemon zest, and lemon juice in a small bowl. Cover and refrigerate.

4. To serve, rinse the salmon under cold water. Pat dry with paper towels. Using a very sharp knife, slice the salmon on a slight bias away from the skin into very thin slices. Sprinkle with the remaining chopped dill and serve with the lemon crème fraîche.

FOR THE SALMON

- 1 (2-pound) salmon fillet, with skin
- 3 tablespoons salt
- 2 tablespoons sugar
- 1 tablespoon freshly ground black pepper
- 2 tablespoons juniper berries, coarsely cracked (optional)
- 1 bunch fresh dill, chopped

FOR THE LEMON CRÈME FRAÎCHE

- 1 cup crème fraîche
  Grated zest of 1 lemon
- ¼ teaspoon fresh lemon juice

PREP TIME: 5 minutes

CURING TIME: 3–4 days

Serves 10–15

FISHING IN LAKE MICHIGAN

Native Americans first fished in the waters of the Great Lakes, catching whitefish and other species, well before other populations arrived. In the early 1800s, Scandinavian settlers caught on (literally) and started fishing for whitefish as well, helping develop some of the first commercial fisheries in the area. Today, tribal fisheries subsidized by the government and independent commercial fisheries catch a combined total of roughly 1 million pounds of whitefish a year.

But pollution, environmental degradation, overfishing, and invasive species like zebra and quagga mussels and Asian carp have threatened the lake fish population over the years, drastically reducing trout and salmon populations. Fortunately, whitefish and some other types of fish have again thrived in the cold, deep waters of Lake Michigan and Lake Huron, thanks to important new regulations that prevent overfishing and encourage more sustainable methods that reduce bycatch. For example, fishing for whitefish in particular must stop at the end of October in order to allow the fish to spawn and naturally repopulate.

Several associations and organizations remain dedicated to helping protect and preserve the Great Lakes and Lake Michigan, including Freshwater Future, the Alliance for the Great Lakes, and Eat Wisconsin Fish (University of Wisconsin). Much research goes into determining which fish and how many of them can be harvested from the lakes in order to preserve species. Commercial fisheries represent the most important preservationists because of their commitment to protecting endangered species. As consumers, we also play a role in this preservation when we buy their products. While the numbers for certain species have dwindled, longtime fishing families in the region continue to do their part to both bring the fish to our plates and keep them alive for future generations.

TYPES OF FISH

BURBOT. A little-known delicacy, this eel-like fish had once been decimated by invasive sea lamprey, but thanks to restoration efforts, fisheries can again fish for it out of Lake Michigan. Despite low market demand for the fish, Ken Koyen of K. K. Fiske and The Granary on Washington Island have made burbot their specialty. Some describe burbot as "poor man's lobster" because of its hearty texture and mild, buttery taste when cooked properly and served with extra drawn butter for dipping.

CHINOOK SALMON. In the late 1960s, fisheries introduced Chinook salmon into the Great Lakes in a desperate effort to control alewife populations. You can still find the meaty, hearty fish in Lake Michigan as well as in the Manistee, Pere Marquette, and St. Joseph Rivers.

CHUB. Oily fish with high levels of omega-3 fatty acids, chubs are often brined and/or smoked before sold or eaten. Though stocks fluctuate because of their long gestation period, they usually repopulate after two or three years, offering a nearly constant source of smaller juvenile chubs, which taste great when smoked or panfried like sardines. They're also low in toxic PCB pollutants because of their low fat content, making them safer to eat. Bloater chubs, fished with gill nets, make up the bulk of the chub fishery in Lakes Michigan and Superior, but their availability can be spotty.

COHO SALMON. Like Chinook, coho salmon were introduced to Lake Michigan in the 1960s to help crack down on invasive species. In the spring, you'll find these salmon near the ports of St. Joseph and New Buffalo, but the bulk of coho are located in the Platte River, near Sleeping Bear Dunes farther north.

LAKE TROUT. An invasion of sea lamprey virtually destroyed populations of this late-maturing fish in all of the Great Lakes except for Lake Superior, which is currently the only lake to have a wild-caught commercial fishery for lake trout.

RAINBOW SMELT. Fisheries catch this soft-textured, oily fish introduced to the Great Lakes in the 1930s using gill nets close to shore as they migrate to spawn in rivers. Though the smelt population in Lake Michigan has dwindled in recent years, one trawl fishery in the Two Rivers area specializes in its catch. Smelts taste similar to sardines when panfried in whole form.

WALLEYE. Naturally resilient, this firm whitefish species recovered from a major population decline in the 1990s, but there is a need for more research on continued proper management. Currently, no commercial walleye fisheries exist in the Wisconsin part of Lake Michigan. Michigan tribal fishermen harvest some walleye using gill nets in Lake Huron where it meets with Lake Michigan, but the majority of walleye caught commercially in the Great Lakes come from the Canadian waters of Lake Erie. Scientists have been working on ways to restore the population.

YELLOW PERCH. Yellow perch, also known as lake perch, has a mild, sweet flavor with firm, flaky white flesh. The majority of U.S. perch comes from Lake Erie; however, some fisheries catch it in the waters of Green Bay, and some sustainable farms in Wisconsin raise the perch in outdoor or indoor aquaponic recirculating systems.

WHITEFISH CHOWDER

THE MIDWEST'S ANSWER TO NEW ENGLAND CLAM CHOWDER, *this soup has become a permanent fixture on many menus throughout Door County and even around Traverse City, where fisheries also catch whitefish. For this particular recipe, I paid homage to the chowder at The Cookery in Fish Creek, which has been run by the Skare family since 1977 and focuses on local Midwestern ingredients.*

The splash of hot sauce and Angostura bitters changes things up a bit with a citrusy kick. These add-ins are optional, however; the chowder tastes just as delicious on its own, especially when using fresh local whitefish.

INGREDIENTS

- 3 bacon strips, chopped
- 1 large onion, chopped
- ½ cup finely chopped celery
- ½ cup finely chopped carrots
- 1 garlic clove, minced
- 1¼ pounds Yukon gold potatoes
- 2 (8-ounce) bottles clam juice
- 2 bay leaves
- ¾ teaspoon salt
- ¼ teaspoon paprika or smoked paprika
- ¼ teaspoon cayenne pepper or freshly ground black pepper
- 1 cup heavy cream
- 1 pound skinless whitefish fillets, cut into 1½-inch pieces
- 2 dashes hot sauce, or as desired
- 2 dashes Angostura bitters, or as desired

1. Cook the bacon in a large saucepan or Dutch oven over medium heat until crisp. Use a slotted spoon to transfer the bacon to paper towels and set aside.

2. Add the onion, celery, and carrots to the bacon drippings. Sauté until the vegetables begin to soften, about 10 minutes. Add the garlic and cook until fragrant, about 1 minute. Meanwhile, the peel the potatoes and cut into ½-inch pieces.

3. Stir the potatoes, clam juice, bay leaves, salt, paprika, and cayenne into the pan. Bring to a simmer over high heat. Reduce the heat to medium, cover, and simmer until the potatoes are almost tender, about 10 minutes.

4. Stir in the cream and heat through. Stir in the fish and cook uncovered until the fish is opaque, about 8 minutes (do not boil or the soup may curdle). Ladle into soup bowls and top with hot sauce and bitters, if desired. Sprinkle the reserved bacon over the top.

PREP TIME: 20 minutes

COOKING TIME: 35 minutes

Serves 6

PARMESAN-GARLIC BREAD

VISIT MacREADY ARTISAN BREAD COMPANY IN EGG HARBOR *for the amazing fresh-baked breads suitable for this and other recipes in this book. Their Italian semolina bread works particularly well for this dish, but of course you can use any fresh Italian or French bread.*

1. Preheat the oven to 350°F (180°C).

2. Slice the bread into ½-inch-thick slices without slicing all the way through, so the slices fan out. If the bread is round, cut the loaf in half and then slice into ½-inch slices, again not all the way through. Place the bread on a large rimmed baking sheet.

3. Combine the butter, oil, and garlic in a small bowl; spread evenly over and in between slices of the bread. Bake for 10 minutes or until golden brown and heated through. Top with the Parmesan and bake for 5 minutes longer. Slice through bread fully to separate the pieces.

INGREDIENTS

- 1 (8-ounce) loaf Italian or French bread
- 4 tablespoons unsalted butter, softened
- 1 tablespoon extra-virgin olive oil
- 4 garlic cloves, minced
- ¼–½ cup freshly grated Parmesan cheese

PREP TIME: 15 minutes

BAKING TIME: 20 minutes

Serves 6–8

SMOKED TROUT SPREAD

WITH TROUT POPULATIONS IN THE GREAT LAKES *dwindling over the years, most lake trout now comes from Canada and sometimes Lake Superior. However, local smokehouses like Charlie's Smokehouse in Ellison Bay and Schwartz Fish Company in Sturgeon Bay still do their part to make that fish even more delicious. Maple syrup helps balance out the smokiness in this spread, which tastes delicious on grilled bread or even buttery crackers.*

INGREDIENTS

- 2 tablespoons extra-virgin olive oil
- ¼ cup minced shallot or sweet onion
- 2 garlic cloves, minced
- 8 ounces skinless, boneless smoked trout, broken into large chunks
- 1 teaspoon maple syrup
- ¼ teaspoon red pepper flakes
- ⅔ cup crème fraîche or sour cream
- 1 teaspoon finely grated lemon zest
- Grilled or toasted thinly sliced country bread, for serving
- Watercress, for serving

1. Heat the oil in a large skillet. Add the shallot and garlic and cook over medium heat, stirring occasionally, until softened, 3 to 4 minutes. Stir in the trout, maple syrup, and pepper flakes, and cook until the fish is heated through, about 1 minute. Transfer to a food processor and let cool completely. Cover and pulse until coarsely chopped. Add the crème fraîche and lemon zest. Cover and pulse until well combined.

2. Transfer to a serving dish, cover, and refrigerate until chilled, about 30 minutes. Serve with grilled bread and watercress. The spread may be made ahead and refrigerated overnight.

PREP TIME: 10 minutes

COOKING TIME: 10 minutes

CHILLING TIME: 30 minutes

Serves 8

SWEDISH PANCAKES

with Lingonberries

I REMEMBER LOADING UP *on Al Johnson's lingonberry-covered Swedish pancakes and Swedish Meatballs (page 69) with my family as far back as when I was just 5 years old. This recipe was inspired by those memorable meals, even if we had to wait for over an hour to enjoy them. If you can't find lingonberries, substitute sliced fresh strawberries or mixed berries.*

1. Combine the eggs and ½ cup of the milk in a large bowl. Whisk until well combined. Add the flour and whisk until the batter is thick. Add the remaining 1¼ cups milk, the butter, vanilla, cardamom (if desired), and salt. Whisk until the batter is smooth. (The batter will be thin.) At this point, the batter may be covered and refrigerated for up to 2 hours before cooking.

2. Preheat the oven to 200°F (95°C). Heat a 10-inch non-stick skillet over medium heat until hot. Use a measuring cup to spoon ¼ cupful of the batter into the hot skillet. Lift the skillet and rotate so that the batter evenly coats the bottom of the skillet. Cook until the pancake is golden brown, about 1 minute per side. Place on an ovenproof plate and keep warm in the oven while making the remaining pancakes.

3. To serve, fold each warm pancake into quarters and arrange on serving plates. Serve immediately with lingonberries. Sift confectioners' sugar over the top, if desired.

INGREDIENTS

- 3 eggs
- 1¾ cups whole milk
- 1 cup plus 2 tablespoons unbleached all-purpose flour
- 4 tablespoons unsalted butter, melted and cooled
- 1 teaspoon vanilla extract
- ½ teaspoon ground cardamom (optional)
- ¼ teaspoon salt
- Bottled lingonberries or lingonberry jam, for serving
- Confectioners' sugar, for serving (optional)

PREP TIME: 15 minutes

COOKING TIME: 15 minutes

Makes 12–15 pancakes

Al Johnson's
Swedish Restaurant
SISTER BAY, WISCONSIN

A TRIP TO DOOR COUNTY MUST INCLUDE a visit to see the goats at Al Johnson's Swedish restaurant in Sister Bay. The tufted-haired, goatee-sporting billy goats perched on the green, grassy roof of the restaurant have marked the memories of all Door County residents and visitors alike. Opened over 65 years ago by Al Johnson and now with sons Rolf and Lars Johnson and daughter Annika continuing the legacy, the landmark eatery — decorated with red and white patterned linens and woodcarvings — has become a respite for locals and many travelers, welcoming them with a wood-carved *Välkommen* sign above the main doorway. Fill up on Swedish pancakes and meatballs, and then shop for Swedish clogs, houseware items, and decorative trinkets in the attached store. Most recently, Al Johnson's has extended its space to include an indoor/outdoor bar next door, with extra grass for the goats to roam closer to ground level.

SWEDISH MEATBALLS

THESE SPICE-FORWARD LITTLE NUGGETS *arrive tableside at Al Johnson's Swedish Restaurant steaming in their own pewter dish and blanketed with a rich and creamy gravy. This recipe was inspired by my memories of this popular dish. Serve as a main course or as a side to Swedish Pancakes (page 67).*

1. For the meatballs, preheat the oven to 375°F (190°C). Combine the beef, egg, breadcrumbs, milk, sugar, salt, pepper, nutmeg, cinnamon, ginger, and cloves, if using, in a large bowl and mix well. (The meat mixture will be soft.) Shape to form 12 balls. Place on a rimmed baking sheet and coat the meatballs with cooking spray. Bake for 12 to 14 minutes, until no longer pink in the center.

2. Meanwhile, for the sour cream gravy, melt the butter in a large skillet over medium heat. Add the flour; cook and stir until bubbly, about 1 minute. Add the broth, salt, pepper, and Worcestershire; cook, stirring frequently, until thickened and bubbly. Simmer for 1 minute. Turn off the heat and stir in the sour cream until well blended. Add the cooked meatballs to the sauce, and cook over medium-low heat until the meatballs are heated through, stirring occasionally. Serve over hot cooked noodles and garnish with parsley, if desired.

VARIATION: For appetizer meatballs, form the meat mixture into 1-inch balls, place on a rimmed baking sheet, coat with cooking spray, and bake in a 375°F (190°C) oven for 10 to 12 minutes, until no longer pink in the center. Heat in the prepared sauce and keep warm in a chafing dish over a low flame. Serve with frilly wooden picks.

FOR THE MEATBALLS

- 1 pound lean ground beef
- 1 egg
- 1 cup soft breadcrumbs (preferably rye or multigrain)
- 1/3 cup milk
- 1 teaspoon brown sugar
- 3/4 teaspoon salt
- 1/4 teaspoon freshly ground black pepper
- 1/4 teaspoon ground nutmeg
- 1/4 teaspoon ground cinnamon
- 1/8 teaspoon ground ginger (optional)
- 1/8 teaspoon ground cloves (optional)
- Nonstick cooking spray

FOR THE SOUR CREAM GRAVY

- 2 tablespoons butter
- 2 tablespoons unbleached all-purpose flour
- 1 cup reduced-sodium beef broth
- 1/2 teaspoon salt
- 1/4 teaspoon freshly ground black pepper
- 1 tablespoon Worcestershire sauce
- 1 cup full-fat sour cream

FOR SERVING

- Hot cooked noodles
- Chopped fresh parsley (optional)

PREP TIME: 20 minutes

COOKING TIME: 20 minutes

Serves 4

STANDING RIB ROAST

with Yorkshire Pudding and Horseradish Cream Sauce

THIS UNIQUE RECIPE REMAINS A TRADITION IN MY FAMILY. *It was inspired by the prime rib and creamy horseradish sauce you might find at places like The Mill in Sturgeon Bay and other supper clubs in Wisconsin on Saturday nights, or at The English Inn in Fish Creek. Slow-roasting the rib roast makes the meat turn out juicy and succulent, with seared, herb-crusted outer edges and a bright red, warm center, just like any well-cooked prime rib should be. Yorkshire pudding, a rich, English pan bread of sorts made using the prime rib drippings, does not reflect the traditions of the many Scandinavian and German immigrants who settled in Door County, but nevertheless, it makes for a special family meal or impressive entertaining supper if prime rib is on the menu.*

FOR THE ROAST

- 1 (6- to 7-pound) standing rib roast (3 ribs)
  Freshly ground black pepper

FOR THE HORSERADISH CREAM SAUCE

- 1 cup heavy cream
- ⅓ cup prepared horseradish
- 2 teaspoons balsamic vinegar
- 1 teaspoon dry mustard
- ⅛ teaspoon salt

FOR THE YORKSHIRE PUDDING

- 1 cup whole milk
- 2 eggs
- ½ teaspoon salt
- 1 cup unbleached all-purpose flour
- ¼ cup reserved drippings from roast or melted unsalted butter

1. For the roast, preheat the oven to 450°F (230°C). Sprinkle the roast all over with pepper. Place the roast, bones side down, in a shallow roasting pan. Place the pan in the oven and roast for 15 minutes. Reduce the oven temperature to 325°F (160°C) and continue roasting until the internal temperature reaches 120° to 130°F (49–54°C) for rare or 135° to 140°F (57–60°C) for medium doneness, about 18 minutes per pound. (The temperature of the roast will rise upon standing by 5 to 10 degrees.) Meanwhile, prepare the horseradish cream sauce and Yorkshire pudding ingredients.

PREP TIME: 20 minutes

COOKING TIME: 2 hours 35 minutes

CHILLING TIME (SAUCE): 1–8 hours

STANDING TIME: 30 minutes

Serves 6–8

2. For the horseradish cream sauce, whip the cream to stiff peaks using a handheld electric blender or a food processor. Fold in the horseradish, vinegar, dry mustard, and salt. Cover and chill for at least 1 hour or up to 8 hours before serving.

3. For the Yorkshire pudding, about 1 hour before the roast is done, process the milk, eggs, and salt in a food processor or blender for 15 seconds. Add the flour and process or blend for 2 minutes. Let the batter stand at room temperature for at least 30 minutes or up to 1 hour.

4. When the roast reaches the desired temperature, remove it from the pan, place on a carving board, and tent with aluminum foil. Let stand for at least 30 minutes for easier carving.

5. Raise the oven temperature to 450°F (230°C). Remove ¼ cup beef drippings from the pan and pour into an 8- or 9-inch square baking pan. Bake for 5 minutes. Process the pudding batter for 5 seconds to recombine and immediately pour the batter into the hot drippings, but do not stir. Return to the oven and bake for 20 minutes. Reduce the oven temperature to 350°F (180°C) and continue baking for 10 minutes longer or until puffed and deep golden brown.

6. Carve the roast and transfer the slices to warmed serving plates. Cut the Yorkshire pudding into squares. Serve with the roast beef and horseradish cream sauce.

SWISS CHEESE FONDUE

THIS IS AN ADAPTION OF A CLASSIC SWISS FONDUE *I once enjoyed during a cheese trip that included a stop at Emmi Roth-Kase's Wisconsin facility in Monroe. For some, the dish might signal memories of the ooey-gooey appetizer (or mini meal) at Alpine Resort's The Hof Restaurant in Egg Harbor, where the fondue comes with garlic cheese bread rather than just plain old chunks of French bread. You can find good-quality cheese for this dish at Schoolhouse Artisan Cheese in Ellison Bay (see page 31).*

INGREDIENTS

- ¾ cup dry white wine, such as Sauvignon Blanc
- 8 ounces Swiss cheese, shredded
- 4 ounces Gruyère cheese, shredded
- 1 tablespoon cornstarch
- 1 tablespoon kirsch liqueur
- ¼ teaspoon salt
- ⅛ teaspoon freshly ground white pepper (optional)
- 1 recipe Parmesan-Garlic Bread (page 65)
- 6 cups cut-up vegetables, such as asparagus, broccoli, and cauliflower, blanched

1. Heat the wine in a medium saucepan over medium-low heat until bubbly around the edges. Toss the cheeses with the cornstarch in a bowl, then gradually whisk the cheeses into the wine. Cook, whisking frequently, until the mixture is smooth, about 5 minutes. Remove from the heat and stir in the kirsch, salt, and pepper.

2. Transfer to a fondue pot and keep warm over an open flame. Serve with the garlic bread and vegetables, using long-handled skewers for dipping.

PREP TIME: 25 minutes

COOKING TIME: 5 minutes

Serves 4 as a main dish or
8 as an appetizer

MAPLE GRANOLA

with Nuts and Seeds

IT'S NICE TO HAVE SOME GRANOLA AROUND FOR A LIGHT BREAKFAST *or even a quick, portable snack for car rides. I used to make my granola with raw honey, but then I learned that baking it in the oven zaps the important antioxidants and nutrients from this natural superfood. So I switched to maple syrup, which, farmers tell me, is not negatively affected by heat — it's boiled in production, after all. Now I actually prefer the richer, earthier taste of the maple syrup, and if I want the nutrients from honey, I just drizzle a little over my bowl of maple granola, seasonal berries, and farm-fresh yogurt. Local maple syrup is pretty easy to find in Wisconsin or Michigan, where it's not uncommon to stumble upon a sugar shack from time to time. Flip to page 74 to learn more about how raw honey and maple syrup are made in the Midwest.*

1. Preheat the oven to 300°F (150°C).

2. Mix the maple syrup and butter together in a large bowl. Add the oats, both seeds, nuts, and salt, and fold together to combine.

3. Spread the granola mixture in an even layer on a rimmed baking sheet. Bake for about 40 minutes, stirring every 10 to 15 minutes, or until the granola is toasted. Remove from the oven, stir in the dried fruit, and bake for 10 minutes longer.

4. Remove the granola from the oven and let cool completely before serving or storing in an airtight container for up to 1 month.

INGREDIENTS

- ¾ cup maple syrup
- ½ cup (1 stick) butter or coconut oil, melted
- 3 cups old-fashioned rolled oats
- 1 cup raw hulled pumpkin seeds
- 1 cup raw hulled sunflower seeds
- 1¼ cups raw pecans, walnuts, and/or almonds, coarsely chopped
- Pinch of sea salt
- 1–2 cups dried fruit, such as cranberries, cherries, and/or blueberries

PREP TIME: 5 minutes

BAKING TIME: 50 minutes

Makes about 7 cups

Sweet Mountain Farm

WASHINGTON ISLAND, WISCONSIN

BEES ARE FASCINATING, HIGHLY INTELLIGENT CREATURES that live in an orderly society. We're lucky to be able to enjoy the fruits of their labor, because they make more honey than they actually need (hence the term *busy bee*). It's up to the beekeeper, however, to make sure the bees have enough honey (aka food) to last them through cold, harsh winters and to sustain the development of new bees from the queen bee in the hive.

True artisan beekeepers like Sue Domkpe of Sweet Mountain Farm not only carefully maintain the health of their bees, but also strive to maintain the health properties of the honey itself by not over-filtering and heating the product. Raw honey, when filtered only to remove extra honeycomb but never heated past 110°F (43°C), contains many natural antioxidants and minerals that, in addition to their nutritional benefits, contribute to the food's value as a medicine; topical application of raw honey can even heal burns and other abrasions and fade scars.

The other fascinating thing about honey is the terroir it has, just like wine, cheeses, and crops. The taste and aroma of honeys vary based on what the bees pollinate. The flavor may even change during the season within one hive, as bees pollinate whatever plants are in season around them.

Washington Island's cold, harsh winters can be too much for some bees, so Domkpe has turned to Russian bees, which can withstand the freezing temperatures. These bees also have two queens per hive, something no other type of bee has and which dramatically increases their honey production. At their peak, 140 hives can produce about 2,000 pounds of honey a year.

Domkpe's bees also favor the wild lavender and other flowers and plants on the island, which gives her honey a highly aromatic and uniquely floral profile. By spreading her hives out across four locations, she enables her bees to pollinate everything on Washington Island, including the sugar maple and basswood trees.

Those sugar maple trees also produce sap, which Domkpe uses to make small batches of maple syrup during the winter when the honeybees are dormant. She gathers the sap with buckets and runs it through a wood-fired evaporator to boil off the water. Honey and maple syrup make great additions to gift baskets. And both are delicious in granola (page 73). Purchase Domkpe's honey and maple syrup at The Danish Mill on Washington Island, on her farm, or online.

Cherry-Chocolate OATMEAL COOKIES

ONE OF THE BEST COOKIES I EVER HAD *came from the little blue landmark house that is Krista Olson and Don Jervis's Town Hall Bakery in Jacksonport, Wisconsin. This recipe is my best attempt to re-create that delicious, giant buttery oatmeal cookie spiked with dried Door County cherries, but with my own twist of white and dark chocolate chips. Store the cookies in an airtight container at room temperature, or freeze for up to 3 months.*

1. Preheat the oven to 350°F (180°C). Beat together the butter and both sugars in the large bowl of an electric mixer until light and fluffy. Add the egg and vanilla and beat until well blended. In a small bowl, combine the flour, baking soda, cinnamon, and salt, mixing well. Add to the mixer and beat until the dough is well blended. Add the cherries, chocolate chips, and walnuts, if using, and beat for 30 seconds.

2. Drop the batter by scant ¼ cupfuls onto ungreased baking sheets 3 inches apart. Bake for 12 to 13 minutes, until the cookies are golden brown. Let stand on the baking sheets for 2 minutes, and then transfer to wire racks to cool completely.

INGREDIENTS

- 1¼ cups (2¼ sticks) unsalted butter, softened
- ¾ cup firmly packed light brown sugar
- ½ cup granulated sugar
- 1 egg
- 2 teaspoons vanilla extract
- 1½ cups unbleached all-purpose flour
- 1 teaspoon baking soda
- 1 teaspoon ground cinnamon
- ½ teaspoon salt
- 3 cups quick-cooking or old-fashioned oats
- 1 cup dried tart cherries
- 1 cup white chocolate chips or semisweet chocolate chips
- ¾ cup chopped walnuts (optional)

PREP TIME: 20 minutes

BAKING TIME: 13 minutes

Makes about 24 cookies

Death's Door Spirits

MIDDLETON, WISCONSIN

WAVES SEVERAL FEET HIGH CRISSCROSS BACK AND FORTH, splashing up against boats doing their best to cross the 6-mile-wide strait where the waters of Lake Michigan and Green Bay clash. If you've ever taken the Island Clipper ferry from Gills Rock in Door County to Washington Island, you've seen the uniquely choppy waters of Death's Door. They don't call it that for nothing; for centuries, the treacherous waters have tested sailors and fishermen. Many lost their lives. Nowadays, the sturdy passenger ferries (and their captains) are strong and skilled enough to bring us — and our cars — safely to Washington Island.

Death's Door Spirits founder Brian Ellison first worked with wheat growers on Washington Island to produce Capital Brewery's Island Wheat Ale, but he wondered what else he could do with the surplus wheat, which today comes from about 1,000 acres. That led to vodka, with its mildly sweet and aromatic scent, and later to gin and white whiskey made from the same hard winter grain. Death's Door's highly floral gin also uses the juniper berries that grow on the island; in fact, the distillery's annual juniper harvest in September has become a regular event for bartenders, cocktail artists, chefs, and other curious folk nationwide. Death's Door Spirits also donates a portion of its revenue to Great Lakes causes that support the health of the waters.

DEATH'S DOOR CAIPIROSKA

THE CAIPIRINHA, BRAZIL'S MOST POPULAR COCKTAIL, *is made from cachaça (a sugarcane liquor), sugar, and lime. This recipe swaps in vodka — in this case, the Death's Door spirit made from wheat grown on Washington Island. Rosemary sprigs balance out the sweetness and add an extra herbal note to the already fragrant vodka.*

1. For the brown sugar simple syrup, place the brown sugar and water in a small saucepan and heat over medium heat until dissolved, stirring occasionally. Pour into a glass or other container and refrigerate until cool. The syrup will keep in the refrigerator for up to 3 months.

2. For the drink, place the lime quarters in the bottom of a mixing glass, add ¾ ounce of the brown sugar simple syrup, and muddle using a muddler or wooden spoon. Add the vodka and several ice cubes, and lightly stir. Strain into a martini glass. Garnish with a fresh rosemary sprig.

FOR THE BROWN SUGAR SIMPLE SYRUP

- 1 cup firmly packed light brown sugar
- 1 cup water

FOR THE DRINK

- ½ lime, quartered
- 2 ounces Death's Door vodka
  Ice cubes
- 1 fresh rosemary sprigs, for garnish

PREP TIME: 10 minutes

Serves 1

ERICAN CLUB, KOHLER, WIS.

Chapter 2

SHEBOYGAN and KOHLER

WINTER IN WISCONSIN MAKES ME THINK OF THE CITY OF SHEBOYGAN and its village to the west, Kohler, which boasts the five-star resort The American Club. Though The American Club sees plenty of loyal visitors year-round, most of my many childhood memories stem from trips there during the winter holiday season.

To this day, the resort conjures up images of gently falling snow, cross-country skiing, long hikes warmed by mugs of beer cheese soup, cozy lunches at River Wildlife, and a little reading time by the fireplace back in the Club's Lincoln Room. During the cooler months, you'll often see a picturesque horse-drawn carriage parked in front of the Club's awning-covered front doors, the bells on the horses' manes ringing as they take off to give sightseers a ride around town.

In the summertime, more beaches and resorts open up along the Sheboygan shores, perfumed with the smell of grilling Sheboygan bratwurst. And all year round, the city draws hungry patrons looking for classic German fare, or a fine meal of handmade pasta at the acclaimed Trattoria Stefano. Of course, a visit to the area wouldn't be complete without a stop to see the fancy tubs and bathrooms at the iconic Kohler museum.

Beer-Braised

BRATWURST AND ONIONS

BRATWURSTS IN WISCONSIN ARE SO MUCH MORE THAN JUST GERMAN SAUSAGES.
Aside from cheese, they're the signature food of the state, and people have strong beliefs about how they should be prepared. For this recipe, I tried a combination of both braising in beer and grilling. If you're feeling ambitious, try making the brats yourself (page 84).

INGREDIENTS

1   (12-ounce) bottle German-style beer or light lager (such as New Glarus Spotted Cow)

2   tablespoons butter

1   large yellow onion, thinly sliced

4   pork bratwurst links

4   bratwurst buns

2   tablespoons grainy mustard

    Sauerkraut, for serving (optional)

1. To cook on a grill: Prepare a gas or charcoal grill for medium-heat grilling. Place the beer, butter, and onions in a heavy-duty foil pan, set on the grill grate, and bring to a simmer. Nestle in the bratwurst and simmer, covered, until the onions are tender and the bratwurst reaches 160°F (71°C), about 15 minutes. Remove the bratwurst from the pan.

2. Grill the bratwurst on the grill grate until browned on both sides, turning once, about 4 minutes. Grill the buns during the last 1 to 2 minutes to toast them lightly.

3. To cook on the stovetop: Melt the butter in a large skillet over medium heat. Add the onions and cook until just caramelized, about 10 minutes. Pour in the beer and bring to a simmer. Nestle in the bratwurst, cover, and continue to simmer until the bratwurst reaches 160°F (71°C). Remove the bratwurst. Increase the heat to high and simmer the beer and onions until most of the liquid is absorbed and the sauce has a syrupy consistency, about 5 minutes longer. Finish bratwurst by grilling them on an outdoor grill or cast iron grill pan over medium heat until browned, turning once, about 4 minutes. Toast the buns lightly, either under the broiler or in a ridged stovetop grill pan.

4. To serve, spread the buns lightly with mustard. Place the bratwurst in the buns, and top with the onions and the sauerkraut, if desired. If not serving right away, return the grilled bratwurst to the pan with the beer to keep warm.

PREP TIME: 3 minutes

COOKING TIME: 15 minutes

Serves 4

Homemade Sheboygan-Style
BRATWURST

YOU'LL OFTEN SEE CHEF DAVE SWANSON GRILLING HIS HOMEMADE BRATS *outside his restaurant Braise (see page 114) for a quick, alfresco or to-go lunch in the summertime. Chilling the meat, fat, and grinder components prevents smearing, he stresses. This recipe requires a stand mixer with meat-grinding attachments and a kitchen scale; I left some of the measurements in the grams Swanson provided to ensure greater accuracy.*

INGREDIENTS

- 3 pounds pork butt, cut into ¾-inch cubes
- 1 pound veal shoulder, trimmed and cut into ¾-inch cubes
- 1 pound pork fatback, cut into ¾-inch cubes
- 40 grams kosher salt

- 6 grams freshly ground white pepper
- 5 grams ground ginger
- 5 grams ground nutmeg
- 1 16-inch-long natural casing
- 2 eggs
- 1 cup heavy cream

1. Thoroughly chill the meat, fatback, and all components of a standing electric mixer, including the bowl and meat grinder attachment, before preparing the bratwurst.

2. Fit the mixer with the grinder attachment, and grind the pork and veal, alternating between pieces, twice on the medium setting. Add the fatback and grind again.

3. Add the salt, pepper, ginger, and nutmeg to the bowl and, with clean hands, gently mix until just combined, but do not overmix. Cover and refrigerate for 12 to 24 hours.

4. Thoroughly chill the bowl and paddle attachment of the stand mixer. Meanwhile, soak the casings in cold water for 20 minutes. Using the mixer with the paddle attachment, mix the refrigerated meat blend on low speed until the fat is evenly dispersed, 2 to 3 minutes. Add the eggs and cream, and mix for 1 minute longer.

PREP TIME: 45 minutes

CHILLING TIME: 12–24 hours, plus 30 minutes

COOKING TIME: 15 minutes

Makes 4 links

5. Chill the sausage stuffer components of the mixer. Attach the stuffer to the mixer and slide the casing onto the tube. Put the meat mixture into the stuffer and set to low speed, pushing the mixture until it comes through the stuffer. Stop and tie off the end of the casing into a knot. Return to stuffing, extruding the meat into the casing to tightly pack the casing with the meat.

6. Gently twist the sausage into 4-inch links. Cut apart or leave in a string, and refrigerate for at least 30 minutes or up to 2 days, or until ready to cook. You can also freeze the fresh sausage in resealable plastic bags.

7. The bratwursts are ready for use in the Beer-Braised Bratwurst and Onions (page 82). Or you may simply grill them as is. You can also poach the brats in simmering water until the internal temperature reaches 160°F (71°C), 12 to 15 minutes, before grilling to brown on all sides.

TANGY POTATO SALAD

THIS IS ONE OF MY FAMILY'S FAVORITE SIDE DISHES *when we're grilling brats come summertime. The lemon juice and crème fraîche or sour cream brighten up the traditional salad and give it a little extra tang. Tossing the potatoes with the lemon juice before adding the mayonnaise and crème fraîche helps prevent the creamy sauce from "breaking" because of the acid, plus it helps evenly flavor the potatoes. I like to add the salt to the water so it infuses the potatoes evenly and doesn't cover up the other flavors added later. Sometimes I'll also throw in some cooked green beans if they're in season. In the spring, garlic scapes make a delicious addition to this mix, but they're strong, so a little goes a long way.*

INGREDIENTS

3	pounds new potatoes
	Salt
2	tablespoons fresh lemon juice
1 or 2	celery stalks, thinly sliced
2	scallions, thinly sliced
¼	cup thinly sliced fresh chives, plus more for garnish (optional)
2	tablespoons chopped fresh thyme leaves
1	cup good-quality or Homemade Mayonnaise (page 87)
½	cup crème fraîche or sour cream
3	tablespoons stone-ground mustard
¼	teaspoon freshly ground black pepper
¼	teaspoon paprika

1. Place the potatoes in a large pot of heavily salted cold water and bring to a boil over high heat. Reduce to a gentle boil and cook until tender when pierced with a knife, 20 to 25 minutes. Drain and allow to cool. When cool enough to handle, slice the potatoes into ½-inch pieces. Discard any skin that comes off the potatoes. Toss the potato slices with the lemon juice and refrigerate or allow to cool to room temperature, about 30 minutes.

2. Combine the celery, scallions, chives, thyme, mayonnaise, crème fraîche, mustard, pepper, and paprika in a large bowl. Add the potato slices and, using a rubber spatula, gently fold them in the mayonnaise mixture to coat. Refrigerate for at least 1 hour or up to 24 hours. Serve chilled, with extra chives sprinkled on top if desired.

PREP TIME: 30 minutes

CHILLING TIME: 1 hour 30 minutes

Serves 6–8

HOMEMADE MAYONNAISE

MAYONNAISE IS EASY TO MAKE YOURSELF, *and there's nothing like this silky, rich DIY condiment, especially when used in salads like my Tangy Potato Salad (page 86). Squeamish about using raw eggs? Use the freshest farm-raised egg you can find and take comfort in the research that shows eggs — especially those from clean, well-maintained coops with sanitary conditions and well-treated chickens — rarely contain harmful bacteria. If you're especially concerned or will be feeding those with weak immune systems, use pasteurized eggs.*

1. Add the egg yolk, lemon juice, mustard, and salt to a food processor or blender. Pulse to blend. Add the oil in a thin steady stream, processing until smooth and creamy.

2. Alternatively, to make the mayonnaise by hand, whisk together the egg yolk, lemon juice, mustard, and salt in a large bowl until blended. While constantly and vigorously whisking with one hand, slowly pour in the oil, a few drops at a time, until the mixture thickens. You may set the bowl on a kitchen towel to keep it from moving while you whisk.

3. Cover and refrigerate the mayonnaise for up to 2 days.

INGREDIENTS

1 egg yolk, at room temperature

1 teaspoon fresh lemon juice

¼ teaspoon Dijon mustard

Pinch of sea salt

¾–1 cup sunflower, grape-seed, walnut, avocado, or olive oil

PREP TIME: 5 minutes

Makes about 1 cup

WURST SOUP

with Homemade Herb-Parmesan Croutons

HAVE LEFTOVER BRATS? TRY THIS SOUP. *Even though it's super simple, use the best vegetables you can find. There's nothing like sweet Wisconsin carrots and onions in the fall and winter, and the freshness will show in the end result.*

FOR THE SOUP

4	tablespoons butter
1	pound smoked bratwurst, cut into bite-size pieces
2	medium onions, diced
2	carrots, peeled and thinly sliced
1	cup thinly sliced celery
1	tablespoon fennel seeds
1	tablespoon smoked paprika or hot paprika
5	cups reduced-sodium beef broth

FOR THE CROUTONS

¼	cup finely grated Parmesan cheese
1	garlic clove, minced
2	tablespoons chopped fresh thyme or 1 teaspoon dried
2	tablespoons chopped fresh rosemary
1	teaspoon dried oregano
1	teaspoon dried basil
½	teaspoon freshly ground black pepper, plus more as needed
¾	cup extra-virgin olive oil
1	loaf Italian bread or day-old baguette, cut into ¾-inch cubes
	Sour cream, for serving

PREP TIME: 5 minutes

COOK TIME: 45 minutes to 1 hour

Serves 6–8

1. For the soup, melt 2 tablespoons of the butter in a large saucepan over medium heat. Brown the bratwurst on all sides. Remove and set aside. Melt the remaining 2 tablespoons butter in the pan and add the onions, carrots, and celery. Sauté until the onions are soft and translucent.

2. Add the fennel seeds and paprika, and stir and toast, about 1 minute. Add the bratwurst and broth and simmer over medium-low heat until the vegetables are tender, 30 to 45 minutes.

3. Preheat the oven to 400°F (200°C). Line a baking sheet with aluminum foil.

4. For the croutons, whisk together the Parmesan, garlic, thyme, rosemary, oregano, basil, pepper, and oil in a large bowl. Add the bread cubes and toss to coat. Spread the bread cubes on the baking sheet and bake for about 20 minutes, until golden, stirring once. This makes more croutons than you need for the soup. The extra croutons will keep in an airtight container or resealable plastic bag in the refrigerator for about 1 week, or longer in the freezer.

5. Divide the soup among bowls and serve hot with the croutons and a dollop of sour cream.

BEER CHEESE SOUP

THIS RECIPE DRAWS INSPIRATIONS FROM A CREAMY, TANGY SOUP *I enjoyed at the Horse and Plow tavern in The American Club (see page 94). Going to the American Club and eating this soup was an annual holiday-time tradition when I was a child. I remember coming inside after playing in the snow or skating on the ice and warming up with a steaming cup of this soup (good thing that alcohol cooks off!) loaded with crunchy croutons. Avoid buying packages of preshredded cheese for this soup because the cheese is often laced with potato starch to prevent caking, and this can make the soup grainy. It also hinders the cheese's melting capability. Serving a larger group? This recipe is easily doubled.*

NOTE: *If you like, make your favorite grilled cheese sandwich, let it cool, and cut it into small squares to use as croutons.*

1. Melt the butter in a medium saucepan over medium heat. Add the flour and cook for 1 minute, whisking constantly. Whisk in the milk, broth, beer, Worcestershire, and cayenne. Bring to a boil over high heat, stirring occasionally. Reduce the heat and simmer for 10 minutes, stirring occasionally.

2. Remove the pan from the heat and stir in the cheese until completely melted. Ladle into soup bowls and add toppings as desired.

INGREDIENTS

- 4 tablespoons butter
- ⅓ cup unbleached all-purpose flour
- 1 cup whole milk or half-and-half
- 1 cup reduced-sodium chicken broth
- 1 (12-ounce) bottle pilsner-style beer, such as Lakefront Brewery's Klisch, New Glarus's Edel Pils, or even Milwaukee's Schlitz
- 1 tablespoon Worcestershire sauce
- ¼ teaspoon cayenne pepper (optional)
- 2 cups shredded extra-sharp cheddar cheese

OPTIONAL TOPPINGS: croutons or garlic croutons, popcorn, chopped fresh chives, cooked crumbled bacon, or a diced grilled cheese sandwich (see Note)

PREP TIME: 10 minutes

COOKING TIME: 15 minutes

Serves 4

DUCK BREAST *with Cranberry-Port Sauce*

MY FAMILY WENT TO THE AMERICAN CLUB'S EXCLUSIVE RIVER WILDLIFE *hunting club year after year for their pheasant, quail, duck, or other game fowl dish, which was always perfectly cooked and usually accompanied by a chutney or gastrique of sorts made with seasonal fruit and local vegetables. I developed this recipe with that dish in mind. When purchasing duck, I reach for duck from Maple Leaf Farms in Milford, Indiana (they distribute pretty widely throughout the Midwest). If using frozen duck, make sure to thoroughly thaw it before cooking. Serve this with Green Bean Casserole with Kale (page 96) or another seasonal vegetable.*

1. Use a sharp knife to score the skin of the duck breasts into a crisscross pattern (about 5 slashes each way), taking care not to cut into the meat. Turn the breasts over and season with the rosemary, salt, and pepper.

2. Heat a large skillet over medium heat until very hot. Add the duck, skin side down. Cook until the skin is well browned, 7 to 8 minutes. Turn the duck breasts over and continue to cook until the duck is medium-rare, about 5 minutes longer, or medium, about 7 minutes longer.

3. Meanwhile, while the duck is browning, transfer 1 tablespoon of the duck drippings to a medium skillet over medium heat. Add the shallots and sauté for 3 minutes. Add the water and sugar, mixing well. Stir in the cranberries and simmer for 5 minutes. Stir in the wine and simmer until the mixture thickens, about 3 minutes.

4. Transfer the duck to a carving board, tent with aluminum foil, and let stand for 3 minutes. If desired, store the duck drippings in the refrigerator for up to 2 weeks (or freeze for up to 6 months) for another use, such as sautéing potatoes. Carve the duck crosswise into thin slices and transfer to warmed serving plates. Spoon the cranberry sauce over the duck.

INGREDIENTS

- 4 duck breast halves (5–7 ounces each), with skin
- 1 teaspoon dried rosemary, crushed
- ¾ teaspoon coarse sea salt or kosher salt
- ¾ teaspoon freshly ground black pepper
- ⅓ cup chopped shallots or sweet onion
- ¼ cup water
- 3 tablespoons sugar
- 1 cup chopped fresh cranberries (see Note)
- ½ cup port wine

NOTE: *If fresh cranberries are not in season, purchase frozen cranberries and pulse in a food processor to coarsely chop them.*

PREP TIME: 10 minutes

COOKING TIME: 15 minutes

Serves 4

BEEF POT ROAST

with Seasonal Root Vegetables and Parsley Gremolata

THE ARRIVAL OF COOL WEATHER MEANS IT'S TIME TO REVISIT THE POT ROAST,
a perfect fall or winter dish. Most Midwesterners grew up on pot roast, but not everyone was lucky enough to have fresh root vegetables straight from a nearby farm. Nowadays, with all the farmers' markets and access to great local product, finding fresh local produce is much easier. I added the parsley gremolata to balance out the richness with a bright, citrusy, herby finish.

Have leftovers? Make a beef pot roast sandwich like the one we devour at Everyday People Café in Douglas with smoked Jack cheese; horseradish, mustard, and sour cream sauce; and Pickled Red Onions (page 44). Or, make a poutine like one you might see at the Duke of Devon pub in Sheboygan; top Belgian-Style Hand-Cut Fries (page 47) with the beef, juices, and a smattering of fresh cheese curds.

FOR THE POT ROAST AND VEGETABLES

- 1 boneless beef chuck roast (2¾–3 lb)
- 2 teaspoons dried thyme leaves
- 1 teaspoon coarse sea salt or kosher salt
- 1 teaspoon freshly ground black pepper
- 2 tablespoons olive oil
- 1 large onion, chopped
- 4 garlic cloves, minced
- 2 cups unsalted beef broth or stock
- ½ cup dry red wine

- 3 large parsnips, cut into 1-inch pieces
- 3 large carrots, cut into 1-inch pieces
- 3 medium turnips, peeled and cut into 1-inch chunks
- 2 small kohlrabi or 1 small celery root (celeriac), peeled and cut into 1-inch chunks

FOR THE PARSLEY GREMOLATA

- ½ cup chopped fresh parsley
- 2 garlic cloves, minced
- 2 teaspoons finely grated lemon zest

1. Preheat the oven to 325°F (160°C). For the pot roast, season the roast with the thyme, salt, and pepper. Heat the oil in a Dutch oven or stockpot over medium heat. Add the roast and brown well, about 4 minutes per side. Transfer to a plate. Add the onion and garlic to the drippings in the pot and sauté until softened, 6 to 8 minutes. Add the broth and wine, and bring to a boil. Return the roast to the pot. Cover, transfer to the oven, and braise for 1 hour 45 minutes.

PREP TIME: 10 minutes to start the roast

COOKING TIME: 3 hours

Serves 6–8

2. Transfer the roast to a plate and add the parsnips, carrots, turnips, and kohlrabi to the liquid in the Dutch oven. Place the roast over the vegetables, cover, and continue to braise in the oven for 50 minutes longer or until the beef and vegetables are tender.

3. Meanwhile, for the parsley gremolata, combine the parsley, garlic, and lemon zest, and refrigerate until serving time.

4. Transfer the cooked roast to a carving board and tent with aluminum foil. Use a slotted spoon to transfer the vegetables to a large serving bowl and cover with foil to keep warm. Bring the sauce in the pot to a boil over high heat. Reduce the heat and simmer until the sauce is slightly thickened, 8 to 10 minutes. Taste the sauce and add additional salt and pepper to taste. Carve the roast into ½-inch-thick slices and transfer to serving plates. Spoon some of the sauce over the roast and the rest over the vegetables. Top with the gremolata and serve immediately.

The American Club

KOHLER, WISCONSIN

THE AMERICAN CLUB, marked by its signature, Tudor Revival architecture, was built in 1918 by Walter J. Kohler to provide comfortable living quarters for single men who had come to this country from Europe and Russia to work in the Kohler Company factory. Founded in 1873 by Kohler's father, John Michael Kohler, the Kohler Company began by making the first American bathtubs and later expanded to plumbing products, furniture, cabinetry, tile, engines, and generators.

The Club, in addition to providing food (in the dining hall now called The Wisconsin Room) and housing, also assisted with learning English and achieving citizenship. According to the June 23, 1918, dedication, "The name, American Club, was decided upon as it was thought that, with high standards of living and clean healthful recreation, it would be a factor in inculcating in men of foreign antecedents a love for their adopted country." The Club's fine-dining restaurant, the Immigrant, also pays homage to this history.

In 1978, 60 years after it was dedicated, The American Club became part of the National Register of Historic Places. In 1981, after renovations to preserve the historical features, it was rededicated and opened as a five-star resort and spa. Today it boasts two fine-dining restaurants, a popular pub, and a full-service spa, as well as indoor and outdoor event spaces for grand weddings, conferences, and other large-scale events. At the same time, the surrounding village of Kohler continued to blossom thanks to that first group of immigrants from The American Club, who went on to become citizens, start families, and build the close-knit community that still exists today.

GREEN BEAN CASSEROLE

with Kale

THIS IS NOT YOUR TYPICAL CASSEROLE *with cream of mushroom soup, commercially fried onions, and green beans from a can. This clean, modern approach was adapted from a dish made by chef Paul Smitala of Black Wolf Run at The American Club. Fresh green beans and a sauce spiked with healthy kale freshen up the typically indulgent side dish.*

FOR THE BEANS AND SAUCE

- 1 pound green beans, trimmed and cut in half
- 3 cups kale leaves
- 1½ tablespoons butter
- 8 ounces cremini mushrooms, cut into ¼-inch pieces
- 1½ tablespoons unbleached all-purpose flour
- ⅔ cup reduced-sodium chicken or vegetable broth
- ⅓ cup heavy cream
- ¼ teaspoon salt
- ¼ teaspoon freshly ground black pepper
- ¼ teaspoon ground nutmeg

FOR THE ONION TOPPING

- 1 large sweet or yellow onion
- ¼ cup unbleached all-purpose flour
- ¼ teaspoon salt
- ¼ teaspoon freshly ground black pepper
- 1½ tablespoons grape-seed or other neutral oil, plus more as needed

1. For the beans and sauce, preheat the oven to 400°F (200°C). Bring a pot of water to a simmer and blanch the green beans until crisp-tender, about 5 minutes. Drain in a colander, return to the pot, and add cold water to cover. Set aside.

2. Bring a pot of water to a simmer and blanch the kale until just tender, 30 seconds to 1 minute. Drain, rinse with cold water, and thoroughly pat dry. Coarsely chop the kale and set aside.

PREP TIME: 35 minutes

COOKING TIME: 25 minutes

Serves 6

3. Melt the butter in a deep 10-inch, ovenproof skillet over medium heat. Add the mushrooms and sauté until they give up their juices, about 5 minutes. Sprinkle the flour over the mushrooms and sauté for 1 minute. Add the broth and cream, and cook, stirring frequently, until the sauce thickens, about 4 minutes.

4. Drain the green beans and stir them into the sauce along with the kale, salt, pepper, and nutmeg, and heat through. Transfer the pan to the oven and bake for 12 to 14 minutes, until bubbly.

5. For the onion topping, while the casserole is baking, peel the onion and cut in half through the core. Place cut sides down and cut crosswise into very thin strips. Dredge the onion pieces in a shallow bowl with the flour, salt, and pepper until evenly coated, and transfer to a plate.

6. Heat the oil in a large skillet over medium heat. Shake the excess flour off the onions and add them to the pan, working in batches as needed so as not to overcrowd the pan. Cook the onions until golden brown, flipping once, 1 to 2 minutes per side, adding more oil to the pan as needed. Transfer the onions to paper towels to drain. Top the casserole with the fried onions.

Wisconsin Ham and Swiss
BRUNCH STRATA

THIS RICH AND INDULGENT STRATA NEVER FAILS TO WARM US UP *on a cool fall or winter morning. Though this particular recipe was inspired by a recipe from the Wisconsin Milk Marketing Board, I've also seen similar stratas served at The American Club's elaborate Sunday brunch. Edelweiss Creamery makes a beautiful Swiss cheese, as does Roth Wisconsin (the artisan branch of Emmi Roth-Kase).*

INGREDIENTS

- 4 tablespoons butter, softened
- 1 tablespoon Dijon mustard
- 8 slices brioche bread or white bread
- 6 ounces Swiss cheese, thinly sliced (about 8 slices)
- 8 slices deli ham (such as Nueske's)
- 3 eggs
- 2 cups whole milk

1. Butter a 9-inch square glass baking dish. Combine the butter and mustard. Spread it evenly over one side of each of the bread slices. Top 4 slices of the bread with 1 slice cheese, 1 slices ham, and another slice of cheese. Close the sandwiches with the remaining 4 slices bread. Cut each sandwich into quarters. Arrange the sandwiches, pointed sides up, in the baking dish.

2. Beat the eggs in a medium bowl. Stir in the milk until well combined. Drizzle evenly over the sandwiches, coating all the bread. Cover with plastic wrap and refrigerate for at least 2 hours or up to overnight.

3. Preheat the oven to 350°F (180°C). Remove the plastic wrap and bake for 50 minutes or until puffed and golden brown. Re-cut into quarters and serve warm.

PREP TIME: 25 minutes

CHILLING TIME: 2 hours

BAKING TIME: 50 minutes

Serves 6

PEANUT BUTTER BITES

A LONG RIDE REQUIRES SNACKS LIKE THESE, *whether you're in your car or on your bike. These portable bites remind me of the ones my husband and I would snatch up at La Grange General Store in Whitewater, Wisconsin, after we spent a picturesque afternoon biking the trails in Kettle Moraine State Forest. We've also made these bites, frozen them, and packed them in our bags for a quick snack (they thaw out to the perfect temperature on the ride) while biking the trails through Sheboygan and farther north, in Door County's Peninsula State Park. You can also pack the bites in your beach bag if you're spending the day at Lake Michigan.*

1. Line a rimmed baking sheet with waxed paper. Combine the peanut butter, almond meal, dates, flaxseed, if using, and cinnamon in a food processor. Process until the mixture is well combined and forms a ball.

2. Roll the mixture into sixteen 1½-ounce balls. Roll the bites in the cocoa powder and/or the coconut flakes, if desired.

3. Place the bites on the baking sheet and freeze for 1 to 2 hours before transferring to a resealable plastic bag for longer storage.

INGREDIENTS

1½ cups peanut butter

1 cup almond meal flour

8 ounces Medjool dates, pitted

1 tablespoon ground flaxseed (optional)

1 teaspoon ground cinnamon, or more as desired

Unsweetened cocoa powder or cacao powder, for rolling (optional)

Unsweetened coconut flakes, for rolling (optional)

PREP TIME: 10 minutes

FREEZING TIME: 1–2 hours

Makes 16 (1½-inch) bites

Cheddar, Cherry, and Pistachio
CHEESE BALL

NOTHING SAYS A HOLIDAY PARTY IN THE MIDWEST LIKE A GIANT CHEESE BALL. *Am I right? This variation, which you should scoop up in generous heaps with sturdy crackers or apple slices, combines Wisconsin-made cream and cheddar cheeses. I prefer the artisan-style Hook's or Carr Valley, and I always grate the cheese myself. If I'm really feeling spunky, I might throw in some of Willi Lehner's bandaged cheddar (see page 33) for an extra dose of sharp richness, to be balanced out by the sweetness of the cherries and pistachios.*

INGREDIENTS

- 1 (8-ounce) package cream cheese, softened
- 2 cups shredded Wisconsin sharp cheddar cheese
- ⅓ cup dried cherries or dried cranberries
- ½ cup finely chopped lightly salted pistachios

  Crackers, for serving

  Red apple slices, for serving

1. Beat the cream cheese with a wooden spoon until smooth. Stir in the cheddar cheese and cherries, mixing well. Place the mixture on a large sheet of plastic wrap. Bring up the ends of the wrap over the cheese mixture and shape into a ball. Refrigerate the ball for at least 1 hour.

2. Remove the plastic wrap and roll the cheese ball in the nuts. Let stand at room temperature for at least 30 minutes before serving with crackers and apple slices.

PREP TIME: 20 minutes

CHILLING TIME: 1 hour

STANDING TIME: 30 minutes

Serves 12

SOFT PRETZELS

with Cheddar and Gouda Beer Sauce

HERE'S MY ATTEMPT TO EXPERIENCE THE HAPPINESS I FELT AS A CHILD *as my family and I hungrily tore apart pieces of chewy, warm pretzel at a German brewpub in Sheboygan, which has sadly since closed. We used the pretzel pieces to mop up a beer-laden cheese sauce not unlike the bowls of Beer Cheese Soup (page 89) we had already consumed that week at the Horse and Plow. For the Gouda, I like Marieke Gouda from Holland's Family Cheese.*

FOR THE PRETZELS

- 1½ cups warm water (120–130°F/49–54°C)
- 1 packet active dry yeast (not rapid rising)
- 1 tablespoon sugar
- 1 teaspoon fine salt
- 4 cups unbleached all-purpose flour, plus more for kneading
- 1 egg, beaten
- ½ teaspoon coarse sea salt or kosher salt

FOR THE SAUCE

- 1 tablespoon butter
- 1 tablespoon unbleached all-purpose flour
- ½ cup mild beer, such as wheat beer, blonde ale, or pilsner
- ¼ cup milk
- ¾ cup shredded sharp or extra-sharp cheddar cheese
- ¾ cup shredded smoked Gouda cheese
- 1 tablespoon grainy mustard

1. For the pretzels, combine the warm water and yeast in a large bowl, mixing until the yeast dissolves. Stir in the sugar and fine salt. Add the flour, 1 cup at a time, and mix thoroughly until the dough is thick and no longer sticky. Transfer the dough to a large floured surface and knead for 5 minutes, adding more flour if needed. Place in an oiled bowl, turn the dough over, and cover with plastic wrap. Let stand in a warm place for 50 minutes or until the dough has doubled in size.

PREP TIME: 20 minutes

RISING TIME: 50 minutes

COOKING TIME: 20 minutes

Makes 6 pretzels

2. Preheat the oven to 425°F (220°C). Line a large baking sheet with parchment paper. Punch the dough down and divide into 6 equal pieces. On a large floured surface, roll and stretch each piece of dough with your hands into a 30-inch length, holding the ends and slapping the middle of the rope on the counter as you stretch. Make a U shape, and holding the ends of the rope, cross them over each other and press onto the bottom of the U to form a pretzel shape. Place on the baking sheet. Brush the beaten egg heavily over the dough and sprinkle with the coarse salt. Bake the pretzels for 18 to 20 minutes, until deep golden brown. Let cool slightly on a wire rack.

3. Meanwhile, for the sauce, melt the butter in a small saucepan over medium heat. Whisk in the flour and cook for 1 minute. Gradually add the beer, whisking constantly. Gradually whisk in the milk. Gradually add the cheeses, whisking occasionally. Remove the sauce from the heat and stir in the mustard. Serve the warm pretzels with the sauce for dipping.

RAVINE DRIVE, LAKE PARK

Chapter 3

MILWAUKEE

BREW CITY HAS CHANGED DRAMATICALLY IN RECENT YEARS, with its influx of chefs, restaurateurs, and food artisans amid community developers intent on reviving urban culture. Once a center for beer and baseball, Milwaukee now draws all types of visitors, from Harley-Davidson riders congregating at the nation's first major motorcycle museum to food and drink enthusiasts in search of the best cheese curds and cocktails to artists gathering at Third Ward galleries and musicians and music lovers catching tunes at Summerfest.

Craft breweries have built up new followers alongside big-name breweries, while artisan cheese makers, chocolatiers, and coffee roasters have set up shop in the burgeoning Walker's Point neighborhood. The once blue collars of the town might have turned white, orange, pink, and everything in between, but don't be fooled — that old-school Midwestern sentiment still pervades.

CITY HALL

SOUVENIR OF
MILWAUKEE
"THE CITY BEAUTIFUL"

WISCONSIN

BEER-BATTERED CHEESE
CURDS *with Homemade Ranch Dip*

YOU CAN'T SET FOOT IN WISCONSIN WITHOUT SEEING FRIED CHEESE CURDS SOMEWHERE. *I've certainly had my share of these deep-fried delights all over the state, but the best I ever had were at Branded, a bar in Milwaukee's Iron Horse Hotel. The curds came out piping-hot in a basket charmingly lined with faux newspaper. As I dipped them in the accompanying homemade ranch dressing and sipped on locally brewed Lakefront Brewery beer, I was in heaven. This recipe is my best attempt to re-create that version, which used more of a light, tempura batter meant to put more emphasis on the very creamy, larger-than-normal cheese curds from nearby Clock Shadow Creamery (page 110), which is the curd of choice for Iron Horse.*

Regardless of which cheese curds you use (Renard's in Sturgeon Bay is another favorite), it's important to freeze them before frying; otherwise, they'll melt all over the place. I usually take day-old curds that have lost their "squeak" and place them, spaced apart (so they don't stick together), on a small lined sheet tray before freezing. Once frozen, I transfer them to a resealable plastic bag for longer-term storage. Also, you'll notice I don't call for salt in the batter; cheese curds are salty enough by their nature.

INGREDIENTS

Canola oil, for frying

FOR THE RANCH DIP

- 1 garlic clove, minced
- 1 teaspoon Worcestershire sauce
- ½ teaspoon white vinegar
- ¼ teaspoon kosher salt
- ½ teaspoon freshly ground black pepper
- ¼–½ teaspoon paprika
- ⅛ teaspoon cayenne pepper, or a dash of hot sauce
- ¼ cup finely chopped fresh parsley
- 1 tablespoon finely chopped fresh dill
- 2 tablespoons finely chopped fresh chives

- 1 cup good-quality mayonnaise (or Homemade Mayonnaise, page 87)
- ½ cup sour cream
- 2 tablespoons buttermilk, or as needed

FOR THE BATTER

- ½ cup unbleached all-purpose flour
- ¼ cup cornstarch
- 1 tablespoon baking powder
- 1 teaspoon baking soda
- 1 teaspoon kosher salt
- ½ teaspoon freshly ground black pepper
- ½ teaspoon garlic powder
- ½ teaspoon onion powder
- ½ teaspoon smoked paprika
- ¼ teaspoon cayenne pepper (optional)
- 1 cup Wisconsin light lager beer
- 2 (12-ounce) packages cheddar cheese curds (white, yellow, or a mix), frozen

PREP TIME: 15 minutes

COOKING TIME: 5–7 minutes

Serves 4–6

Recipe continues on page 108

1. Pour the oil into a large stockpot or Dutch oven to a depth of 3 inches and heat to 350°F (180°C).

2. For the ranch dip, combine the garlic, Worcestershire, and vinegar in a medium shallow bowl. Season with the salt, black pepper, paprika, and cayenne. Add the parsley, dill, and chives, and whisk to combine. Fold in the mayonnaise and sour cream to combine with the herbs and seasonings. Add the buttermilk to thin out the dip to the desired consistency.

3. For the batter, whisk together the flour, cornstarch, baking powder, baking soda, salt, black pepper, garlic powder, onion powder, paprika, and cayenne, if using, in a medium bowl. Pour in the beer and stir to combine until frothy.

4. Working in small batches, dip the curds into the batter, and using a slotted spoon, transfer to the oil. Fry the curds until golden brown, stirring occasionally to prevent sticking, 30 seconds to 1 minute. Using a slotted spoon or long-handled skimmer, transfer the curds to paper towels to drain. Serve hot with the ranch dip.

Wisconsin QUARK CHEESECAKE

WHEN I TRIED QUARK FOR THE FIRST TIME AT CLOCK SHADOW CREAMERY (*see page 110*), *it was unlike anything I had ever tasted. The flavor compares slightly to a whole-milk ricotta — the really good kind, imported from Italy — but tangier and more citrusy, perhaps like a yogurt cheese or farmers' cheese, although much creamier, smoother, and denser. Quark has its roots in Germany and northern Europe, where for centuries people have used the soft fermented white cheese (made without rennet) in everything from breakfast dishes to spaetzle and desserts. In cheesecake, quark makes the popular dessert more savory and rich than sickly sweet.*

If you can't find quark (Clock Shadow in Milwaukee is one supplier), you can substitute good-quality whole-milk ricotta mixed with cream cheese for more smoothness, though it won't be quite the same.

1. For the crust, preheat the oven to 325°F (160°C). Butter a 9-inch pie plate. Mix the graham crackers, granulated sugar, melted butter, and cinnamon in a large bowl until well blended. Spread the mixture evenly over the bottom and up the sides of the pie plate. Bake for 5 minutes. Remove from the oven and let stand on a wire rack while making the filling.

2. For the filling, beat the eggs with both sugars until light. Add the lemon zest and juice, vanilla, and salt, mixing well. Fold in the quark until fully combined. Pour the filling into the crust. Bake for 1 hour or until the center is set. Transfer to a wire rack and let cool fully. Cover and refrigerate until cold before serving.

FOR THE CRUST

- 8 ounces graham crackers, crushed
- 1⅓ cups granulated sugar
- ⅔ cup (10 tablespoons plus 2 teaspoons) unsalted butter, melted
- Ground cinnamon, as desired

FOR THE FILLING

- 3 eggs
- ½ cup granulated sugar
- ¼ cup firmly packed light brown sugar
- Zest and juice of ½ lemon, or ½ teaspoon almond extract
- ½ teaspoon vanilla extract
- ⅛ teaspoon salt
- 1 pound fresh quark cheese

PREP TIME: 25 minutes

BAKING TIME: 1 hour

CHILLING TIME: 1–2 hours

Serves 8

Clock Shadow Creamery

MILWAUKEE, WISCONSIN

MILWAUKEE-BORN-AND-RAISED CEDAR GROVE CHEESE FOUNDER Bob Wills founded Clock Shadow Creamery in April 2012 as one of Milwaukee's first small-scale urban cheese companies. "When we opened, there were more than 2,600 cheese factories in Wisconsin, but none in Milwaukee," Wills says.

The creamery has filled that niche by accommodating farmers and itinerant cheese makers who want to produce and market smaller batches of specialty artisan cheese varieties, from cow's milk cheese to sheep's milk and goat cheeses. The company even sources some milk from a small herd of cows at the Milwaukee County Zoo.

Located on the ground floor of a "green" building in the Walker's Point neighborhood, Clock Shadow regularly opens its door to Milwaukee residents and visitors alike who want to see and learn about artisan cheese making firsthand and understand the nutrient value of fresh dairy products sourced from local, sustainable small farms. The company gets its name from the iconic Allen-Bradley (Rockwell) clock tower just a few blocks north. Since opening shop in 2012, Clock Shadow Creamery has helped lead the way toward transforming Walker's Point, once a stretch of abandoned buildings and warehouses, into a new community of artisan food and beverage producers. Nearby, you'll find Anodyne Coffee, Milwaukee Brewing Company, Purple Door Ice Cream, Indulgence Chocolatiers, and more. Clock Shadow is most known for its cheese curds, which are some of the freshest, squeakiest curds I've ever had. Any curds not pressed into blocks of cheddar become those highly addictive nuggets of creamy, squeaky young cheese.

QUARK SOUFFLÉS

"WE'RE VERY PROUD OF OUR SOUFFLÉ," *said chef-owner Peter Sandroni of La Merenda when providing this recipe. The use of quark gives this version a rich, tangy taste. Soufflé is no easy dish to make, but if you have time and patience, the results make for a memorable dessert for a family meal or dinner party.*

Opened in 2007, La Merenda is a casual tapas restaurant and bar that has been a fixture in Milwaukee's Walker's Point neighborhood since well before the area's recent development. Sandroni has made it his mission to combine local foods with international flavors and techniques, so it's no surprise he's been working with Clock Shadow Creamery (located just two blocks away) since its inception.

1. Preheat the oven to 375°F (190°C). Melt the butter in a medium saucepan over medium heat. Stir in ¼ cup of the flour and cook, stirring constantly, for 1 to 2 minutes. Whisk in the half-and-half, cream, sugar, and vanilla bean seeds or extract. Bring to a simmer, then whisk in the cheese until melted. Remove from the heat and let stand for 10 minutes to cool.

2. Meanwhile, whip the egg whites to medium peaks. Whisk the egg yolks slowly into the cheese mixture. Gently fold the egg whites into the mixture.

3. Butter four 8-ounce soufflé molds or ramekins. Combine the cocoa powder and remaining 2 tablespoons flour, and sprinkle over the buttered molds. Turn the molds to coat the sides and bottom, and tap out any excess mixture.

4. Fill the molds three-quarters full with the cheese mixture. Arrange the molds in a shallow baking pan and carefully fill the pan with hot water to come halfway up the sides of the molds. Transfer the pan to the oven and bake for 50 to 60 minutes, until the soufflés are golden brown in color and a wooden pick inserted in the center comes out dry. Serve immediately.

INGREDIENTS

- 4 tablespoons unsalted butter
- ¼ cup plus 2 tablespoons unbleached all-purpose flour
- 1 cup half-and-half
- ¾ cup heavy cream
- ⅓ cup sugar
- ½ vanilla bean pod, split, seeds removed, or 1 teaspoon vanilla extract
- 5½ ounces fresh quark cheese
- 4 eggs, separated
- 2 tablespoons unsweetened cocoa powder

PREP TIME: 30 minutes

BAKING TIME: 50–60 minutes

Serves 4

Boone Brandy OLD-FASHIONED

THIS UNOFFICIAL STATE COCKTAIL *has been served at supper clubs statewide for many years as a sort of mascot. At Boone and Crockett bar in Milwaukee, craft cocktails take front and center attention, but the Wisconsin old-fashioned (always made with brandy, not whiskey) remains a familiar favorite. Owner John Revord maintains the traditional use of Korbel brandy and Angostura bitters, sometimes storing batches of the cocktail in charred oak barrels to introduce a smoky, aged taste. In place of a bright red maraschino cherry, he garnishes his old-fashioneds with a dark, slightly bitter Amarena cherry and an orange slice. If you can't find Amarena cherries, try authentic maraschino cherries imported from Italy (I prefer Luxardo brand).*

INGREDIENTS

- 2 ounces Korbel brandy or Old Forester bourbon
- 1 ounce simple syrup made with turbinado sugar
- 6 dashes Angostura bitters

  Ice cubes

  Amarena cherry, for garnish

  Orange slice, for garnish

Stir the brandy, simple syrup, and bitters together in a double old-fashioned glass, and add ice cubes. Garnish with an Amarena cherry and an orange slice.

PREP TIME: 5 minutes

Serves 1

ASPARAGUS SAUTÉ

with Green Garlic and Herbs

THE FIRST OF SPRING'S SWEET ASPARAGUS AND SPICY GREEN GARLIC *emerging from the earth elicit a sigh of relief from Midwestern farmers after a long stretch with snow-covered ground. Chef-owner Dave Swanson of Braise (see page 114) combines that bounty with fresh herbs from the restaurant's rooftop garden. This and the Green Garlic Custard (page 115) showcase the special taste of just-harvested spring produce.*

1. Trim off the ends of the asparagus, leaving 7-inch stalks. (Save the trimmings for soup.) Bring a pot of water to a simmer and blanch the asparagus for 2 minutes. Drain well.

2. Heat the oil in a large skillet over medium-high heat. Add the green garlic, asparagus, and butter. Sauté until the asparagus is crisp-tender, 6 to 8 minutes depending on the thickness of the stalks. Season with salt and pepper to taste and transfer to serving plates. Top with the herbs.

INGREDIENTS

- 1 pound fresh asparagus
- 1 tablespoon olive oil
- ½ cup thinly sliced green garlic or garlic scapes (white and green parts)
- 2 tablespoons butter

  Salt and freshly ground black pepper
- 2 tablespoons chopped fresh basil, thyme, rosemary, or a mix of all three

PREP TIME: 15 minutes

COOKING TIME: 8 minutes

Serves 4

Braise and RSA

MILWAUKEE, WISCONSIN

MILWAUKEE HAS SEEN A CULINARY RENAISSANCE in recent years, and Dave Swanson of Braise restaurant and cooking school has led the charge with his longtime support of local sustainable farms. He even grows his own herbs and vegetables in the restaurant's rooftop garden, which has a beehive for honey, too.

A former fine-dining chef who has earned nominations for Best Chef: Midwest, from the James Beard Foundation, Swanson started his mission with the school, founding Braise on the Go Traveling Culinary School in 2004. The restaurant came later, in December 2011, when Swanson found the perfect space in the burgeoning Walker's Point neighborhood to house both the cooking school and full-service dining: a conjoined 1907 brick building and 1940s former bowling alley.

One of my most memorable cooking classes (outside of going to culinary school) happened at Braise, when Swanson taught us how to make handmade tagliatelle using good-quality ingredients, our hands, a manual pasta roller, and some TLC. We tossed the toothsome noodles with an herb pistou we blended up using fresh basil from the rooftop garden, lemon

zest, good olive oil, and local Parmesan. The dish couldn't have been any simpler, yet it remains one of my most memorable lunches to this day, reminiscent of the lovely and light lunches I've enjoyed in Italy.

When he's not running the restaurant or cooking school, Swanson oversees a successful RSA (Restaurant-Supported Agriculture), providing Milwaukee-area restaurants with produce and other foods from a network of small local farms. Similar to a CSA, the RSA provides the same harvest to community restaurants. Each week, Swanson's team picks up the goods from different farmers, brings them back to the restaurant for cleaning and processing, and then delivers them to more than 100 restaurants as well as a small handful of Milwaukee residents who got on the list early, when the program first started.

GREEN GARLIC CUSTARD

SERVE THIS CREAMY AND UNIQUE CROWD-PLEASING APPETIZER *with toast points or crackers for dipping.*

1. Preheat the oven to 325°F (160°C). Purée the cream, milk, and green garlic in a blender until fairly smooth. Add the egg, egg yolks, and salt. Purée until well combined. Strain the mixture and discard the solids.

2. Butter a 6- by 9-inch earthenware dish or shallow casserole dish. Pour the egg mixture into the dish. Place the dish into a larger baking pan, and carefully add boiling water to the pan until the water reaches halfway up the sides of the dish.

3. Bake for 28 to 30 minutes, until the custard is firm around the edges but still jiggles in the center. Let cool completely on a wire rack. Refrigerate until chilled.

4. Garnish the custard with basil, if desired. Serve with toast points or crackers.

INGREDIENTS

- 1 cup heavy cream
- 1 cup whole milk
- 1 cup thinly sliced green garlic (white and green parts)
- 1 egg
- 2 egg yolks
- 1 teaspoon salt
- Chopped fresh basil, for garnish (optional)
- Toast points or crackers, for serving

PREP TIME: 15 minutes

BAKING TIME: 30 minutes

Serves 6–8

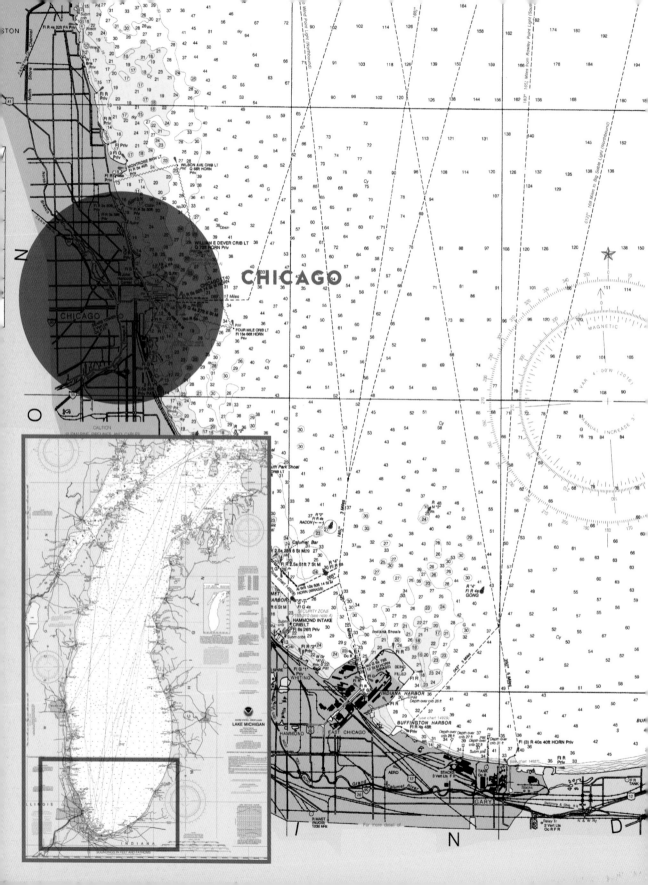

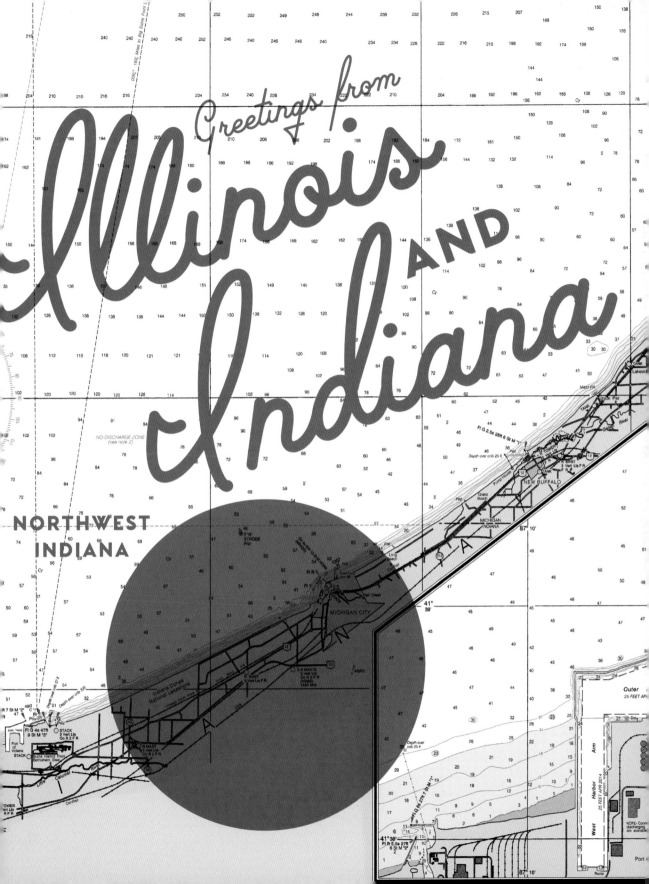

Greetings from

Illinois

AND

Indiana

NORTHWEST INDIANA

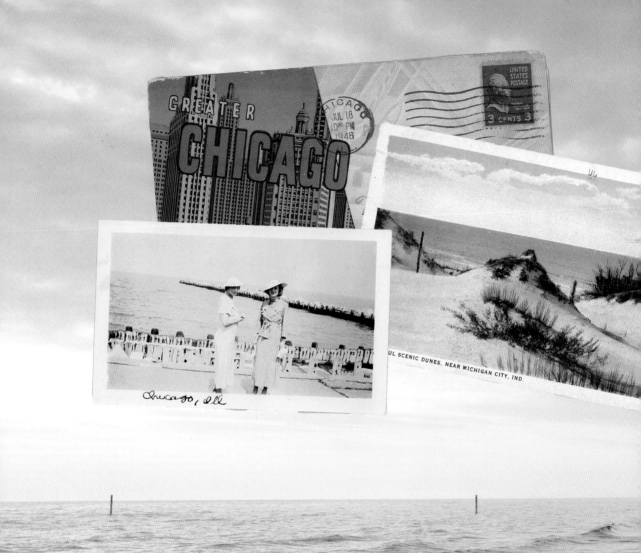

GREATER **CHICAGO**

UNITED STATES POSTAGE
3 CENTS 3

CHICAGO
JUL 18
10³⁰ PM
1946

Chicago, Ill.

UL SCENIC DUNES, NEAR MICHIGAN CITY, IND.

CHICAGO *and* NORTHWEST INDIANA

THE SCENIC LAKE SHORE DRIVE, running alongside miles of sandy and sunny beaches, forever serves as the iconic and picturesque image most of us have in our minds when we think of Chicago. The beaches, with their soft waves and sun-drenched blue waters, represent one of the Windy City's greatest assets to locals and tourists alike.

In the summertime, you'll see beaches lined with suit-clad swimmers and loungers like a modern-day interpretation of Seurat's *A Sunday Afternoon on the Island of La Grande Jatte*, which you can view in person at the Art Institute downtown. Just west of the beach and in the heart of grassy Lincoln Park sits the Green City Market, Chicago's largest farmers' market and the inspiration for three waves of acclaimed chefs in the city, who have made it their mission to showcase the bounty of the Midwest. For the past two decades, chefs and farmers have come together to elevate the

city's food scene from overindulgent deep-dish pizza pies to sophisticated creations using the best produce, meat, cheese, and more from the region.

At the end of the chapter, you'll find three dishes connected to the tiny patch of land in Indiana that connects South Chicago with Michigan's Harbor Country. This area sees thousands of tourists a year, many of whom flock to the white sandy Indiana Dunes near Michigan City. Farmers in this region grow some of the sweetest crops in all the Midwest, thanks to the fertile soil and Lake Effect breeze.

Abigail's Miso SWEET CORN SUNRISE *with Poached Eggs*

ENJOY THIS EASY RECIPE IN THE PEAK OF SUMMER *as a comforting breakfast, side dish, or light lunch. The miso adds savory notes as well as extra nutrients. If you can't live without bacon, that's a tasty add-in, too. Buttered toast is great for sopping up the egg yolks.*

One tip: If you plan to barbecue and want extra smoky flavor, blister the shucked and cleaned corn on the grill before scraping the kernels off the cobs. And, whenever possible, use the freshest, straight-from-the-farm eggs you can find for best results.

INGREDIENTS

- 2 teaspoons white vinegar
- 1 teaspoon salt
- 3 tablespoons butter
- 2 tablespoons minced shallot
- 2 garlic cloves, minced
- 3 cups fresh sweet corn kernels (from about 3 ears)
- ¼ cup unsalted chicken stock
- 2 tablespoons white miso
- 2 tablespoons fresh lime juice
- ⅓ cup chopped fresh cilantro, plus more for garnish
- 2 tablespoons grated Parmesan cheese, plus more for garnish
- ¼ teaspoon freshly ground black pepper
- 2 eggs, cold

1. Fill a wide, deep saucepan with 2 to 3 inches of water. Add the vinegar and salt and bring to almost a boil; reduce the heat to a gentle simmer with just a few bubbles.

2. While the water is heating, melt the butter in a medium skillet over medium heat, and cook the shallots until soft and translucent, about 2 minutes. Add the garlic and cook until fragrant, about 30 seconds. Add the corn, stirring to coat it with the butter. Cook until beginning to turn golden brown, about 5 minutes.

3. In a small bowl, whisk together the chicken stock and miso. Add the mixture to the skillet with the corn. Stir well and simmer until the liquid has reduced and the corn has a glazed consistency, 3 to 5 minutes. Remove from the heat and stir in the lime juice, cilantro, Parmesan, and pepper. Divide the corn mixture between two plates and keep warm.

4. One at a time, crack each egg into a small bowl, ramekin, or measuring cup and gently slide it into the simmering water by lowering the bowl or cup partially into the water. Coax the egg whites closer to the yolk to maintain the eggs' shape after setting them in the water. Poach for 3 minutes. Remove each egg with a slotted spoon and place 1 egg atop each plate of corn. Serve immediately with more Parmesan and cilantro on top.

PREP TIME: 5 minutes

COOKING TIME: 25 minutes

Serves 2

Abigail's American Bistro

HIGHLAND PARK, ILLINOIS

TUCKED IN THE HEART of Highland Park's quaint Ravinia neighborhood near the musical venue Ravinia Festival, chef-owner Michael Paulsen named this popular eatery after his daughter. Opened in 2009, the small, bright, and airy dining room packs many regular customers, who enjoy dishes made with local meats and produce at the peak of their season, often with some Asian elements. In the spring, the menu has featured dishes like soft shell crab with ramp aioli, pickled ramps, and micro radish, while heartier dishes might feature house-made pork sausage with kimchi, poached egg, black garlic, and cilantro. In the summertime, Paulsen favors sweet peppers, tomatoes, and of course, being in Illinois, sweet corn. Paulsen has one advantage being outside the city in the northern Chicago suburbs — he's only a stone's throw from Lincolnshire, where farmers at Didier Farms grow incredibly sweet corn.

CREAMED CORN *with Bacon*

SUMMER MEANS SWEET CORN IN ILLINOIS AND WISCONSIN, *when we grab it by the bushels at farmers' markets and roadside stands and eat it straight off the cob after a quick grill and a hearty swath of farm fresh butter. Here's another classic — if not indulgent — way to eat fresh corn alongside Grilled Waseda Farms Rib Steak (page 53), fried chicken, whitefish, or just by itself.*

1. Cook the bacon in a 10-inch skillet over medium heat until crisp. Use a slotted spoon to transfer the bacon to a paper towel; set aside.

2. Meanwhile, cut off the kernels of corn (if you have a Bundt pan, stand each ear in the center of the ring and cut down, letting the kernels fall into the pan).

3. Add the shallots to the drippings in the skillet and sauté for 5 minutes. Stir in the corn along with its milky juices and sauté for 2 minutes longer. Stir in the cream, salt, and pepper.

4. Transfer half of the mixture to a blender or food processor and blend until creamy. Stir the blended mixture into the corn in the skillet and cook for 2 minutes or until heated through. Serve topped with the reserved bacon. Garnish with chives, if desired.

INGREDIENTS

- 2 bacon strips, diced
- 6 ears fresh corn on the cob, shucked
- ⅓ cup chopped shallots or onion
- ⅓ cup heavy cream or half-and-half
- ¼ teaspoon salt
- ¼ teaspoon freshly ground black pepper

  Chopped fresh chives, for garnish (optional)

PREP TIME: 20 minutes

COOKING TIME: 10 minutes

Serves 4

GRILLED SUMMER CORN AND VEGGIE SALAD

with Goat Cheese and Tomato-Dill Vinaigrette

I LIKE TO MAKE THIS SALAD AFTER A STOP AT THE GREEN CITY MARKET *on Saturday mornings in the summer. I make it when we already have the grill going for a barbecue so I can grill the corn and the veggies, and even the tomatoes, for the dressing. The grilling doesn't take long, but it makes a huge difference in the salad and really brings out the bright and sweet flavors of the summer harvest. I make a plain vinaigrette with some local raw honey and fresh dill to keep the emphasis on the taste of those amazing summer tomatoes, but the dill helps tone down the acidity of the tomatoes and adds another dimension.*

Feel free to swap in any other fresh summer vegetables you have on hand. If you can't find romaine or other sturdy lettuce, you can use butter lettuce and just tear it without grilling for the base of the salad. Before serving, I always put the salad plates or bowls in the freezer to chill them.

FOR THE VEGETABLES

- 2 medium or large heirloom tomatoes (about 1 pound)
- 3 ears fresh sweet corn, shucked
- 1 medium zucchini, sliced lengthwise into ½-inch-thick pieces
- 1 medium yellow summer squash, sliced lengthwise in ½-inch-thick pieces
- 2 bell peppers (red, orange, and/or yellow), halved and seeded
- 1 bunch green or other local bulb onion, green stalks included
- 1 head romaine or green leaf lettuce, halved lengthwise through the core

  Olive oil, as needed

FOR THE VINAIGRETTE

- ½ cup extra-virgin olive oil
- 2 tablespoons local raw honey
- 1 tablespoon sherry vinegar

  Pinch of sea salt

  Freshly ground black pepper
- 2 tablespoons finely chopped fresh dill

- ½–1 cup crumbled plain or herbed artisan goat cheese
- ¼ cup chopped fresh chives or basil, for garnish (optional)

1. Prepare a gas or charcoal grill for medium-high-heat grilling.

2. Blacken the heirloom tomatoes on the hot side of the grill, uncovered, and set aside.

Recipe continues on next page

PREP TIME: 10 minutes

COOKING TIME: 20 minutes

Serves 4

TOMATO PRESERVING TIPS

When it's nearing the end of tomato season and you hate to see it go, stock up on local fresh tomatoes. Ask farmers just before the close of your local farmers' market for the "ugliest," and even any bruised, tomatoes they may not want to take back with them. At home, roast the tomatoes on a foil-lined baking sheet in a 400°F (200°C) oven until the skin starts to peel back and the flesh is tender and releasing juice. Remove them from the oven and, when cool enough to handle, peel as much skin off the tomatoes as you can.

Transfer the tomatoes with their juices by lifting the foil and pouring everything into a food processor or blender, then blend until they are the desired consistency. Pour batches of the purée into resealable plastic bags, then place the bags on small sheet trays or other flat surfaces in the freezer until frozen into flat and thin bricks. Then store the bricks stacked on top of each other in the freezer to save space. These bricks of sunshine become the base for sauces and salsas in the dead of winter when you want a taste of summer.

3. Blister the corn on all sides. When cool enough to handle, cut off the kernels and place in a large bowl. Set aside.

4. Coat the squashes, peppers, onion, and lettuce lightly with olive oil. Grill the lettuce, cut side down, until slightly charred and wilted, turning occasionally, about 2 minutes. Set aside. Grill the other vegetables, covered, turning occasionally, until charred and tender, 10 to 15 minutes.

5. Peel the blackened skin off the peppers and cut into large dice. Add to the bowl with the corn. Dice the squash and slice the onions and add to the bowl. If desired, chill the grilled vegetables in the refrigerator for at least 30 minutes to 1 hour. The grilled vegetables can be prepared 1 day ahead.

6. In the meantime, make the vinaigrette. Peel and crush the grilled tomatoes over a blender jar to catch the juices. Discard the cores. Blend the tomatoes with the olive oil until puréed. Add the honey, vinegar, salt, and pepper to taste and blend until smooth. Fold in the dill. Refrigerate for 15 to 20 minutes to chill. The vinaigrette may be made ahead and stored in the refrigerator for about 2 weeks.

7. To serve, chop the lettuce halves in half and divide among four plates. Top each plate with one-quarter each of the grilled vegetable mixture and one-quarter of the goat cheese. Drizzle 1 to 2 tablespoons dressing over each plate and garnish with the chives, if desired.

SWEET CORN CORNBREAD

with Honey Butter

HERE'S ANOTHER USE FOR ILLINOIS SWEET CORN *at the height of the season. Twin Garden Farms in Harvard, Illinois, developed Mirai, a type of hybrid corn that's even more candy-sweet than traditional sweet corn. Buy it at farmers' markets in the city and suburbs. If you can't find Mirai, you can substitute another sweet corn variety, such as Butter and Sugar or Silver Queen.*

1. Preheat the oven to 400°F (200°C). Place ¼ cup (½ stick) of the butter in a 9-inch baking pan. Let the remaining ½ cup (1 stick) butter sit at room temperature to soften. When the oven reaches temperature, place the pan in the oven and bake for 4 to 5 minutes, until the butter is sizzling and light golden brown. Let stand at room temperature for 5 minutes to cool.

2. Meanwhile, combine the flour, cornmeal, sugar, baking powder, and salt in a large bowl and mix well. Add the half-and-half, the butter from the pan, the eggs, and the corn. Mix just until the dry ingredients are moistened. (Do not overmix or the cornbread will be tough.) Spread the batter into the baking pan and bake for 20 to 22 minutes, until golden brown. Let cool in pan on a wire rack for at least 10 minutes.

3. For the honey butter, mix the softened ½ cup butter with the honey until well blended. Serve the warm cornbread with the honey butter.

INGREDIENTS

- ¾ cup (1½ sticks) unsalted butter
- 1¼ cups unbleached all-purpose flour
- ¾ cup yellow cornmeal
- 1-2 tablespoons sugar, as desired
- 1 tablespoon baking powder
- ½ teaspoon salt
- 1 cup half-and-half or buttermilk
- 2 eggs, lightly beaten
- 1 cup fresh (or roasted) sweet corn kernels
- ¼ cup honey

PREP TIME: 20 minutes

BAKING TIME: 22 minutes

Serves 8

ROAST ACORN SQUASH

with Toasted Pecans

PECANS FROM THREE SISTERS GARDEN in Kankakee, Illinois, are more buttery, richer, and more tender than any supermarket pecan. While I can easily pop them in my mouth raw or just toasted, I like to combine them with seasonal acorn squash for a perfect fall side dish or even meatless main. Pair with Red Wine–Braised Brisket (page 56) for a fuller meal. If you can find black walnuts in Wisconsin or Michigan, those are a great substitute for the pecans.

INGREDIENTS

- 2 acorn squash (1-1¼ pounds each), stems trimmed, halved crosswise, seeds discarded (see Note)
- 2 tablespoons maple syrup
- 2 tablespoons unsalted butter, melted
- 2 tablespoons bourbon (optional)
- ½ teaspoon ground cinnamon
- ½ teaspoon coarse sea salt or kosher salt
- ¼ cup chopped pecans, toasted

NOTE: *If the ends of the squash are pointed, cut them off so that the squash will lay flat when turned over. This will make cutting easier.*

1. Preheat the oven to 375°F (190°C). Place the squash, cut sides down, in a large shallow baking dish. Add ¼ inch water to the dish. Bake for 35 minutes or until almost tender when pierced with a sharp knife.

2. Meanwhile, combine the maple syrup, butter, bourbon (if desired), and cinnamon, and mix well. Turn the squash over and spoon the butter mixture evenly over the edges of the squash, letting the excess drip into the hollow. Return to the oven and bake for 10 minutes longer, or until the squash is tender and glazed. Sprinkle the salt over the squash and top with the pecans.

PREP TIME: 15 minutes

BAKING TIME: 45 minutes

Serves 4

HEIRLOOM TOMATO SALAD

with Balsamic Vinegar and Basil

"DO NOT SKIMP ON THE QUALITY OF THE INGREDIENTS — THAT IS THE KEY TO THIS RECIPE," *says acclaimed chef Bruce Sherman, one of the very first chefs in the city to work with local farms. With such a simple salad, Sherman reaches for the best tomatoes he can find, many from Leaning Shed Farm in Berrien Springs, Michigan (see page 167). A wide variety of heirloom tomatoes, like Pruden's Purple, yellow Kellogg's Breakfast, Aunt Ruby's German Green, White Beauty, and Sun Gold cherry tomatoes, make the colors in this bright and fresh, sweet summer salad pop. Remember: Never refrigerate the tomatoes, as they will become mealy and lose their beautiful flavor.*

1. Cut each heirloom tomato into 4 slices. In the center of each serving plate, arrange the slices overlapping in a fan shape. Arrange the yellow cherry tomatoes on the top portion of the plate and the red cherry tomatoes on the bottom.

2. Drizzle the olive oil over the tomatoes, then follow with the balsamic vinegar. Sprinkle salt and pepper to taste over the tomatoes and garnish with the basil leaves. Garnish with the cheese.

INGREDIENTS

- 1 red heirloom tomato
- 1 yellow heirloom tomato
- 1 green heirloom tomato
- 1 pint yellow cherry tomatoes. halved
- 1 pint red cherry tomatoes, halved
- ¼ cup highest-quality extra-virgin olive oil
- 4 teaspoons aged balsamic vinegar

  Fleur de sel or coarse sea salt

  Freshly cracked black pepper
- 4 fresh green or purple opal basil sprigs, leaves sliced
- 2 ounces good-quality aged Parmesan cheese

PREP TIME: 15 minutes

Serves 4

CHICKEN SHAWARMA BURRITOS

THESE AREN'T JUST ANY BURRITOS. *Nick LaCasse from Half Acre Beer Company (see page 133) flexes his creative culinary muscles with pineapple-infused pork shoulder, Asian-inspired rice noodles, mushrooms, long beans, sesame and sweet soy glaze, and even slow-roasted, guajillo-spiced goat. Burritos may sound like a funny pairing with beer, but the intent was to differentiate from the pub grub and burgers found at many craft breweries in town and elsewhere with food "that's fun to eat," says LaCasse. This recipe takes some time, but the final result will impress and the elements of the dish can be served separately, if desired.*

FOR THE CHICKEN AND BRINE

- 2 cups water
- 1 tablespoon kosher salt
  Grated zest of 1 lemon
- 1 teaspoon red pepper flakes
  Fresh herb sprigs, such as oregano, thyme, and/or parsley (optional)
- 6 boneless, skinless chicken breast halves (2 to 2½ pounds total)

FOR THE TABBOULEH SALAD

- 1 cup bulghur wheat
- 1½ cups boiling water
- ¼ cup extra-virgin olive oil
- ¼ cup fresh lemon juice
- 1½ teaspoons kosher salt
- 1 cup finely diced tomato
- 1 cup minced fresh parsley
- ½ cup minced fresh mint
- 1 teaspoon sambal oelek (optional)
- ½ teaspoon freshly ground black pepper

FOR THE HUMMUS

- 2 garlic cloves, peeled
- 2 (16-ounce) cans chickpeas, rinsed and drained, or 3½ cups cooked chickpeas
- ⅓ cup drained bottled peppadew peppers or roasted red bell peppers
- ¼ cup tahini
- 3 tablespoons fresh lemon juice
- 2 tablespoons olive oil
  Rice vinegar, as needed
  Salt and freshly ground black pepper

FOR THE JERUSALEM SALAD

- 1 cup plain Greek yogurt
- ⅓ cup tahini
- 1 tablespoon sambal oelek (optional)
- ½ teaspoon kosher salt
- 1 medium cucumber, seeded and finely diced (2 cups)

PREP TIME: 15 minutes, plus additional time for brining the chicken

BRINING TIME: 2–4 hours

COOKING TIME: 30 minutes

Serves 8

FOR THE SHAWARMA SPICE RUB AND VEGETABLES

1 tablespoon fennel seeds	2 teaspoons kosher salt
1 tablespoon coriander seeds	1 large Vidalia or other sweet onion, coarsely chopped
1 tablespoon cumin seeds	
1 tablespoon black peppercorns	1 each: large red bell pepper and yellow bell pepper, coarsely chopped
¼ cup paprika (not smoked)	8 (9-inch) flour tortillas or large sun-dried tomato or spinach wraps)
1½ teaspoons granulated garlic	

1. For the chicken and brine, combine the water, salt, lemon zest, pepper flakes, and herb sprigs in a large bowl. Submerge the chicken in the brine and refrigerate for 2 to 4 hours. While the chicken is brining, prepare the tabbouleh salad, hummus, and Jerusalem salad.

2. For the tabbouleh salad, place the bulghur in a large bowl. Stir in the boiling water and let stand for 10 minutes. Stir in the olive oil, lemon juice, and salt. Let stand at room temperature for 1 hour. Stir in the tomato, parsley, mint, sambal oelek (if using), and pepper. Tabbouleh salad will keep, covered and refrigerated, for up to 1 week. (This makes 4 cups.)

3. For the hummus, drop the garlic through the feed tube of a large food processor while the motor is running and process until minced. Add the chickpeas, peppers, tahini, lemon juice, and olive oil. Process until the mixture is smooth, stopping once and using a rubber spatula to scrape down the sides of the bowl. If the mixture is very thick, thin with a little rice vinegar. Season with salt and pepper to taste. Hummus will keep, covered and refrigerated, for up to 1 week. (This makes 3 cups.)

4. For the Jerusalem salad, combine the yogurt, tahini, sambal oelek (if using), and salt in a medium bowl. Mix well, and fold in the cucumber. Refrigerate until serving time. (This makes 2½ cups.)

5. Preheat the oven to 325°F (160°C).

6. For the rub, grind the fennel seeds, coriander seeds, cumin seeds, and peppercorns in a spice or coffee grinder. Transfer to a small bowl. Add the paprika and granulated garlic and mix well. Spread out on a small shallow roasting pan and bake for 6 to 7 minutes, until the spices are fragrant and toasted. Stir in the salt. Leftover spice rub may be transferred to a small jar and stored at room temperature for up to 3 months.

Recipe continues on next page

7. Drain the chicken and discard the brine. Pat the chicken dry with paper towels and rub 2 tablespoons of the spice mixture over both sides of the chicken. Arrange the chicken on one side of a rimmed baking sheet.

8. Combine the onion and red and yellow bell peppers with 1 tablespoon of the spice rub. Spread out the mixture onto the baking sheet next to the chicken. Bake for about 30 minutes or until the internal temperature of the chicken reaches 160°F (71°C) and the vegetables are tender, turning the chicken once and stirring the vegetables after 15 minutes to mix with the juices. Let cool on the pan for 10 minutes. Slice the chicken into strips and toss with the vegetable mixture.

9. To serve, for each burrito, spread ⅓ cup hummus evenly over the tortilla, leaving a ½-inch border. Layer ½ cup tabbouleh over the hummus. Spoon 1 cup of the sliced chicken breast and vegetables into an oval down the center of the tortilla. Use a spoon to make a trench down the center of the chicken and vegetables. Spoon ¼ cup of the Jerusalem salad into the trench.

10. Roll up the tortilla, tightly folding in the edges. If desired, place the burrito in a grill pan over medium heat, turning until warm and grill marks appear. Cut diagonally in half and serve immediately.

Half Acre Beer Company

CHICAGO, ILLINOIS

FOUNDED IN 2006 BY GABRIEL MAGLIARO and originally brewing their beer in Black River Falls, Wisconsin, Half Acre Beer Company has become a fixture in Chicago's Lincoln Square neighborhood on the north side of the city. Business has been good, enabling them to open a second location farther north and increase their distribution outside Illinois. They've also begun serving food at their original, formerly bring-your-own-food, taproom.

The chef at the taproom is Nick LaCasse, a protégé of top chefs Shawn McClain (see page 148) and Charlie Trotter. LaCasse has earned serious accolades in Chicago, in part for his versatility and dedication to Midwestern farmers. Having once developed a new menu every week with celebrity cocktail partner Charles Joly at The Drawing Room, he later went on to focus on Spanish-style seafood at the restaurant mfk.

He now pairs elevated street food with craft beer at Half Acre. Instead of serving the usual burgers, wings, and other brewpub fare, LaCasse has developed a changing lineup of creative burritos and small plates. Look for a barbecue brisket burrito with buttermilk biscuit, cheddar, and arugula stuffed inside, and one with pineapple- and pepper-laden pork fried rice. Plates range from addictive hush puppies topped with caramelized apple purée and butternut squash to chimichurri hummus with crudités and a sinful short rib French onion soup.

TEMPURA ASPARAGUS

WITH A CONSISTENCY SLIGHTLY THINNER THAN PANCAKE BATTER, *the tempura batter makes for a lighter fry. Umami-rich sesame seeds balance the natural sweetness of the Midwest-sourced vegetable. When shopping at the Green City Market in Chicago's Lincoln Park, I always reach for Mick Klug's asparagus when in season. Located in St. Joseph, Michigan, Mick Klug Farm — known for its strawberries, blueberries, grapes, peaches, nectarines, apples, and more grown in Michigan's fruit belt — also has the sweetest asparagus and peas around, thanks to their fertile soil and cooling Lake Michigan breezes.*

1. For the dipping sauce, combine the soy sauce, vinegar, mustard, ginger, jalapeño, and sriracha; whisk well and set aside.

2. For the batter, combine the flour, cornstarch, baking powder, baking soda, and salt in a medium bowl, mixing well. Stir in the club soda (the batter should be a little thinner than pancake batter). Stir in the sesame seeds.

3. For the asparagus, trim the stalks to 5 inches in length. Reserve the ends for making stock. Pour enough oil into a medium saucepan to come 1 to 2 inches up the sides of the pan. Heat over medium-high heat until the temperature reaches 350°F (180°C) on a deep-frying thermometer clipped to the edge of the pan. Adjust the heat to keep the temperature even during the frying.

4. Use tongs to dip the asparagus, one spear at a time, into the batter, coating well. Add to the hot oil without crowding. Fry until golden brown, 2 to 3 minutes. Transfer to paper towels to drain. Continue frying the remaining asparagus. Serve immediately with the dipping sauce.

FOR THE SPICY-SWEET DIPPING SAUCE

- ¼ cup soy sauce
- ¼ cup rice vinegar
- 1 tablespoon Dijon mustard
- 1 teaspoon minced fresh gingerroot
- 1 teaspoon minced seeded jalapeño, or as desired
- 1 teaspoon sriracha sauce or hot chili-garlic sauce

FOR THE BATTER

- ½ cup unbleached all-purpose flour
- ¼ cup cornstarch
- 1 tablespoon baking powder
- 1 teaspoon baking soda
- 1 teaspoon kosher salt
- ¾ cup club soda
- 1 tablespoon toasted sesame seeds

FOR THE ASPARAGUS

- 1 pound medium-thick asparagus spears

  Vegetable oil or peanut oil, for frying

PREP TIME: 20 minutes

COOKING TIME: 3 minutes per batch

Serves 4

Local Foods

CHICAGO, ILLINOIS

ANDREW LUTSEY, BROTHER OF MATT LUTSEY OF WASEDA FARM (see page 55), partnered with former Green City Market farm forager/grass-fed beef rancher Dave Rand and former technology consultant Ryan Kimura to open Local Foods, Chicago's first distribution hub sourcing and supplying produce, meat, cheese, and other foods from sustainable and organic Midwestern farms.

Since opening in 2015, the 27,000-square-foot supermarket has grown to include an in-store butcher shop run by former chef and restaurateur-turned-sustainable butcher Rob Levitt and Local Foods Café, a 16-seat diner. Levitt and his wife Allie closed their acclaimed farm-to-table restaurant, Mado, years ago to lead the charge in whole animal butchering when it was beginning to take shape in Chicago. Having moved his shop to Local Foods, Levitt continues to serve as a model for sourcing humanely and sustainably raised meats from farmers in the Midwest.

In the produce section, which seems to have expanded after every visit, rows and rows of shelving and displays hold produce, local grains, honey, jams, breads, and other artisan-quality foods, many of which come from vendors who also sell at Chicago's Green City Market and the Logan Square farmers' market. There are also heirloom tomatoes, lettuces, and other vegetables grown year-round from a prominent Chicago greenhouse, as well as a wide selection of specialty cheeses from Wisconsin, Illinois, and Michigan.

HBFC Original FRIED CHICKEN SANDWICH

THE CHICKEN IS FIRST SOAKED IN BUTTERMILK TO TENDERIZE *and then double-dredged before frying, for delicious results. The 40 pounds of chicken sold each week (1,300 pieces per day) at Honey Butter Fried Chicken (HBFC) come from Miller Produce, an Indiana-based supplier of chicken raised on Amish farms throughout the region, farms known for their antibiotic-free, humane treatment of animals.*

When frying the chicken, use a deep-frying thermometer to more accurately test the doneness of the chicken.

FOR THE BRINE

- 2 quarts water
- ⅓ cup coarse kosher salt
- ¼ cup sugar
- ⅛ teaspoon red pepper flakes
  Peel of 1 lemon
  Peel of 1 orange

FOR THE CHICKEN

- 8 boneless, skinless chicken thighs

FOR THE CHILE MAYO

- 2 medium jalapeños, cut into ¼-inch rounds
- 2 medium Fresno chiles or jalapeños, cut into ¼-inch rounds
- ½ cup water
- ½ cup sugar
- 1 cup mayonnaise
  Kosher salt

FOR THE CRUNCHY SLAW

- 1 cup shredded green cabbage
- 1 cup shredded red cabbage

PREP TIME: 50 minutes

BRINING TIME: 8–12 hours

COOKING TIME: 10 minutes

Serves 8

- ½ cup Pickled Red Onions (page 44)
- 3 scallions, sliced into thin rounds
- ¼ cup red wine vinegar (or the juice from the pickled red onions)
- 2 tablespoons extra-virgin olive oil
- 1 teaspoon honey
  Kosher salt and freshly ground black pepper

FOR THE DREDGING MIXTURE

- 1¾ cups unbleached all-purpose flour
- ¼ cup rice flour
- 1½ teaspoons coarse kosher salt
- 1½ teaspoons freshly ground black pepper
- 1½ teaspoons garlic powder
- 1 teaspoon onion powder
- ¼ teaspoon baking powder
- ⅛ teaspoon cayenne pepper
- ⅛ teaspoon smoked paprika

FOR THE BATTER, FRYING & ASSEMBLY

- 4 cups buttermilk
  Canola or rice bran oil, for frying
  Kosher salt
- 1 tablespoon smoked paprika
- 8 buttery buns (or challah or brioche-type buns), split, lightly toasted, if desired

1. For the brine, combine the water, salt, sugar, pepper flakes, and citrus peels in a large pot. Heat over medium heat and stir until the sugar and salt dissolve. Cool the brine completely.

2. Cut each chicken thigh lengthwise into 3 strips. Place the chicken pieces in the brine and refrigerate for 8 to 12 hours. Remove from the brine and dry excess moisture with paper towels.

3. For the chile mayonnaise, combine the chiles, water, and sugar in a saucepan over high heat until it boils. Reduce the heat to maintain a simmer and cook until the chiles are soft, 20 to 30 minutes. Cool the chiles to room temperature in their syrup. Remove the chiles from the syrup and transfer to a food processor. Use on-off pulses until the chiles are chopped but still a little chunky. Whisk the candied chiles into the mayonnaise in a medium bowl. Season to taste with salt. If you prefer a spicier flavor, stir in a little of the candied chile syrup. Refrigerate until ready to use.

4. For the slaw, combine the cabbages, red onions, and scallions in a large bowl. Add the vinegar, olive oil, honey, and a good sprinkling of salt and pepper. Toss to combine and season to taste. Refrigerate until ready to use.

5. For the dredging mixture, combine the flours, salt, black pepper, garlic powder, onion powder, baking powder, cayenne, and paprika in a shallow bowl and mix well.

6. Pour the buttermilk into a second shallow bowl. Batter one piece of chicken at a time. Submerge the chicken first in the buttermilk. Lift the chicken out of the buttermilk and let drip slightly, and then place into the dredging mixture. Ensure that the chicken is evenly and fully coated, but do not let the coating become too thick. Place the battered chicken on a plate.

7. To fry the chicken strips, heat the oil in a large pot over medium heat to 340°F (171°C) on a deep-frying thermometer. Fry the chicken in batches and adjust the heat as needed so the oil will maintain the correct temperature. Place the chicken gently into the hot oil and fry until each piece registers a temperature of at least 165°F (74°C) at its thickest point. When the chicken is cooked, remove carefully from the oil and place on a wire rack over a baking sheet or on paper towels.

8. Dust the top side of the just-fried chicken with a sprinkle of salt and a sprinkle of the smoked paprika. Let rest for 1 minute, then flip the chicken and dust the other side with salt and smoked paprika.

9. To assemble the sandwiches, slather chile mayo on each side of the buns. Place 3 fried chicken strips on the bottom bun, then top with crunchy slaw and the top bun.

Prairie Grass Cafe

NORTHBROOK, IL

CHEFS GEORGE BUMBARIS, FORMER RITZ-CARLTON HEAD CHEF, and Sarah Stegner, long-time founding board member of Chicago's Green City Market, partnered with television news anchor and personality Bill Kurtis to open this north suburban hotspot years ago. One of the pioneers of the local food movement in Chicago, Stegner has cultivated strong relationships with Midwestern farmers and artisan producers over the years, and it shows on the restaurant's menu.

Seasonal vegetables show up in salads, atop sandwiches, and as sides to mains like house-made lamb sausage and crispy Amish chicken. Prairie Grass also serves steaks and burgers made with Kurtis's Tall Grass Beef from his 50,000-acre ranch in Kansas.

In the wintertime, Stegner and Bumbaris's commitment to farmers doesn't end; when summer heirloom tomatoes run scarce, they supplement with other supersweet versions sourced from an indoor hydroponic garden in the city.

Turnip, Squash, and Scallion
VEGETABLE PLATTER
with Soppressata and Mint

THIS RECIPE COMBINES FRESH VEGETABLES with rich, dry-cured soppressata sausage and fresh mint leaves. In Chicago, find a variety of charcuterie and salumi from West Loop Salumi on Randolph or at Publican Quality Meats in Fulton Market. The Butcher & Larder at Local Foods (see page 136) also carries some select charcuterie.

1. Prepare a gas or charcoal grill for medium-heat grilling.

2. Peel and trim the turnips and cut into wedges. Bring a saucepan of water with 1 teaspoon salt added to a boil over high heat. Blanch the turnips and greens for 1 to 2 minutes, and drain well. Heat 2 tablespoons olive oil in a large skillet over medium heat, and sauté the turnips and greens until tender and golden, about 5 minutes. Season with salt and pepper and set aside.

3. Cut the soppressata into thin slices. Wipe out the skillet and sauté the soppressata over medium-high heat until crispy, flipping once.

4. Cut the zucchini, pattypan squash, and scallions in half lengthwise. Toss with olive oil to coat and season to taste with salt and pepper. Grill over high heat, turning occasionally, until the vegetables are charred and crisp-tender and the green parts of the scallions are wilted, 7 to 10 minutes.

5. To serve, arrange the vegetables on a serving platter and top with the soppressata and the drippings from the skillet. Remove the mint leaves from their stems, coarsely chop, and sprinkle over the platter to garnish.

INGREDIENTS

- 8 baby turnips with greens
- Salt and freshly ground black pepper
- Olive oil, as needed
- 8 ounces soppressata or other Italian-style salumi
- 3 zucchini
- 3 pattypan squash
- 4 scallions
- 6 fresh mint sprigs

PREP TIME: 15 minutes

COOKING TIME: 20 minutes

Serves 4–6

ROLLED OAT *and* MAPLE SYRUP SCONES

BREAD TELLS JUST PART OF THE STORY *of Hewn Bakery in Evanston (see page 146). Artisan baker Ellen King also lines her display case with a range of baked goods and pastries, which her loyal following of regulars snatches up daily. She offers this easy scone recipe using a bourbon barrel–aged maple syrup from B&E's Trees out of the Driftless Area in Wisconsin, though any real maple syrup could be used. She uses traditional rolled oats from Hazzard Free Farm in Pecatonica, Illinois, but any organic oats (and flour, if available) also work well for the scones.*

For the flour, King is able to source locally grown, heritage (heirloom) wheat that's freshly milled at the farm. Check your local farmers' market. When selecting heritage wheat flour for this recipe, look for a light, sifted version closer to all-purpose flour than to bread flour.

FOR THE SCONES

- 3 cups unbleached all-purpose flour
- 2 cups old-fashioned rolled oats
- 1 cup dried blueberries
- 1 tablespoon baking powder
- ½ teaspoon baking soda
- ¼ cup sliced almonds, toasted
- ½ teaspoon salt
- 1 cup plus 2 tablespoons (2¼ sticks) unsalted butter, cut into small cubes
- ¾ cup crème fraîche
- ¼ cup heavy cream
- 1 cup maple syrup
- 1 egg
- 1 teaspoon ground cinnamon
- 1 teaspoon vanilla extract

FOR THE ICING

- 1 cup confectioners' sugar
- 2 tablespoons maple syrup
- 2 teaspoons water

1. For the scones, preheat the oven to 350°F (180°C). Line a large rimmed baking sheet with parchment paper or a silicone baking liner.

2. Combine the flour, oats, blueberries, baking powder, baking soda, almonds, and salt in the bowl of an electric mixer, and mix on medium-low for 10 seconds. With the mixer on low speed, slowly add the butter until it is combined and pea-size, about 1 minute.

Recipe continues on page 144

PREP TIME: 5 minutes

BAKING TIME: 20 minutes

Makes 12 scones

3. Whisk the crème fraîche, cream, maple syrup, egg, cinnamon, and vanilla in a medium bowl. With the mixer on low speed, slowly pour the crème fraîche mixture into the dry ingredients, and mix just until the dry ingredients are moistened, about 20 seconds.

4. The dough will be very wet, so I like to use an ice cream scooper. Scoop the scones 1 inch apart onto the prepared baking sheet. Bake for 12 minutes. Rotate the pan so the back is in front and the front is in back, and bake for 8 minutes longer or until golden.

5. Meanwhile, for the icing, place the confectioners' sugar in a small bowl. Using a whisk, slowly mix in the maple syrup and water until the icing falls into the bowl like a satiny caramel ribbon when you lift the whisk up.

6. Gently spoon the icing over the scones while still warm, adding as much or as little as desired. Serve warm or at room temperature. Leftovers may be stored in an airtight container for 2 to 3 days.

MORNING GLORY MUFFINS

THESE SIGNATURE MUFFINS *use locally grown carrots and other flavorful add-ins for the perfect morning pick-me-up with coffee. Use locally grown and freshly milled heritage (heirloom) wheat flour, if possible, for the healthiest, most delicious base.*

1. Preheat the oven to 375°F (190°C). Line 12 standard muffin cups with liners or grease them generously.

2. Cover the golden raisins with hot tap water and let stand for 5 to 10 minutes to soften. Combine the flour, brown sugar, baking soda, cinnamon, ginger, and salt in a large bowl, mixing well. Stir in the carrots, pear, walnuts, flaxseed, and sunflower seeds. Drain the raisins and stir them in.

3. Whisk together the eggs, oil, pineapple, and vanilla in a medium bowl. Pour into the dry ingredients and mix just until the dry ingredients are moistened.

4. Fill each of the muffin cups evenly with the batter and top with a sprinkling of coarse sugar and oats, if desired. Bake for 25 to 28 minutes, until a wooden pick inserted in the center comes out clean.

5. Allow the muffins to cool in the tin for 15 minutes. Transfer them to a wire rack to cool completely.

INGREDIENTS

- ½ cup golden raisins
- 2 cups unbleached all-purpose flour
- 1 cup firmly packed dark brown sugar
- 2 teaspoons baking soda
- 2 teaspoons ground cinnamon
- ½ teaspoon ground ginger
- ½ teaspoon salt
- 2 cups peeled and grated carrots
- 1 large pear, peeled, cored, and grated
- ½ cup chopped walnuts
- ⅓ cup flaxseed
- ⅓ cup hulled sunflower seeds or pumpkin seeds
- 3 eggs
- ⅔ cup vegetable oil
- ¼ cup canned crushed pineapple
- 2 teaspoons vanilla extract
- Coarse sugar, for topping (optional)
- Old-fashioned rolled oats, for topping (optional)

PREP TIME: 25 minutes

BAKING TIME: 28 minutes

Makes 12 muffins

Hewn Bakery

EVANSTON, ILLINOIS

ELLEN KING MOVED ACROSS COUNTRY FROM THE BAY AREA to follow love, quitting her day job at a restaurant to bake at home while raising her young son. But her "for fun" underground bake club soon turned into a business venture when friends and huge numbers of fans insisted she make a career out of baking her fermented, chewy, fresh, and aromatic breads. Such breads, though plentiful in San Francisco, were lacking at the time in the Midwest.

King uses only the finest-quality and healthiest flours, starters, and other ingredients. She stays far away from the commercial flours that are laced with pesticides and other chemicals, which she believes have ties to the rising incidence of gluten sensitivities and other digestive issues. Rather, she works with sustainable grain farmers to source the best-quality grains possible, and with artisan millers who turn the grains into flour using age-old milling techniques.

Such mills were once popular all over the Midwest, but they started to close in the late 1800s, when the burgeoning railroad system helped farmers from all over the region send off their wheat for mass processing. When the mills closed, so too disappeared those delicious nuances between different grains and the way they were milled in their respective towns. By supporting local artisan millers, King is hoping to revive that dying trade.

King works with different mills and farms that source and grow heritage wheat varieties from Wisconsin and Illinois. She uses this type of wheat to make Hewn's flavorful and aromatic Orleans, Marquis, and Turkey Red wheat breads, as well as a country bread that's naturally fermented for 17 hours with a decades-old starter. Other breads feature different seeds, polenta, pumpkin, ancient grains, and even spent grains collected from Evanston breweries.

Using heritage grains is so important to King that she has partnered with sustainable grains farmer Andy Hazzard of Hazzard Free Farm in Pecatonica to start the Midwestern Bread Experiment. It's an ambitious three-year undertaking that King hopes will help revitalize heritage wheat crops grown in the region and create bread as it was 100 years ago, before industrialization.

King has also been working with Harold Wilken of Janie's Organic Farm in Danford, Illinois, who opened the state's first stone-ground milling operation for freshly milled, nutritious, and flavorful flour. The first year did not produce enough wheat to meet Hewn's volume, but King looks forward to the coming years and these exclusive partnerships. One of the breads she plans to make is a higher-protein, hearty bean bread using Wilken's wheat as well as the beans he grows alongside the crop through a sustainable, polyculture farming method that allows him to avoid the use of pesticides. "Every crop and the way and place where it's grown makes the bread taste different," King says. Proof that even bread, like wine, has terroir.

Green Zebra GREEN SALAD

THIS SALAD IS A MAINSTAY ON THE GREEN ZEBRA MENU. *When Green Zebra opened in 2001, chef Shawn McClain was way ahead of his time. Not only did he serve an all-vegetarian menu, but he also insisted on using only local Midwestern produce, much of it from small farms in the area. One such location is Werp Farms in Buckley, Michigan, just outside the Traverse City area and inland from Lake Michigan. This salad comes with a variety of the farm's lettuces, from red oak to arugula, Little Gem, and Ruby Streak mustard greens. A light sherry vinaigrette gets an extra kick with smoky Spanish paprika, crunchy pumpkin seeds, and nutty ricotta salata cheese. BelGioioso (based in Brownsville, Wisconsin) makes a ricotta salata that's not too difficult to find throughout the state.*

FOR THE SHERRY VINAIGRETTE

- ½ cup minced shallots
- 2 garlic cloves, minced
- 2 cups vegetable oil
- 1 tablespoon sweet smoked paprika
- 1 cup sherry vinegar
- 2 tablespoons extra-virgin olive oil
- 2 tablespoons kosher salt

FOR THE SALAD

- 1 head red oak lettuce
- 1 head Little Gem lettuce
- ½ cup green beans, blanched or raw
- ¼ cup baby Ruby Streak mustard greens
- ¼ cup Sylvetta arugula or regular arugula
- ¼ cup pea tendrils
- ¼ cup pumpkin seeds, toasted
- 4 radishes, very thinly sliced

  Kosher salt and freshly ground black pepper
- 1 ounce ricotta salata cheese, shaved with a vegetable peeler

1. For the vinaigrette, combine the shallots and garlic with the vegetable oil in a small saucepan and bring to a simmer. Turn the heat to low and cook until the shallots and garlic are translucent. Remove from the heat and stir in the paprika. Cool to room temperature. Combine the oil mixture and the vinegar, olive oil, and salt in a blender. Cover and blend until smooth. Refrigerate the vinaigrette until serving time. The vinaigrette will keep for up to 1 week.

2. For the salad, combine the lettuces, green beans, mustard greens, arugula, pea tendrils, pumpkin seeds, and radishes in a large bowl. Toss to combine. Drizzle 3 to 4 tablespoons of the vinaigrette over the salad and toss to coat. Season to taste with salt and pepper. Place in shallow serving bowls, and arrange the cheese shavings over the top.

PREP TIME: 25 minutes

Serves 4–6

Griddle-Style
DOUBLE CHEESEBURGERS

IT'S HARD TO RE-CREATE THE ÜBER-VELVETY CHEESE SAUCE *you get on a burger at Redamak's in New Buffalo, Michigan, but a second-best attempt uses pub cheese — the packaged kind made by Heston Supper Club in La Porte, Indiana, that you can buy at local grocery stores in the area. While your kitchen probably lacks the commercial, grease-laden flat top grill that gives the burgers their signature caramelized edges, a cast-iron or stainless steel skillet with some butter can get you close enough at home.*

1. In a medium to large bowl, gently combine the chuck and sirloin without overmixing. Gently divide the meat into 8 balls about 2 inches high (do not form into patties).

2. Heat two 12-inch cast-iron or stainless steel skillets (not nonstick) over medium-high heat. Add 1 teaspoon butter to each skillet, and swirl to spread the butter evenly. When the skillets are very hot, add the meat, leaving plenty of room around each ball. Use a stiff metal spatula to press down firmly several times, forming each ball into a patty about 4½ inches wide and ½ inch thick. Season the patties with the salt and pepper. Cook without moving the patties until a crust forms on the bottom, about 2 minutes.

3. Use the spatula to scrape up the patties and turn them over. Press down on the patties with the spatula and place 1 tablespoon of the cheese over each patty. Continue to cook for 2 minutes longer or until the patties form a crust on the bottom.

4. Place 2 patties inside each bun. Serve with condiments, lettuce, tomato, and onion, as desired.

INGREDIENTS

- 12 ounces ground beef chuck
- 12 ounces ground beef sirloin
- 2 teaspoons butter
- 1 teaspoon kosher salt
- 1 teaspoon freshly ground black pepper
- ½ cup pub cheese (such as Heston Supper Club)
- 4 good-quality hamburger buns, such as brioche or onion rolls, split, lightly toasted

  Homemade Mayonnaise (page 87) or assorted condiments, as desired

  Lettuce leaves, sliced tomatoes, and sliced onion, for topping, as desired

PREP TIME: 20 minutes

COOKING TIME: 4 minutes

Serves 4

Iron Creek Farm

LAPORTE, INDIANA

ROWS OF BULGING RED AND YELLOW TOMATOES and bell peppers greet you as you walk into the warm and humid sprawling greenhouse at Iron Creek Farm. In the center, you can hear the trickling of the water in the hydroponic system feeding the delicate green lettuce heads, their leaves flickering from the light fan overhead.

The tomatoes are planted in the rich, fertile soil off the farm, and it shows: their vines wind up toward the ceiling, packed full of leaves and fruit like a mini orchard. Farmers Tamera and Patrick Mark are blessed with their location, just south of New Buffalo and west of Highway 12. The deep black soil, moist and naturally rich in minerals and organic matter, makes for extra-sweet crops when planted.

Five generations and a century of organic farming and crop rotating have only helped enrich the terroir. Outdoors, other vegetables, including squash, cucumbers, potatoes, green beans, and sweet corn, take root in the healthy earth, making for an even sweeter taste. As such, residents and chefs in Chicago have clamored to get their hands on the Marks' amazing produce. As have I.

CREAMY GAZPACHO

CUCUMBERS, TOMATOES, AND PEPPERS AT THE PEAK OF THE SEASON — *especially when they come from Iron Creek Farm's sweet-tasting bounty — make for some amazing gazpacho. Blending the veggies with a generous amount of good-quality olive oil creates that smooth, velvety texture that cream would offer. This is a lighter version.*

1. Seed and coarsely chop the bell pepper. Finely chop 3 tablespoons and reserve for garnish. Peel, seed, and coarsely chop the cucumber. Finely chop 3 tablespoons and mix with the reserved red pepper for garnish.

2. In a large bowl, combine the coarsely chopped bell pepper and cucumber, the tomatoes, onion, bread, jalapeño, garlic, salt, and vinegar. Place half of the mixture in a blender. Pour in half of the oil. Cover and process until very smooth, for several minutes. Transfer to a clean large bowl. Repeat with the remaining ingredients and the oil and transfer to the large bowl. Refrigerate for at least 2 hours before serving. Garnish with the reserved bell pepper and cucumber.

INGREDIENTS

- 1 large red bell pepper
- 1 medium cucumber
- 2 pounds heirloom tomatoes, cored and coarsely chopped (do not discard seeds and juices)
- ½ small red onion, coarsely chopped
- 1 slice white bread or egg bread, torn into 1-inch pieces
- 1 small jalapeño, seeded and coarsely chopped
- 1 garlic clove, peeled
- 1 teaspoon salt, or more as needed
- 3 tablespoons sherry vinegar
- ¾ cup extra-virgin olive oil

PREP TIME: 25 minutes

CHILLING TIME: 2 hours

Serves 6

Harvest Ratatouille CROSTINI

THIS CROWD-IMPRESSING APPETIZER *is my favorite to make at the height of the summer, when I've gotten my hands on as much Iron Creek produce as possible that morning at the Green City Market. Leftovers taste just as great the next day and make for an incredible salad or pasta dish when tossed with some more fresh herbs and perhaps a little Parmesan cheese. The ratatouille also freezes well for when you want a reminder of summer on a cool fall day. It is adapted from a family recipe shared with me by Tamera Mark of Iron Creek Farm (see page 150).*

INGREDIENTS

- 1   large red bell pepper
- 2   large or 4 small tomatoes
- 3   tablespoons olive oil
- 1   small onion, chopped
- 1   small eggplant, unpeeled, cut into ½-inch cubes (2 cups)
- 1–2   tablespoons balsamic vinegar
- 2   tablespoons chopped fresh basil leaves
- ¼   teaspoon salt
- ¼   teaspoon freshly ground black pepper
- 1   long French baguette, cut into ½-inch-thick slices
- 1 or 2   large garlic cloves, peeled and cut in half

    Shaved Parmesan cheese or aged goat cheese, for topping

1. Preheat the oven to broil. Line a rimmed baking sheet with aluminum foil. Cut the bell pepper lengthwise into quarters and discard the stem and seeds. Place skin side up on the baking sheet. Place the tomatoes around the pepper quarters and broil 4 inches from the heat source for 5 minutes. Use tongs to turn the tomatoes over. Continue to broil until the pepper skins are blackened and the tomato skins are split, about 2 minutes. Cool to room temperature.

2. Meanwhile, heat 2 tablespoons of the oil in a large deep skillet over medium heat. Add the onion and eggplant and sauté for 5 minutes.

3. Peel and discard the skins from the tomatoes, and break into pieces over a bowl to catch the juices. Remove and discard the skins from the bell pepper quarters, and cut the peppers into ½-inch pieces. Add the tomatoes and pepper with their juices from the bowl and foil to the skillet and sauté until the vegetables are tender, about 10 minutes. Remove from the heat and stir in 1 tablespoon of the balsamic vinegar and the remaining 1 tablespoon oil. Stir in the basil, salt and pepper. Taste and add additional balsamic vinegar, salt, and pepper to taste.

4. Lightly toast the baguette slices. While still warm, rub a halved piece of garlic over one side of each toast. Spoon the ratatouille over the toasts and top with the shaved Parmesan.

PREP TIME: 25 minutes

COOKING TIME: 20 minutes

Serves 8–10

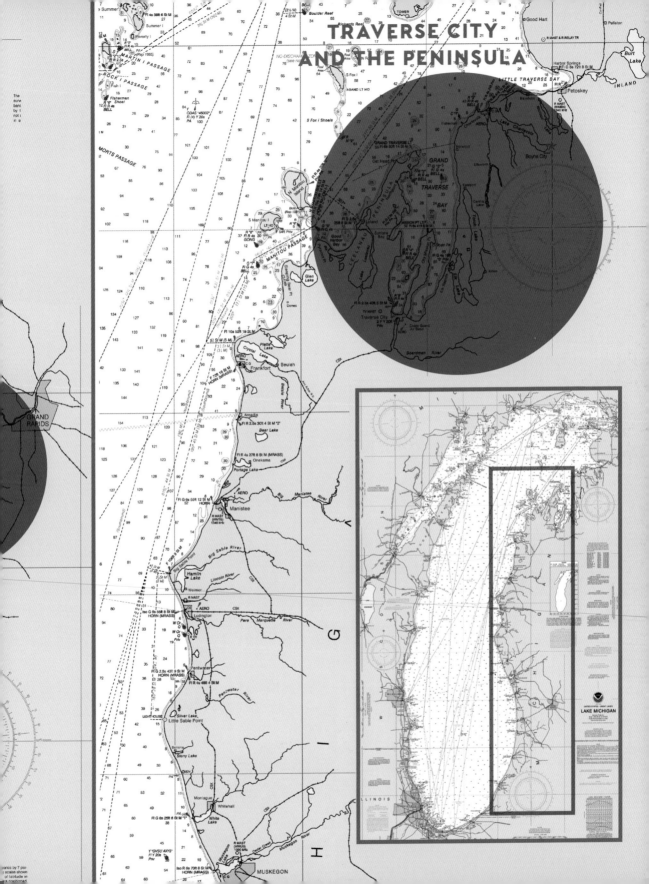

Chapter 5

HARBOR COUNTRY

THE LONG STRETCHES OF BEACHFRONT AND THE DUSTY WHITE SANDS have made the 15-mile southwesternmost strip of Michigan, nicknamed Harbor Country, a tourist haven for Michiganders and Chicagoans alike. Year-round, you'll find more people moving to this area permanently, including a number of transplants from the city less than two hours away.

In between the beaches you'll find marinas and boats, which bring truth to this area's name and give way to the resort culture of the small, close-knit community. In just the past several years, Harbor Country has earned a reputation for something else: great food and drink. You'll find increasing numbers of well-trained chefs, artisans, butchers, distillers, and brewers setting up shop in an area that once truly needed it. Towns include Michiana, Grand Beach, New Buffalo, Union Pier, Lakeside, Harbert, Sawyer, and Three Oaks.

New Buffalo Bill's

WOOD-SMOKED BBQ RIBS

TO RE-CREATE THE AMAZING, SMOKY FLAVOR *of ribs you get at New Buffalo Bill's (see page 162), add a smoker box full of soaked wood chips to the grill when cooking over low temperatures, or wrap the chips in heavy-duty foil with some holes punched through the top. These ribs are so well seasoned, moist, and tender — thanks to the rub and the apple juice basting spray — that they really don't even need sauce, but sometimes I like a little on the side for dipping. Purchase an artisan-style sauce or try my recipe for Simple Barbecue Sauce (page 160). To round out the meal, pair these ribs with Creamy Coleslaw (page 15) and Sweet Potato and Pineapple Salad (page 161), Beach House Cheesy Potatoes (page 170), or Tangy Potato Salad (page 86).*

This recipe takes some time and patience and works best for those weekend or vacation days when you're looking to relax outside with some beers.

FOR THE RUB

- 1 cup granulated or firmly packed brown sugar (or a mixture)
- ¼ cup smoked paprika
- 2 tablespoons garlic powder
- 2 tablespoons onion powder
- 2 tablespoons salt
- 2 tablespoons freshly ground black pepper

FOR THE BASTING SPRAY

- 1 cup apple juice
- ¼ cup apple cider vinegar

FOR THE RIBS

- 2 full racks pork baby back ribs (about 24 ribs), each rack cut in half

1. For the rub, combine the sugar, paprika, garlic and onion powders, salt, and pepper in a small bowl and mix well. For the basting spray, fill a clean, empty spray bottle with the apple juice and vinegar and shake to blend.

2. For the ribs, preheat the grill. If using a charcoal grill, prepare the grill for two-zone heat. Remove the top grate and arrange the coals on either side of the grill, leaving a cool zone in the middle. Replace the grate. If using a gas grill, heat the grill to medium-low heat. Place a smoke box (or a foil packet as noted in the headnote) filled with presoaked, food-safe wood chips (maple, cherry, hickory, apple, oak, or a mixture) over one of the hot coal sides or in the corner of the gas grill with the heat on that side turned up.

Recipe continues on next page

PREP TIME: 5 minutes

COOKING TIME: 2½–3 hours

Serves 4 (half rack of ribs per person)

3. Place a drip pan one-third full with water on the cold side of the grill to catch drippings and prevent flare-ups as well as to add moisture while cooking and prevent the ribs from drying out.

4. Just prior to smoking the ribs, cover both sides of the ribs with the dry rub (2 to 3 tablespoons per rack). Reserve any remaining rub in an airtight container for future use.

5. Place the ribs, bone side down, on the grate opposite the heat source over the drip pan. Cover the grill, making sure the top vents are positioned over the ribs so smoke moves across the meat.

6. Place a kettle grill vent thermometer in one of the top vents so you can monitor the temperature without lifting the cover too often. Adjust the heat by using the dampers on the bottom of your grill to achieve and maintain a cooking temperature of 225°F (107°C).

7. Check the ribs every hour and spray with the basting mixture. If you are using a charcoal grill, you will need to replenish the coals as well to maintain the temperature. The ribs will be done when, if you pick up a rack with tongs in the middle, the meat begins to break apart between each rib and there is a light reddish hue under the skin. This smoking method takes 2½ to 3 hours.

Simple BARBECUE SAUCE

THIS IS A SWEETER SAUCE, *so if you prefer any heat or smoke, add hot sauce, cayenne, and/or smoked paprika to taste.*

INGREDIENTS

- 1 cup ketchup
- ½ cup firmly packed light brown sugar
- 3 tablespoons soy sauce
- 3 tablespoons Worcestershire sauce

Combine the ketchup, brown sugar, soy sauce, and Worcestershire in a bowl or jar. Mix well. Store in the refrigerator for up to 3 weeks.

Makes about 2 cups

SWEET POTATO *and* PINEAPPLE SALAD

THIS REFRESHING AND BRIGHT SALAD *makes a great addition to any summer barbecue or picnic meal. Don't be alarmed at the added sugar in the recipe — it may sound like a strange addition given the sweetness of the sweet potato and the pineapple, but it actually helps boost those flavors and create a silky texture for the dressing. The salad is a favorite at the Washburne Culinary Institute in Chicago, where Reynolds served as provost for many years. For smaller groups, halve the ingredient amounts.*

1. Preheat the oven to 350°F (180°C).

2. For the dressing, combine the oil, vinegar, lemon juice, sugar, salt, and pepper in a blender and process until smooth, or whisk vigorously by hand until emulsified.

3. For the salad, spread the sweet potatoes on a baking sheet and roast in the oven until tender, about 30 minutes. Let cool slightly.

4. Gently toss the warm potatoes, pineapple, celery, red onion, dates, and cashews in a large bowl with the dressing. Chill for at least 1 hour before serving.

FOR THE DRESSING

- ¼ cup canola oil
- ¼ cup apple cider vinegar
- 2 tablespoons fresh lemon juice
- 1 tablespoon sugar
- ½ teaspoon salt
- ¼ teaspoon freshly ground black pepper

FOR THE SALAD

- 2 pounds sweet potatoes, peeled and diced
- 1½ cups diced pineapple
- ¾ cup diced celery
- ¾ cup diced red onion
- ½ cup chopped pitted dates
- ½ cup coarsely chopped cashews

PREP TIME: 20 minutes

COOKING TIME: 30 minutes

CHILLING TIME: 1 hour

Makes 8 cups

New Buffalo Bill's

NEW BUFFALO, MICHIGAN

TAKE ONE STEP INSIDE NEW BUFFALO BILL'S and you'll be instantly greeted by the comforting smells of wood smoke and barbecued meats. This charming smokehouse and 50-seat casual restaurant (complete with a cozy fireplace and brisk take-out business) sits across from the legendary burger joint Redamak's in New Buffalo.

The brainchild of Bill Reynolds, a chef-instructor for the past 25 years at the Culinary Institute of America and the former provost of City Colleges of Chicago's Washburne Culinary Institute, this constantly packed barbecue joint has become a fixture in the city's culinary community. At New Buffalo Bill's, all the mains — from the ribs to the pulled pork, brisket, chicken, and even salmon and vegetarian-friendly tofu and portobello mushroom — are rubbed with a variety of spices and smoked the old-fashioned way for up to 16 hours in a smoker burning a mixture of hickory, oak, and applewood. Pair them with traditional, delicious sides like mac and cheese and creamy coleslaw.

ENCHILADAS *de Berrien Springs*

THESE ENCHILADAS ARE UNLIKE ANY YOU HAVE HAD BEFORE. *Tomatoes and peppers at the peak of the summer season, plus extra-sweet onions and spicy garlic create an even bolder, fresh taste. Warning: The sauce is a touch time-consuming, so consider making extra and freezing it, or make it the day ahead. Serve the enchiladas with chopped cilantro, diced avocado, and sour cream. if desired.*

INGREDIENTS

- 6 dried guajillo chiles (about 2 ounces)
- 6 large poblano chiles (about 1¼ pounds)
- Vegetable oil or corn oil, for frying
- 1 large candy onion, chopped (2 cups)
- 12 garlic cloves, chopped
- 2 cups halved yellow cherry tomatoes (about 10 ounces)
- 2 cups water
- 3 tablespoons fresh lime juice
- 1 tablespoon agave nectar or maple syrup
- 1 tablespoon ground cumin
- Kosher salt
- 12 corn tortillas
- 3 cups shredded Cotija or Chihuahua cheese
- 3 cups shredded sharp cheddar cheese
- ½ cup finely chopped red onion

1. Soak the dried guajillo chiles in hot water to cover for at least 30 minutes to soften them. Drain the chiles and discard the water. Discard the stems and seeds from the chiles and cut into chunks. Set aside.

2. Meanwhile, preheat the broiler to high. Line a baking sheet with aluminum foil. Cut the poblano chiles in half lengthwise and discard the stems and seeds. Press cut sides down onto the baking sheet to flatten. Broil 4 to 5 inches from the heat source until the skins are evenly blackened, about 8 minutes. Wrap the poblanos in the foil from the baking sheet and let stand at room temperature for 20 minutes. Peel and discard the blackened skins and cut the chiles into chunks.

Recipe continues on next page

PREP TIME: 2 hours
BAKING TIME: 25 minutes
Serves 6–8

3. Heat 2 tablespoons of the oil in a large saucepan over medium heat and sauté the candy onion until soft, about 4 minutes. Add the garlic and sauté for 3 minutes. Add both of the chopped chiles and the tomatoes to the saucepan. Add the water and bring to a boil over high heat. Reduce the heat to maintain a simmer. Cook until the vegetables are very tender, about 20 minutes. Use an immersion blender or a food processor to blend until fairly smooth. Stir in the lime juice, agave nectar, cumin, and salt to taste. You should have about 4 cups sauce. Set aside 2 cups of the sauce to cool and then freeze up to 3 months. Spoon ¼ cup of the remaining sauce onto the bottom of a 9- by 13-inch baking dish. Pour 1 cup of the sauce into a shallow pie plate.

4. Preheat the oven to 375°F (190°C). Heat ½ inch of the oil in a small skillet over medium heat until very hot. Fry each tortilla in the oil for about 10 seconds, turning once. Transfer to paper towels to drain. Use tongs to pick up each fried tortilla and dip it into the sauce in the pie plate on both sides, letting excess drip back into pie plate. Transfer to a large sheet of waxed paper.

5. In a large bowl, combine 2 cups of the Cotija cheese with the cheddar cheese and red onion. Spoon ⅓ cup of the cheese mixture down the center of each coated tortilla. Roll up and place seam side down in the baking dish. Spoon the remaining sauce from the saucepan over the enchiladas. Sprinkle the remaining 1 cup Cotija cheese over the enchiladas. Bake for 20 to 25 minutes or until heated through.

Leaning Shed Farm

BERRIEN SPRINGS, MICHIGAN

BRIGHT RED BELLS. LITTLE RED ZINGERS. Twisty capsicums of all shapes, sizes, and names. Waxy purple tomatillo orbs wrapped in leafy shells. When Dave and Denise Dyrek of Leaning Shed Farm show up at Chicago's Green City Market with their first batch of hot and sweet peppers, tomatoes, and tomatillos, you learn the definition of the term *summer bounty*. They bring with them endless rows of crates overflowing with more than 70 tomato and 20 pepper varieties, from the very sweet and mild to the most flavorful and hot, and many with some pretty funky, exotic names.

The Dyreks bought their 30-acre farm in Berrien Springs, Michigan, years ago during Dave's self-described "midlife crisis," when he just wanted to be back in the area and near the beach. He didn't realize that he would work harder than he ever had in his life. But it's all worth it; his rich, fertile soil and hot, dry, shade-free acreage lend themselves well to heat-seeking tomatoes and peppers, providing bountiful harvests that feed many loyal customers in Michigan and across the border.

POACHED EGGS

with Leaning Shed Summer Salsa

THERE IS LITTLE IN LIFE AS CONSISTENTLY SATISFYING AS A SOLID MEXICAN BREAKFAST — *eggs (cooked any way) with a tomato-based spicy sauce or salsa and some warm corn tortillas. You can add rice and beans, onions, cheese, and fried tortilla chips, but the backbone is a great salsa made with fresh produce (such as that from Leaning Shed Farm; see page 167). Keep extras in your fridge for topping just about anything, or freeze for longer-term storage through the winter.*

FOR THE SALSA

- 2 large tomatoes
- 1 large red bell pepper
- 1 large poblano chile
- 1 jalapeño chile
- 2 tablespoons vegetable oil
- 1 cup chopped sweet onion
- 3 garlic cloves, minced
- 2 teaspoons ground cumin
- ½ teaspoon salt
- 1 cup unsalted chicken stock or broth

FOR THE EGGS

- 6 eggs
- 2 tablespoons chopped fresh cilantro, for garnish (optional)

1. For the salsa, preheat the broiler to high. Line a baking sheet with aluminum foil. Place the tomatoes on the baking sheet. Cut the bell pepper in half lengthwise, discard the stem and seeds, and place cut side down on the baking sheet. Place the poblano and jalapeño chiles on the baking sheet.

2. Broil the vegetables 3 to 4 inches from heat source for 5 minutes. Turn the tomatoes and chiles (not the bell pepper) with tongs and continue to broil for 4 to 5 minutes longer or until the skins are brown. Remove from the broiler and let stand for 10 minutes, covered loosely with a clean kitchen towel or foil. Peel and discard the skins and seeds from the vegetables and chop into ¼-inch pieces.

PREP TIME: 15 minutes

COOKING TIME: 30 minutes

Serves 3 (makes 2½ cups sauce)

3. Meanwhile, heat the oil in a large saucepan over medium heat and sauté the onion until soft, about 4 minutes. Add the garlic and sauté for 3 minutes. Stir in the bell peppers, chiles, cumin, and salt, and cook for 2 minutes. Stir in the tomatoes and chicken stock. Remove from the heat and allow to cool slightly. Transfer the salsa to a food processor or in two batches to a blender. Process until just slightly chunky. The salsa will keep for up to 1 month in the refrigerator.

4. For the eggs, return the salsa to the saucepan over medium heat. Bring to a low simmer and cook until the salsa has thickened slightly and is reduced by one-third. Crack the eggs, one at a time, directly into the salsa, making sure to space them evenly. Cover and simmer until the eggs are just set and the whites are cooked through, 7 to 10 minutes. Garnish with the cilantro, if desired, and serve immediately.

Beach House CHEESY POTATOES

WE MAKE THESE EXTREMELY INDULGENT BUT UNFORGETTABLE *cheesy potatoes when grilling steaks or ribs at my sister-in-law's family beach house in Grand Beach, just south of downtown New Buffalo. It's such a treat to get an invitation to the house in the summer for some beach time.*

INGREDIENTS

- 2 pounds russet or Yukon gold potatoes (about 3 large)
- 4 tablespoons unsalted butter
- 2 garlic cloves, minced
- 1 cup heavy cream
- 1 (8-ounce) block sharp cheddar cheese, grated
- 1 (8-ounce) block Havarti or butterkäse cheese, grated
- ¾ teaspoon salt
- ¾ teaspoon freshly ground black pepper

1. Preheat the oven to 375°F (190°C). Using a sharp knife or mandoline, cut the potatoes into ¼-inch slices and, as they are cut, add to a large bowl filled with cold water.

2. To make the cheese sauce, melt the butter in a large saucepan over medium heat. Add the garlic and cook until fragrant, 1 to 2 minutes. Add the cream, bring to a simmer, and cook for 2 minutes.

3. Combine the cheeses in a medium bowl. Transfer half of the cheese to a smaller bowl and set aside. Add the remaining cheese to the saucepan and stir until melted. Remove from the heat.

4. Drain the potatoes, and dry with a clean kitchen towel or paper towels. Butter a 9- by 13-inch baking dish. Layer one-third of the potato slices over the bottom of the dish. Sprinkle ¼ teaspoon each salt and pepper lightly over the potatoes. Spread one-third of the cheese sauce over the potatoes. Repeat the layering with potatoes, salt and pepper, and sauce two more times.

5. Cover the dish with aluminum foil and bake for 45 minutes. Uncover and top with the reserved cheeses. Continue baking, uncovered, for 15 minutes longer, or until the potatoes are cooked through (check with a sharp knife) and the sauce is bubbly. Let stand at room temperature for 10 minutes before serving.

PREP TIME: 40 minutes

BAKING TIME: 1 hour

Serves 6–8

PORK RILLETTES
with Pickled Cherries

I'VE MADE THIS RECIPE FOR MANY DINNER PARTIES *and always get a pat on the back from friends as a result. Thanks to Pat Mullins. This recipe requires some advance planning: The cherries need to marinate for at least a day and up to a week before serving. Serve this with crackers, toast points, or baguette slices, along with assorted mustards.*

1. For the pickled cherries, combine the vinegar, sugar, cloves, and peppercorns in a medium stainless steel saucepan. Bring to a boil over high heat, stirring occasionally. Reduce the heat and simmer until the sugar is dissolved, about 2 minutes. Cool to room temperature.

2. Place the cherries in a large bowl. Pour the vinegar mixture over the cherries. Cover and refrigerate for at least 1 day and up to 1 week before serving.

3. For the pork, combine the pork shoulder, pork fat, water, salt, and bay leaf in a large saucepan. Bring to a boil over high heat. Stir well, reduce the heat, cover, and simmer until the pork is falling apart, about 4 hours.

4. Discard the bay leaf. Strain and reserve the cooking liquid from the pork. Place the pork in a large bowl, add the pepper, and begin to pull or mash the pork together (alternatively, this can be done in an electric mixer with a paddle attachment). Gradually add the cooking liquid and stir until incorporated. Taste and add more salt if needed. Place in a serving container or mason jar and allow to cool. Cover and refrigerate to chill before serving with the pickled cherries.

FOR THE PICKLED CHERRIES

4¼ cups white wine vinegar

1½ cups sugar

½ teaspoon whole cloves

½ teaspoon black peppercorns

2 pounds pitted sweet cherries

FOR THE PORK

2 pounds boneless pork shoulder, cut into 1-inch chunks

8 ounces pork fat (fatback or trimmings), cut into 1-inch chunks

1 cup water

2 tablespoons salt

1 bay leaf

1 teaspoon ground black pepper

PREP TIME: 30 minutes

COOKING TIME: 4 hours

Serves 8–10

SPICY FENNEL SAUSAGE AND PEPPERS

with Garlicky Heirloom Tomato Sauce

THIS DISH, INSPIRED BY THE CLASSIC SAUSAGE-AND-PEPPERS DISH *gracing old school Italian restaurants in Chicago, uses spicy fennel sausage made by Pat Mullins of Patellie's Pizza (formally P.&E. Mullins butcher shop), though you can substitute another good local Italian sausage. A nice bottle of red wine might not be a bad idea for a pairing. If you don't have balsamic vinegar on hand, use a little of the wine to deglaze the pan. Leaning Shed Farm (see page 167) also has wonderful supersweet tomatoes and peppers, perfect for this dish. Serve with crusty bread or your favorite pasta, if you like.*

FOR THE SAUCE

- 1 pound heirloom tomatoes
- 4 garlic cloves, unpeeled

FOR THE SAUSAGE

- 2 tablespoons olive oil
- 1 pound Italian-style or fennel sausage, links or cut into 4 links
- 1 medium yellow or sweet onion, halved and sliced
- 2 medium red bell peppers, halved, seeded, and cut into 1-inch strips
- 1 tablespoon good-quality balsamic vinegar or red wine vinegar
- ⅓ cup grated Parmesan cheese
- ⅓ cup thinly sliced fresh basil

1. For the sauce, preheat the oven to broil. Line a baking sheet with aluminum foil. Broil the tomatoes and garlic on the baking sheet until partially blackened, turning occasionally. Remove the garlic cloves. Peel the skins from the tomatoes, and transfer the tomatoes and juices to a blender by lifting the foil. When cool enough to handle, squeeze the garlic flesh out of the blackened peels into the blender. Purée until smooth.

2. For the sausage, heat 1 tablespoon of the oil in a large skillet over medium heat. Add the sausage and brown on all sides, about 5 minutes. Remove the sausage from the skillet. Add the remaining 1 tablespoon oil and the onions, and cook until soft and translucent, about 2 minutes. Add the peppers and cook until the onions begin to brown and the peppers begin to soften, about 5 minutes. Add the vinegar and cook until reduced by half, about 1 minute, stirring frequently to deglaze the pan. Return the sausages to the pan and pour the tomato-pepper sauce over them. Simmer over medium heat until the vegetables are tender and the sauce has thickened, 10 to 15 minutes. Serve topped with the Parmesan and basil.

PREP TIME: 5 minutes

COOKING TIME: 35 minutes

Serves 4

DEVILED EGGS *Two Ways*

HERE'S MY ATTEMPT AT RE-CREATING THE PERFECT PROTEIN-PACKED SNACKS *or entertaining appetizers from Froehlich's Deli, which offers deviled eggs with its lineup of hearty sandwiches and impressive party platters. For a special treat, top the classic ones with a little spoonful of Collin's Caviar (see page 187). If taking them on the road for a snack or picnic, you can do what Froehlich's does — press two deviled eggs together, filling to filling, with the whites on the outside like a mini sandwich, for mess-free transfer.*

FOR THE EGGS

12 eggs

FOR THE TRADITIONAL FILLING

½ cup mayonnaise

1 tablespoon pickle relish

2 teaspoons Dijon mustard

½ teaspoon dried dill (optional)

¼ teaspoon salt

Paprika, for sprinkling

FOR THE HERBED FILLING

⅓ cup mayonnaise

2 teaspoons Dijon mustard

2 tablespoons chopped fresh parsley, plus more for garnish (optional)

2 tablespoons chopped fresh tarragon

2 tablespoons chopped fresh chives

¼ teaspoon salt

1. For the deviled eggs, place the eggs in a large saucepan or deep skillet in one layer. Cover with cold water by 1 inch. Cover and bring to a boil over high heat. Uncover, reduce the heat to medium-low, and simmer gently for 10 minutes. Drain the eggs, leaving them in the pan. Run cold tap water over the eggs. Add ice cubes to the pan to cool the eggs faster. When the eggs are cool enough to handle, peel and halve each egg lengthwise. Use a small spoon to transfer the egg yolks to a medium bowl.

2. For the traditional filling, mash the yolks with the mayonnaise, pickle relish, mustard, dill (if using), and salt. Mound the mixture into the egg whites or pipe in using a pastry bag or plastic bag with one of the corner tips cut off to create a small hole. Dust the eggs with paprika. Arrange on a serving dish and refrigerate for at least 30 minutes before serving.

3. For the herbed filling, mash the yolks with the mayonnaise, mustard, parsley, tarragon, chives, and salt. Mound the mixture into the egg whites or pipe in using a pastry bag or plastic bag with one of the corner tips cut off to create a small hole. Garnish with more parsley, if desired. Arrange on a serving dish and refrigerate for at least 30 minutes before serving.

PREP TIME: 20 minutes

COOKING TIME: 10 minutes

CHILLING TIME: 30 minutes

Serves 12

Froehlich's Deli

THREE OAKS, MICHIGAN

FROEHLICH'S DELI IS A REGULAR STOP FOR SANDWICHES, fresh homemade bagels, and jarred pantry goodies like artisan jams, spreads, and other preserves and sauces made on-site. Colleen Froehlich opened the shop and deli in 1992 after buying and restoring an old building on North Elm Street. She's since expanded her artisan food and home goods empire with a renovated bakery at the original location and Froehlich's Kitchen and Pantry just across the street.

SMOKED LEEK SAUSAGE FRITTATA

with Summer Squash and Goat Cheese

I DEVELOPED THIS RECIPE AFTER A SAUSAGE RUN *to the former P.&E. Mullins Local in New Buffalo. If you can't get their smoked leek or fennel sausage, try another smoked sausage, such as kielbasa. If you go to the store, you can also pick up the farm-fresh eggs, summer produce, and goat cheese for this recipe. Serve for brunch, lunch, or a light dinner.*

INGREDIENTS

- 1 tablespoon vegetable oil or grape-seed oil
- 4 links smoked leek (or fennel) pork sausage, sliced on the bias into ½-inch-thick pieces
- 2 tablespoons butter
- 1 medium leek, sliced (white and light green parts separated)
- 1 medium yellow squash, cut into ¼-inch rounds, then sliced in half
- 1 medium zucchini, cut into ¼-inch rounds, then sliced in half
- 1 garlic clove, finely chopped
- 12 eggs
- Pinch of salt, or more as needed
- ¼ teaspoon freshly ground black pepper
- ¼ cup chopped fresh chives, plus more for garnish
- ½ cup crumbled goat cheese (such as Evergreen Lane Cheese fresh chèvre, page 223)
- 2–3 ounces Parmesan or other hard, nutty cheese, shaved with a vegetable peeler

1. Preheat the oven to 400°F (200°C).

2. Heat the oil in a large deep skillet over medium-high heat. Add the sausage and cook, flipping once, to brown on both sides, 2 to 3 minutes per side. Remove the sausage and set aside. Add 1 tablespoon of the butter, the white parts of the leek, and both squashes to the skillet. Cook, stirring occasionally, until the squash is browned and beginning to soften. Add the garlic and the green parts of the leek, and cook until fragrant, 1 to 2 minutes.

3. Add remaining 1 tablespoon butter and melt in the skillet. Meanwhile, season the eggs with the salt and pepper and beat vigorously with a whisk to fluff up with air. Fold in the chives and goat cheese.

4. Pour the egg mixture into the skillet. Cook just until the bottom and edges are set, about 5 minutes. Layer the Parmesan shavings over the top of the frittata and transfer to the oven. Bake for about 5 minutes, or until the center is set and the cheese has melted. Let the frittata cool for 5 to 10 minutes before slicing. Garnish with additional chives.

PREP TIME: 5 minutes

COOKING TIME: 25 minutes

Serves 4

BRINED PORK CHOPS

with Caramelized Onions and Apples

THANK GOODNESS IT'S NOW ACCEPTABLE TO EAT PORK CHOPS COOKED MEDIUM-RARE.
Thanks to more natural marbling and better care of the animals, we can enjoy juicy, bone-in pork cuts cooked just like steak. It's a far cry from the hockey pucks of the 1980s and '90s. Sweet, buttery onions and apples add even more richness to this dish. Look for the fattier, deeper-flavored Berkshire or Duroc pork chops from Slagel Family Farms. Or, try Jake's Country Meats in Cassopolis, Michigan — a 40-year-old pig farm raising its animals outside on rich, hearty pasture.

1. For the brine, bring the water, salt, and sugar to a simmer in a saucepan, stirring until the sugar dissolves. Cool to room temperature and pour into a large shallow pie plate or baking dish. Add the pork chops, turn over to coat them, and let stand at room temperature for 30 minutes or refrigerate for up to 2 hours.

2. Meanwhile, melt the butter in a large skillet over medium heat. Sauté the onions until they begin to brown, about 15 minutes. Stir in the apples and apple cider and sauté until the apples are tender and the juices have thickened, 6 to 8 minutes.

3. Prepare a gas or charcoal grill for medium-high-heat grilling, or have a stovetop ridged grill pan ready. Drain the pork chops and pat dry with paper towels. Combine the paprika, thyme, pepper, garlic powder, and salt, and rub over both sides of the pork chops.

4. Grill on the covered grill or in a heated grill pan over medium heat until the internal temperature of the pork reaches 135°F (57°C), about 4 minutes per side. Allow the pork to rest for 5 minutes (the temperature will rise about 10 more degrees to 145°F (63°C) for medium-rare doneness). Serve the pork chops with the caramelized onions and apples.

FOR THE BRINE

- 4 cups water
- ¼ cup kosher salt
- ¼ cup firmly packed brown sugar

FOR THE PORK

- 4 bone-in pork loin chops, ¾ inch thick
- 2 tablespoons butter
- 1 medium sweet onion, cut into thin wedges
- 2 small red apples, cored and cut into ¼-inch wedges
- ¼ cup unsweetened apple cider or apple juice
- 1½ teaspoons smoked or sweet paprika
- 1½ teaspoons dried thyme
- ½ teaspoon freshly ground black pepper
- ¼ teaspoon garlic powder
- ¼ teaspoon kosher salt

PREP TIME: 15 minutes

BRINING TIME: 30 minutes–2 hours

COOKING TIME: 30 minutes

Serves 4

Round Barn Winery
and Free Run Cellars
BARODA AND BERRIEN SPRINGS, MICHIGAN

WITH ITS ICONIC ROUND BARN TASTING ROOM and grassy grounds in Baroda, Round Barn Winery has established a loyal following in the southwest Michigan region. Founded in 1992 by winemaker Richard Moersch, it is known for its wide variety of dry (and fruity) wines using locally grown grapes, as well as its line of DiVine vodka and other spirits made from Ugni Blanc grapes. In 2006, Moersch's sons and winemakers-distillers Matt and Christian opened Free Run Cellars, the boutique craft winery offshoot of Round Barn. There, they make smaller batches of wine by hand using local grapes.

In 2005, the Moersch brothers added a brewery to Round Barn, and in 2013, they opened Public House at Round Barn, a casual brewpub with more than 60 handcrafted beers, from aromatic IPAs to lighter, food-friendly session beers to others aged in bourbon and brandy barrels. Culinary director Ryan Thornburg, who has spent the past two decades in the area, first at Tosi's Restaurant and later at Bistro on the Boulevard, helped shape the menu for Round Barn.

In anticipation of the 10-year anniversary of Free Run Cellars in 2016, the Moersch brothers gutted and renovated the winery's tasting room and teamed up with Thornburg to offer an expanded, epicurean-inspired tasting menu. They pair Free Run wines with Thornburg's inventive creations, which involve local peaches, blueberries, asparagus, peas, pork, pickles, apricots, smoked whitefish, tart cherries, and sausages from Zick's Grocery in St. Joseph, among other seasonal foods.

Vitis vinifera grapes grown on the grounds of Free Run are used to produce drier-style white wines like Riesling, Chardonnay, Pinot Grigio, and Pinot Gris, and some red wines like Pinot Noir and Cabernet Franc. The grapes actually prefer the harsh winters and Lake Effect breeze, "which moderates the temperature here so we don't get extreme highs and lows," Matt Moersch explains. As with any crop, the terroir has an impact on the taste. "We have sandier, heavier soil, which helps create a lot of fruit-forward characteristics in the wine, whereas in Europe there is typically more limestone and rock, which leads to more minerality," he says.

In the fall, the staff at Free Run will harvest the grapes by handpicking them rather than using machines so they can be more selective and careful, so the grapes retain more flavor when they are crushed or pressed. Leaving the stems on during pressing adds even more aroma and flavor to the wine. Temperature-controlled tanks maintain natural fermentation, and the reds wines are transferred to French oak barrels to age for up to 24 months, which helps soften out the edges.

Thornburg pairs Free Run Moscato wine, which has light tropical notes, with roasted Michigan peaches, blue cheese, arugula, and pumpernickel toast. He likes the winery's Lake Michigan Shore Syrah with a locally sourced smoked duck breast and whipped goat cheese on puff pastry.

KOREAN PORK BAO SANDWICH

PAIR CARAMELIZED PORK BELLY WITH SOFT, PLIABLE BUNS *and you get this highly addictive sandwich, which is lightened up by a little pickled cucumber and the crunch of peanuts. Richard Moersch (see page 178) recommends pairing this Asian-inspired treat with Free Run's Zinfandel, aged for 18 months in French oak.*

FOR THE PORK

- 4 cups water
- 1½ cups soy sauce
- 1½ cups firmly packed light brown sugar
- 1 tablespoon garlic powder
- 3 scallions, sliced
- 2 pounds skinless pork belly

FOR THE QUICK PICKLES

- 3 small pickling cucumbers, sliced into thin rounds
- 1 tablespoon kosher salt
- 1 teaspoon sugar

FOR THE SANDWICHES

- ½ cup roasted peanuts, chopped
- 1 tablespoon sugar
  - Vegetable oil, as needed
- 6 bao buns or slider rolls
- 3 tablespoons hoisin sauce
- 3 teaspoons chopped fresh cilantro

1. For the pork, combine the water, soy sauce, brown sugar, garlic powder, and scallions in a large bowl. Stir to dissolve the sugar. Place the pork belly in a baking pan large enough to hold the pork. Pour the marinade over the pork. Cover and refrigerate for 24 hours.

2. Preheat the oven to 300°F (150°C). Uncover the pork belly and place in the oven (do not drain the marinade). Bake for about 3 hours, until tender.

3. Remove the pan from the oven and let cool slightly. Place another pan directly on top of the pork belly and weight it down with canned goods to compress the pork belly. Refrigerate for 6 hours or until the pork belly is firm.

PREP TIME: 50 minutes

MARINATING TIME: 24 hours

COOKING TIME: 3 hours

CHILLING TIME: 6 hours

Serves 6

4. To make the quick pickles, place the cucumbers, salt, and sugar in a nonreactive bowl and combine well. Cover and let marinate for at least 1 hour. The pickles can be stored in the refrigerator for up to 1 week.

5. For the sandwiches, crush the roasted peanuts with the sugar and set aside. Slice the pork belly into 3-inch-long blocks, and then into ½-inch-thick rectangles. Add a little oil to a large skillet and place over medium heat until hot. Add the pork belly slices and cook until golden brown, about 2 minutes. Turn over and cook until golden brown and heated through, 2 to 3 minutes longer.

6. Wrap each bun in a damp paper towel and heat in a vegetable steamer or place one at a time in microwave and heat on high for 30 seconds. Open up the steamed buns and spread each with 1½ teaspoons of the hoisin sauce. Add a slice of pork belly to each and top with quick pickles, cilantro, and the crushed peanuts. Refrigerate the remaining pork belly for up to 3 days.

SMOKED WHITEFISH PÂTÉ

with Tart Cherry Jam

SERVE THIS PÂTÉ ON WARM CRUSTY BREAD OR CRACKERS, *topped with the jam and scallions. The cherry jam also tastes delicious as a topping for yogurt or ice cream. Richard Moersch (see page 178) recommends pairing this with their Pinot Meunier rosé, which is fresh and full of red fruit flavors without being overly sweet, of course. Tip: There is no pectin in the jam, so it needs to be reduced by half to thicken properly. Toward the end, you will have to stir frequently to avoid scorching.*

FOR THE WHITEFISH SPREAD

- ½ cup good-quality or Homemade Mayonnaise (page 87)
- 1 tablespoon fresh lemon juice
- 1 celery stalk, minced
- 1 scallion, sliced thinly on the bias, plus more for garnish

  Salt and freshly ground black pepper
- 1 pound smoked whitefish, skinned, boned, and flaked

FOR THE CHERRY JAM

- 1 pound fresh or frozen pitted tart cherries
- 1 cup sugar

  Toasted buttered baguette slices, for serving

1. For the whitefish spread, combine the mayonnaise, lemon juice, celery, scallion, and salt and pepper to taste in a medium bowl. Mix well, and then gently fold in the smoked whitefish to combine. Refrigerate for at least 30 minutes to chill.

2. For the jam, combine the cherries and sugar in a large saucepan over medium-low heat and watch until the mixture starts to release its juices and the sugar has dissolved. Raise the heat to medium-high and cook, watching closely and stirring with a heatproof spatula. The cherries will tend to foam high in the pan, so be careful of boiling over. If this happens, turn the heat down slightly. Maintain a steady boil until the jam has thickened, 15 to 20 minutes. Remove from the heat and let cool. The jam can be stored in the refrigerator for up to 1 month.

3. Serve the pâté on buttered toasted baguette slices, topped with about a tablespoon of the jam and a pinch of scallions.

PREP TIME: 5 minutes

CHILLING TIME: 30 minutes

COOKING TIME: 25 minutes

Serves 6–8

FREE RUN
CELLARS
2016 PINOT MEUNIER
• LAKE MICHIGAN SHORE •
FREE
Run

RED CURRY CHICKEN
SKEWERS *with Apricot Chutney*

MATT MOERSCH AND RYAN THORNBURG (PAGE 178) RECOMMEND PAIRING *these spiced skewers with Free Run's dry Riesling, a crisp and fruity, "lovely anytime wine," as they call it, with just a hint of sweetness in the finish. In the summer, apricots abound in this fruit belt and make for great chutney.*

FOR THE CHICKEN SKEWERS

- ½ cup vegetable oil
- 3   tablespoons Thai red curry paste
- 1   tablespoon sriracha sauce
- 1   teaspoon kosher salt
- 3   pounds boneless, skinless chicken breasts, cut into 1-inch cubes

FOR THE APRICOT CHUTNEY

- 2   pounds fresh apricots, halved and pitted
- ¼   cup finely chopped yellow onion
- 1   garlic clove, minced
- ⅓   cup granulated sugar
- ⅓   cup firmly packed light brown sugar
- ⅓   cup golden raisins
- ⅓   cup apple cider vinegar
- 1   teaspoon grated fresh gingerroot
- ½   teaspoon dry mustard
- ¼   teaspoon ground allspice
- ½   teaspoon kosher salt
- ⅛   teaspoon cayenne pepper

1. For the chicken skewers, stir together the oil, curry paste, sriracha, and salt in a large bowl. Add the chicken, mixing well to coat it. Cover and marinate in the refrigerator for at least 2 hours or overnight.

2. Meanwhile, for the apricot chutney, combine the apricots, onion, garlic, both sugars, raisins, vinegar, ginger, mustard, allspice, salt, and cayenne in a large saucepan. Bring to a boil over high heat, stirring occasionally. Reduce the heat to medium. Cook until slightly thickened, stirring occasionally, about 20 minutes. Remove from the heat and cool completely. The chutney can be stored in the refrigerator for up to 1 month.

3. Prepare a gas or charcoal grill for medium-high-heat grilling. Thread the chicken onto 10 metal skewers, leaving about 1 inch between the chicken cubes. Grill until lightly charred, turning about halfway through, about 8 minutes. Transfer to a platter and serve with the chutney.

PREP TIME: 20 minutes

MARINATING TIME: 2 hours

COOKING TIME: 30 minutes

Serves 10

Spiced BREAKFAST SAUSAGE PATTIES

THE SPICE-FORWARD SAUSAGE PATTIES *we've enjoyed during brunch at Jackie Shen's Café were the inspiration for these breakfast sausages. Make them part of a true farmer's breakfast or brunch with fresh, local farm eggs, toast with good-quality butter, and homemade fruit jam. The patties can be frozen, raw or cooked, for up to 3 months.*

1. Combine the pork, egg, garlic, sage, cardamom, pepper flakes, thyme, salt, and pepper. With wet hands, divide the mixture into 8 pieces and shape to form patties about 2½ inches in diameter and ⅓ inch thick.

2. Heat the oil in a very large nonstick skillet over medium heat. Add the patties and cook until golden brown and cooked through, about 4 minutes per side.

INGREDIENTS

- 1 pound ground pork
- 1 egg, beaten
- 1 large garlic clove, minced
- ¾ teaspoon dried sage
- ½ teaspoon ground cardamom
- ½ teaspoon red pepper flakes
- ½ teaspoon dried thyme
- ½ teaspoon coarse sea salt
- ½ teaspoon freshly ground black pepper
- 2 teaspoons vegetable oil or olive oil

PREP TIME: 8 minutes

COOKING TIME: 8 minutes

Serves 4

MINI HOECAKES

with Great Lakes Golden Caviar

THIS TWIST ON THE CLASSIC BLINI WITH CAVIAR APPETIZER *makes for a perfect enter-taining hors d'oeuvre. Rachel Collins, founder of Flagship Specialty Foods & Fish Market in Lakeside, Michigan (see page 187), and president of her family's business, Collins Caviar, tops just about anything with caviar — from simple crackers and toast points to deviled eggs (page 174) and, for a special treat, thin and round corncakes known as hoecakes.*

INGREDIENTS

- ½ cup unbleached all-purpose flour
- ⅓ cup coarse-grind cornmeal, such as Bob's Red Mill
- 1 tablespoon sugar
- ½ teaspoon salt
- ½ teaspoon baking powder
- ⅔ cup whole milk
- 1 egg, beaten
- 2 tablespoons unsalted butter, melted, plus more for cooking

  Crème fraîche or sour cream, for serving
- 1 (1-ounce) container Carolyn Collins Great Lakes Golden Whitefish Caviar

  Chopped fresh chives or chive blossoms, for garnish (optional)

1. Whisk together the flour, cornmeal, sugar, salt, and baking powder in a medium bowl. Make a well in the center of the dry ingredients. Add the milk and egg. Mix just until the dry ingredients are moistened. Stir in the melted butter.

2. Melt 2 teaspoons butter in a large nonstick skillet over medium heat. Swirl the skillet to coat the bottom with the butter. Pour level tablespoons of the batter into the skillet 2 inches apart. Cook until bubbles appear on the surface, 2 to 3 minutes. Turn over the hoe-cakes with a spatula and cook until the bottoms are browned, about 2 minutes. Transfer the hoecakes to a large serving platter and let cool to room temperature. Continue making the hoecakes, using more butter in the skillet as needed.

3. To serve, spoon a heaping ¼ teaspoon crème fraîche onto each cake and top with a heaping ¼ teaspoon caviar. Garnish with chives, if desired, and serve immediately.

PREP TIME: 10 minutes

COOKING TIME: 5 minutes per batch

Serves 6–8

Flagship Specialty Foods
& Fish Market

LAKESIDE, MICHIGAN

RACHEL COLLINS GREW UP FISHING the waters of Lake Michigan with her mother, Carolyn Collins, helping alongside in the 1980s as she figured out a way to save the beautiful roe from Great Lakes Chinook salmon and trout and produce it into caviar. Now, following a successful run as a personal chef and caterer, Collins has brought the family caviar — and other fresh fish — even more into the public eye with her store, Flagship Specialty Foods & Fish Market, located on Red Arrow Highway in Lakeside, Michigan.

Opened in the summer of 2016, Flagship Specialty Foods offers a lineup of fresh fish and shellfish — including whitefish, salmon, lake trout, walleye, and burbot (lawyer fish) — that is flown in or caught locally daily. The store also carries meals for takeout or eating at a table outside: hot-out-of-the-oven, juicy and monstrous fennel- and rosemary-spiked porchetta sandwiches; fresh fish and chips; pesto-loaded mashed potatoes; homemade triple-chocolate cookies; and more. Customers can also purchase gourmet items like smoked fish spreads and, of course, Collins Caviar.

Collins Caviar is an exclusive producer of American freshwater caviar, purchasing roe from local and national fisheries and Native American tribes. In addition to its most popular whitefish caviar from the Great Lakes, the company also produces caviars from hackleback sturgeon and paddlefish, along with specialty products like caviar cream spread.

Fruit Scene - Berrien Co., So. West Mich.

Greetings from
BENTON
HARBOR
MICHIGAN

Chapter 6

SOUTHWEST MICHIGAN

A DRIVE THROUGH MICHIGAN'S SOUTHWESTERN TERRAIN means passing by countless u-pick farms for blueberries, strawberries, peaches, and more. In the summertime, this bounty overruns crates set out at nearby roadside stands. Further inland, rolling hills carry you through rows upon rows of grapevines and apple trees peppered by farmhouse wineries and cider houses.

This is the Fruit Belt of the nation, considered by some to be the most diverse agricultural area outside of Orange County, California. The rich and fertile soil and temperate climates have — what else? — Lake Michigan to thank. Cooling winds during the first frost of the fall activate the natural sugars of the crops, making them some of the sweetest bounties anywhere. At the northern end of Berrien County, towns include St. Joseph, Benton Harbor, Bridgman, Baroda, Buchanan, Coloma, Niles, and Watervliet.

Grandma's German APPLE PANCAKE

THIS IS NOT YOUR ORDINARY PANCAKE. *Think of it as a fluffy fruit tart, bubbling up with a sweet, caramelized crust. René Gelder of Ellis Family Farms shared this recipe from her grandmother, who used the farm's apples, which always seem to be amazingly crisp, tart, and sweet — all in one complex bite.*

INGREDIENTS

- 4 tablespoons butter
- 3 large apples (about 1½ pounds), such as Jonagold, Golden Delicious, or Melrose, peeled and thinly sliced
- 2 tablespoons ground cinnamon
- ¼ cup sugar
- 3 eggs
- ¾ cup whole milk
- ¾ cup unbleached all-purpose flour
- ¼ teaspoon salt

PREP TIME: 30 minutes

COOKING TIME: 22 minutes

Serves 6–8

1. Preheat the oven to 425°F (220°C). Melt 2 tablespoons of the butter in a 10-inch ovenproof skillet at least 2 inches deep over medium-high heat. Add the apples and sauté until beginning to brown, about 5 minutes. Add the cinnamon and 2 tablespoons of the sugar and toss with the apples until they are well coated with the mixture. Remove from the pan and set aside. Do not wash the pan.

2. Beat the eggs with a fork in a medium bowl. Add the milk and mix well. Add the flour and salt and mix just until the dry ingredients are moistened. Melt the remaining 2 tablespoons butter in the same pan you used for the apples. Pour the milk mixture into the pan and spoon the apples over the batter in a single layer. Transfer the pan to the oven and bake for 20 to 22 minutes, until the batter is puffed and set.

3. Cut into wedges and serve warm or at room temperature.

Ellis Family Farms

BENTON HARBOR, MICHIGAN

RENÉ GELDER AND HER HUSBAND, BRUCE, maintain the 56-acre farm with the help of their children Matthew, Marc, and Mary, and their daughters-in-law, Christina and Laura. It's truly a family affair to grow the asparagus, rhubarb, strawberries, cherries, apricots, blueberries, multicolored raspberries, blackberries, nectarines, peaches, apples, grapes, pears, and even chestnuts that loyal customers clamor for every season. They also travel to Chicago to sell at the Green City Market.

Heirloom APPLE BUTTER

THIS VERSATILE CONDIMENT, *with its strong apple flavor that can vary from sweet with Honey-crisp apples or tart with Jonagold apples, makes regular butter seem boring. Simply spread it on toast, English muffins, or cinnamon-raisin bread, or try it in a sandwich with a little cheddar cheese for a more sweet-and-savory combination.*

1. Peel and core the apples and cut each into 8 wedges. Combine the apples and cider in a large saucepan. Cover and bring to a boil over high heat. Reduce the heat and simmer for 15 minutes. Uncover and simmer until the apples are very tender and the liquid is absorbed, about 10 minutes longer.

2. Place the apples in a food processor and process until smooth. Return to the same saucepan and stir in the brown sugar, cinnamon, allspice, and salt. Simmer uncovered over medium heat until very thick and reduced to 2 cups, about 15 minutes. Cool completely, and store in jars in the refrigerator for up to 1 month.

INGREDIENTS

- 2 pounds apples, such as Wealthy, Cortland, or Empire
- 1 cup unsweetened apple cider or apple juice
- ¼ cup firmly packed brown sugar
- 1 teaspoon ground cinnamon
- ¼ teaspoon ground allspice or cloves
- ¼ teaspoon salt

PREP TIME: 25 minutes

COOKING TIME: 40 minutes

Makes about 2 cups

Apple-Cinnamon FRITTERS

SENT STRAIGHT FROM THE OVEN PIPING-HOT, *the cinnamon- and sugar-speckled nuggets from Apple Holler restaurant in Kenosha would help satisfy my rumbling tummy after an afternoon of apple picking as a child, while I waited for the rest of the feast. These fritters are an homage to that nostalgic treat.*

The fritters will not keep well overnight, but you may refrigerate any remaining batter and save the oil in the saucepan overnight. Let the batter come to room temperature before frying.

INGREDIENTS

Vegetable oil, for frying

¾ cup sugar

2 teaspoons ground cinnamon

1¾ cups unbleached all-purpose flour

2½ teaspoons baking powder

¼ teaspoon salt

2 eggs

¾ cup whole milk

2 tablespoons unsalted butter, melted and cooled

2 large apples, peeled, cored, and cut into ¼-inch pieces

NOTE: *If a deep-frying thermometer is not available, heat the oil just until shimmering and then drop a small amount of the batter into the hot oil. If it browns in less than 1 minute, the oil is ready. If the fritters are getting brown too quickly, adjust the heat under the burner to keep the oil from getting too hot.*

1. Heat 2 to 3 inches of oil in a large heavy saucepan over medium heat until the temperature reaches 350°F (180°C) (see Note).

2. Meanwhile, combine ½ cup of the sugar and the cinnamon in a medium bowl, mixing well. Set aside for rolling the cooked fritters.

3. Mix together the flour, remaining ¼ cup sugar, baking powder, and salt. Beat the eggs in a small bowl with a fork. Stir in the milk and butter. Add to the dry ingredients and mix just until the dry ingredients are moistened. Fold in the apples.

4. When the oil reaches 350°F (180°C), drop the batter, in small batches, by heaping tablespoons into the hot oil. Do not crowd the pot. Fry until deep golden brown, 3 to 4 minutes. If the fritters do not turn by themselves, use a slotted spoon to turn them over. Once they are browned on both sides, transfer with a slotted spoon to paper towels to drain very briefly. Then, one at a time, roll each hot fritter in the cinnamon-sugar mixture. Repeat with the remaining batter. Serve warm or at room temperature.

PREP TIME: 20 minutes

COOKING TIME: 4 minutes per batch

Makes about 36 fritters

Blueberry Sour Cream COFFEE CAKE

THIS MOIST AND BUTTERY CAKE *is an adaption of a recipe in the Seedling Farm (see page 196) archives. Blueberries are a staple in this region, so even if you can't grow them yourself, you can definitely find them at other local farms and farm stands in the area. You might forgo dipping this extra-tender treat into your coffee, but a strong brew on the side is still a must.*

1. Preheat the oven to 350°F (180°C). Grease a 9- by 13-inch baking dish.

2. Combine the walnuts, brown sugar, and cinnamon in a medium bowl, mixing well. Set aside.

3. Beat the butter in the large bowl of an electric mixer until light. Gradually beat in the granulated sugar until fluffy. Beat in the eggs, then the sour cream and vanilla. Combine the flour, baking soda, baking powder, and salt in a bowl. Add half of the flour mixture to the mixer bowl and beat just until the dry ingredients are moistened. Repeat with the remaining flour mixture. Stir in the blueberries by hand.

4. Pour half of the batter into the baking dish. Sprinkle half of the walnut mixture over the batter. Repeat with the remaining batter and walnut mixture.

5. Bake for 35 to 40 minutes, until golden brown and a wooden pick inserted in the center comes out clean. Cool on a wire rack for at least 1 hour before serving. Leftover coffee cake may be covered tightly and stored at room temperature, or frozen for up to 3 months.

INGREDIENTS

- 1 cup coarsely chopped walnuts
- ¾ cup firmly packed light brown sugar
- 2 teaspoons ground cinnamon
- ½ cup (1 stick) unsalted butter
- ¾ cup granulated sugar
- 3 eggs
- 1 cup sour cream (do not use fat-free)
- 1 teaspoon vanilla extract
- 2 cups unbleached all-purpose flour
- 1 teaspoon baking soda
- 1 teaspoon baking powder
- ½ teaspoon salt
- 2 cups fresh blueberries

PREP TIME: 20 minutes

BAKING TIME: 35 minutes

Serves 12

MELON and MINT SALAD

YOU CAN FIND FRESH, SEASONAL MELONS *in the summertime at many roadside farm stands in southwestern Michigan during the summer. This salad is simple, meant to showcase the deliciousness of the fruit by itself. If you can't find the small mozzarella balls, called bocconcini, buy larger ones and cut them into bite-size pieces.*

INGREDIENTS

3 cups cubed melon, such as musk, honeydew, or cantaloupe (¾-inch pieces)

8 ounces small fresh mozzarella balls

¼ cup coarsely chopped fresh mint leaves

2 teaspoons extra-virgin olive oil

2 teaspoons balsamic vinegar

⅛ teaspoon freshly ground black pepper, or more as desired

Coarse sea salt, for sprinkling

1. Toss together the melon, mozzarella balls, mint, oil, vinegar, and pepper in a medium bowl and toss well. Refrigerate for at least 15 minutes or up to 2 hours.

2. Just before serving, spoon the mixture into shallow bowls and sprinkle a pinch of sea salt over each serving.

PREP TIME: 15 minutes

CHILLING TIME: 15 minutes–2 hours

Serves 4

Seedling Farm

SOUTH HAVEN, MICHIGAN

"**S**O THIS IS WHAT A MELON IS SUPPOSED TO TASTE LIKE**," I thought when biting into a sweet, juicy heirloom variety from Seedling Farm for the first time years ago. Over a decade ago, Peter Klein left behind a career in restaurant marketing in Chicago to grow more than 20 varieties of these amazing, colorful melons — along with strawberries, blueberries, stone fruits, cherries, apples, cucamelon cucumbers (above left), and other crops at his 81-acre farm and orchard in South Haven. His fruit has drawn Midwesterners and chefs alike, who flock to the Green City Market in Chicago for the week's picks, along with a jug of freshly made apple cider in the fall.

Klein changes up the selection each year to keep things interesting both for him and his loyal customers, growing anything from a pale honeydew variety called Snow Leopard to three different kinds of cantaloupe, including an aromatic and soft French-style melon. Thanks to the cooling lakefront and rich soil, these fruits grow easily in South Haven. Klein also likes to leave the fruit on the tree or vine for as long as possible, so they're only harvested when super-ripe and sweet, ready for eating plain or in more experimental dishes.

WARM WINTER WASSAIL

THIS FALL-FRIENDLY DRINK *marries apple cider with the acidity of citrus. Stephanie Izard uses Seedling Farm's apple cider for this drink when serving it at her restaurants, but you can use any apple cider you like.*

Bring the cider, juices, chile, cinnamon stick, star anise, cloves, and peppercorns to a boil in a medium saucepan. Turn off the heat and let steep for 30 minutes. If you prefer your beverage spicier, leave the chile in while steeping; if you prefer it less spicy, remove the chile. Strain and serve hot, with cinnamon sticks to garnish.

INGREDIENTS

- 1⅓ cups high-quality apple cider
- ⅓ cup fresh grapefruit juice
- ⅓ cup fresh orange juice
- 1 dried Thai chile
- 1 (2-inch) cinnamon stick, plus more for garnish
- 2 whole star anise
- 2 whole cloves
- 1 teaspoon black peppercorns

COOK TIME: 30 minutes

Serves 2 (makes 24 ounces)

BLACKBERRY-BLUEBERRY JAM

THIS EASY, THREE-INGREDIENT JAM *is ready in less than an hour. It does contain seeds, but you can simply strain the hot mixture through a strainer and discard the seeds for a seedless jam. I use fruit jams like this on nut butter sandwiches, in smoothies, and atop ice cream and yogurt. Because I don't use added pectin in my jams, I boil the fruits longer to help release their naturally occurring pectin as the main thickener. While you can easily find blueberries and blackberries throughout southwestern Michigan's Fruit Belt, feel free to substitute for those fruits with fresh strawberries, strawberries and rhubarb, or apricots, peaches, or other stone fruits. This jam will keep refrigerated for up to 2 months.*

INGREDIENTS

- 1 pint (6 ounces) fresh blackberries (about 1¼ cups)
- 1 pint (6 ounces) fresh blueberries (about 1¼ cups)
- ½ cup unsweetened apple juice concentrate
- ½ cup turbinado sugar

1. Rinse the berries (do not dry them) and place in a medium saucepan. Use a potato masher to mash the berries. Stir in the apple juice concentrate and sugar. Bring to a boil over high heat. Boil hard for 1 minute. Reduce the heat to medium-low and cook at a low boil until thickened and reduced to 1¼ cups, stirring once or twice, about 30 minutes.

2. Cool to room temperature and then transfer to clean mason jars with tops. Store in the refrigerator for up to 2 months.

PREP TIME: 10 minutes

COOKING TIME: 35 minutes

Makes 1¼ cups

BLUEBERRY-MINT SODA

THE FIRST TIME I TRIED THIS REFRESHING AND BRIGHT, *not-too-sweet bubbly, I had just downed a juicy burger at Grange Hall Burger Bar in Chicago. It was the perfect quencher. When making the summery soda at home, I prefer skipping refined sugar for the naturally occurring sweetness of the berries, or I'll sometimes add a touch of raw honey or agave nectar. Make this mocktail into a cocktail by adding a little vodka or light rum (courtesy of Journeyman Distillery in Three Oaks, perhaps?). Have other fruits on hand? Strawberries, raspberries, and/or blackberries also work well for this drink.*

To bring out the aroma of the mint, place the leaves in one hand and slap them a few times with the other hand. In a tall Collins glass, muddle the mint leaves, blueberries, and sweetener, if using, until fragrant and well mixed, about 30 seconds. Add the lemon juice and ice cubes. Pour in the soda water and stir gently. Garnish with a toothpick piercing a few blueberries.

INGREDIENTS

- 8   fresh mint leaves
- ¼   cup fresh blueberries, plus more for garnish
- 1–2   teaspoons raw honey, agave nectar, or raw cane sugar (optional)
- ½   teaspoon fresh lemon juice

  Ice cubes
- 10   ounces soda water

PREP TIME: 3 minutes

Serves 1

Michigan PEACH CRISP

IN MICHIGAN'S FRUIT BELT, PEACHES ARE THE STAR *come midsummer. You'll find the juicy, fuzzy sweets at nearly every roadside farm stand and farmers' market in the area. My favorite peaches come from Ellis Farms (see page 190). They are some of the sweetest, juiciest in the region. Have extra peaches about to over-ripen? Make this crisp.*

INGREDIENTS

- ⅓ cup granulated sugar
- 1 tablespoon unbleached all-purpose flour or cornstarch
- 2 teaspoons ground cinnamon
- 6 large peaches (2–2¼ pounds)
- ½ cup unbleached all-purpose flour
- ½ cup quick-cooking or old-fashioned oats
- ½ cup firmly packed brown sugar
- ¼ teaspoon salt
- ½ cup unsalted butter, cut into chunks, cold
- ½ cup chopped walnuts or pecans
- Vanilla bean ice cream, for serving (optional)

1. Preheat the oven to 375°F (190°C).

2. Combine the granulated sugar, flour, and 1 teaspoon of the cinnamon in a large bowl and mix well. Working over the bowl, cut the peaches into ½-inch slices from top to bottom, stopping at the pit. Let the slices and juices drip into the bowl. When all the peaches are sliced, mix well with the flour mixture. Transfer the mixture to a shallow 1½-quart oval casserole dish.

3. Combine the flour, oats, brown sugar, remaining 1 teaspoon cinnamon, and salt in a medium bowl. Use a pastry blender or two knives to cut the cold butter into the mixture until the crumbs are the size of small peas. Alternatively, combine the flour, oats, brown sugar, remaining cinnamon, and salt in a food processor and pulse until the batter is the size of small peas. Stir in the nuts and sprinkle the mixture evenly over the peaches.

4. Bake for 35 minutes or until the topping is golden brown and the peaches are bubbly. Cool on a wire rack for at least 30 minutes. Serve warm or at room temperature, with ice cream if desired.

PREP TIME: 30 minutes

BAKING TIME: 35 minutes

COOLING TIME: 30 minutes

Serves 8

Strawberry-Rhubarb HAND PIES

THESE TREATS ARE EVERYTHING YOU LOVE ABOUT A CLASSIC PIE, *with a fruity, sweet filling and buttery crust, but in portable hand form. Their small size makes them perfect for a special picnic on the beach, a bike ride, or a day trip through the countryside. Strawberries are grown all over southwestern Michigan's Fruit Belt, with many orchards allowing you to pick your own. While the initial strawberry season can be short at the start of summer in late May or June, many farms enjoy a second, late-season strawberry rush in late July or August, when the berries are even sweeter.*

FOR THE PASTRY

- 1¼ cups unbleached all-purpose flour
- ½ teaspoon salt
- ½ cup (1 stick) unsalted butter, cut into pieces, cold
- 3–5 tablespoons ice water

FOR THE FILLING

- 1 cup chopped fresh rhubarb (½-inch pieces)
- 1 cup sliced strawberries
- ¼ cup granulated sugar
- 1 tablespoon unbleached all-purpose flour

FOR THE GLAZE

- 1 egg, well beaten
- Coarse raw cane sugar, such as turbinado

1. For the pastry, combine the flour and salt in a medium bowl. Add the butter and use a pastry blender or two knives to cut in the butter until it is the size of coarse crumbs. Drizzle 3 tablespoons of the ice water over the top and stir with a fork. Gently knead the mixture with your hands until the dough holds together. If it is dry, add more ice water 1 tablespoon at a time and knead until the dough holds together. Shape into an oval disk, wrap in plastic wrap, and refrigerate for at least 40 minutes.

2. Meanwhile, for the filling, combine the rhubarb, strawberries, and granulated sugar in a small saucepan. Cook, stirring frequently, over medium heat until the fruits release their juices and the mixture begins to thicken. Sprinkle the flour over the mixture and continue to cook until the flour is dissolved and the mixture is very thick, 1 to 2 minutes. Remove from the heat and transfer to a bowl to cool completely.

Recipe continues on next page

| PREP TIME: 40 minutes |
| CHILLING TIME: 40 minutes |
| BAKING TIME: 25 minutes |
| Makes 6 pies |

3. Preheat the oven to 350°F (180°C). Grease a baking sheet or line with parchment paper. Roll out half of the chilled dough on a lightly floured surface to ⅛ inch thick. Use a 3½-inch biscuit cutter or a large glass to cut out 6 circles. Place the circles on the prepared baking sheet. Roll out the remaining dough and cut 6 more circles.

4. Spoon about 2½ tablespoons of the filling in the center of each of the 6 circles on the baking sheet, leaving a ¼-inch rim. Brush some of the beaten egg around the rim. Place the remaining 6 circles over the filling and use a fork to crimp the edges together. (Note: For semicircle pies, cut 12 circles and fold in half, reducing the filling to 1 tablespoon.) Cut several slits in each top circle to let steam escape during baking. Brush the remaining beaten egg over the tops and sprinkle with the coarse sugar.

5. Bake for 23 to 25 minutes, until golden brown. Let cool for at least 20 minutes before serving warm. Cooled pies may be tightly covered and refrigerated for up to 2 days or frozen for up to 2 months.

STRAWBERRY SHORTCAKES

BECAUSE YOU CAN NEVER GET ENOUGH STRAWBERRIES, *make shortcakes. I like to use just-picked berries and real fresh cream from local farms or organic cream. The fresh ingredients give this dish a cleaner, smoother taste that is very unlike the more sugary renditions you might find in a store or mainstream restaurant chain. To save extra strawberries not used for this recipe, freeze them individually by arranging them on a sheet tray in the freezer before transferring them to a resealable plastic bag for longer-term storage. You'll thank yourself come December.*

1. Preheat the oven to 425°F (220°C). Place the strawberries in a medium bowl. Add 2 teaspoons of the granulated sugar and mix well. Cover and refrigerate to allow the strawberries to produce juices.

2. Beat the heavy cream with an electric mixer until soft, firm peaks form. Beat in the confectioners' sugar until almost stiff. Cover and refrigerate until serving time.

3. Combine the flour, baking powder, remaining 2 teaspoons granulated sugar, and salt in a medium bowl. Using a pastry blender or two knives, cut the butter into the flour mixture until coarse crumbs form. Add the milk and vanilla. Mix just until the dry ingredients are moistened. Knead the dough gently right in the bowl six to eight times until the dough holds together in a ball.

4. Place the dough on a lightly floured surface. Pat or roll the dough into a ½-inch thickness. Cut out biscuits with a 3-inch round biscuit cutter and place on a baking sheet. If necessary, leftover dough scraps may be re-rolled. Beat together the egg and water and brush over the biscuits.

5. Bake for 12 to 14 minutes, until the biscuits rise and are golden brown. Cool slightly on a wire rack. Split the warm shortcakes and arrange on serving plates. Spoon two-thirds of the berries and two-thirds of the whipped cream over the bottoms of the shortcakes. Replace the tops of the shortcakes and top with the remaining strawberries and whipped cream. Serve immediately.

INGREDIENTS

- 2 cups sliced strawberries (about 12 ounces)
- 4 teaspoons granulated sugar
- ¾ cup heavy cream
- 1-2 tablespoons confectioners' sugar
- 1¼ cups unbleached all-purpose flour
- 1 tablespoon baking powder
- ⅛ teaspoon salt
- ½ cup (1 stick) unsalted butter, cold
- ½ cup whole milk or buttermilk
- 1 teaspoon vanilla extract
- 1 egg
- 1 teaspoon water

PREP TIME: 25 minutes

BAKING TIME: 14 minutes

Serves 6

LAKE SHORE DRIVE, DOUGLAS, MICH.

6A-H2452

RUSTIC BRIDGE TO LAKE FROM BEACHMONT RESORT - DOUGLAS

Chapter 7

SAUGATUCK, DOUGLAS, and FENNVILLE

SAUGATUCK, WITH ITS ROWS OF SHOPS AND CAFÉS along the water, has earned its reputation as one of the best vacation destinations in the Midwest. Those looking to escape the summer crowds, though, are more apt to flock to neighboring Douglas, home to a beautiful, quiet beach and the popular restaurant Everyday People Café.

More "rural" yet is Fennville, home to a strong artists' community but also to a burgeoning group of food artisans and farmers. While the following pages detail the must-visit sites of Fennville, don't miss a stop at Kismet Bakery for organic artisan treats, Crane's Pie Pantry for cherries galore, or a wine tasting at Fenn Valley Winery next door.

HERB-GRILLED FARM CHICKEN *with Lemon Confit and Greens*

THIS SIMPLE YET FLAVORFUL DISH *gets its great taste from quality ingredients like sustainably raised chicken and local greens. Pietsch (page 216) sources his chicken from CoachStop Farms in Zeeland. I added a buttermilk brine because I find that it makes the chicken incredibly tender and juicy.*

FOR THE BRINED CHICKEN

Whole roasting chicken (about 4 pounds)

4 cups buttermilk

FOR THE LEMON CONFIT

6 lemons, ends trimmed, cut into ½-inch-thick slices

Olive oil

FOR THE VINAIGRETTE

6 scallions, tossed lightly in 1 tablespoon canola or vegetable oil

½ cup fresh lemon juice

¾ cup reserved lemon confit oil

3 garlic cloves, minced

Salt and freshly ground black pepper

FOR SERVING

4–6 cups mixed salad greens

1. For brining the chicken, spatchcock the chicken for more even cooking on the grill, using kitchen shears to cut down both sides of the backbone from top to bottom. Remove and discard the backbone. Turn the chicken over and press firmly on the breast until the chicken is flattened. Submerge the chicken in the buttermilk in a large bowl, glass dish, or resealable plastic bag to fully cover. Refrigerate for at least 4 hours or up to overnight.

2. For the lemon confit, preheat the oven to 325°F (160°C). Place the sliced lemons in an ovenproof casserole dish. Pour enough olive oil over the lemon slices to cover them completely. Bake for 45 minutes to 1 hour, until the lemons are tender but not falling apart. Remove from the oven and cool completely. Strain the lemons, reserving all of the oil.

3. Prepare a gas or charcoal grill for high-heat and low-heat grilling.

Recipe continues on next page

PREP TIME: 1 hour

BRINING TIME: 4–24 hours

COOKING TIME: 2 hours–2 hours 25 minutes

Serves 4–6

Virtue Cider

FENNVILLE, MICHIGAN

WITH ITS SWEEPING APPLE ORCHARDS, Michigan has always been home to cider (both hard and nonalcoholic), but now, on the heels of a burgeoning craft beer industry, a new generation of craft cider makers — with their own cider mills or as part of wineries and breweries — are rediscovering more sophisticated, food-friendly versions far removed from the supersweet Woodchuck and Angry Orchard types. Many of these craft houses are located in towns near Lake Michigan, from southwestern Michigan to Traverse City and farther north.

One of the first such European-style cider makers to open in the Midwest was Virtue Cider, started by Greg Hall (former brewmaster at Goose Island Beer Company) and Stephen Schmakel in 2011. They set up shop in Fennville, the scenic farm and orchard expanse just outside Saugatuck. One of the main reason Hall chose this area, he has said, is because Fennville has similar precipitation patterns, cool temperatures, and growing conditions as the cider-growing areas of Normandy, France; West Country, England; and the Basque Country of Spain.

Hall likes to say that his craft cider operation can be described using ABCs. *A* is for the use of 100 percent Michigan apples, which include Paula Red, Gala, Cortland, Northern Spy, McIntosh, Jonathan, Jonagold, Winesap, and Arkansas Black varieties; *B* is for the French oak and Kentucky bourbon barrels that age the cider; and *C* is for the farm cider house in which the cider is made, just like in Europe. Their debut cider, Red Streak, became an instant hit, drawing loyal drinkers who preferred the tart and crisp taste of the local apples, mostly sourced from neighboring farms in Fennville (including Seedling Farm on page 196) and sometimes from elsewhere in Michigan.

Aside from Red Streak, the other main sellers are The Mitten, a bourbon barrel–aged cider based on the bourbon stout that Hall developed for Goose Island; Lapinette, a slightly funky, French-style cider released in the spring; Percheron, a sweeter French cider released in the summer and early fall; and Cidre Nouveau, Virtue's take on Beaujolais Nouveau using fresh-pressed apples from the height of the apple season in the fall. There are other seasonal or specialty ciders available exclusively at the cider house, like Cherry Mitten, a variation of their popular cider that's spiked with cherries from the farm next door.

Visitors can stop in the barnlike tasting room for a quick visit or event and enjoy glasses of the naturally effervescent refreshment at the bar inside or outside on the grounds, perhaps while enjoying a game of ladder toss. Outside the cider house, Virtue Ciders are available in urban markets like Chicago and Milwaukee, but distribution has been expanding throughout Michigan. Some major grocery stores in the state carry Virtue's Michigan Brut, available in 12-ounce bottles, while specialty stores and craft liquor shops carry other varieties.

FRESH PASTA BOLOGNESE

THIS RECIPE SOUNDS LIKE ANY OTHER BOLOGNESE SAUCE, *but using local meats, cream, and cheese as well as seasonal tomatoes and fresh basil from the garden or farmers' market elevates it to a whole new level. If you're making this in Door County, check out Clario Farms in Algoma for fresh homemade pasta by Claire Thompson. You can buy Clario pasta at the Sturgeon Bay farmers' market and at Renard's and other specialty grocers in Sturgeon Bay.*

INGREDIENTS

1 tablespoon extra-virgin olive oil

8 ounces thickly sliced bacon or pancetta, chopped

8 ounces hot Italian pork sausage (bulk or casings removed)

8 ounces grass-fed ground beef chuck

3½–4 cups puréed roasted heirloom tomatoes (page 172), or 1 (28-ounce) can diced tomatoes, undrained

¼ cup heavy cream

1 pound favorite fresh pasta

Chopped fresh basil, for garnish

Shredded Parmesan cheese, for serving

1. Heat a large deep skillet over medium heat. Add the oil to the pan, swirling to coat the bottom. Add the bacon to the pan. Cook, stirring frequently, until most of the fat is released, about 5 minutes. Add the sausage and cook, breaking up the sausage, for 5 minutes. Add the ground beef and cook, breaking up the beef, until all the meat is cooked through. Drain the fat from the pan and return to the heat.

2. Add the tomatoes and reduce the heat to low. Simmer until the sauce thickens, about 20 minutes. Add the cream and heat through.

3. Bring a large pot of water to a boil and cook the pasta according to the package directions. Spoon the sauce over the hot cooked pasta. Garnish with basil and serve with Parmesan.

PREP TIME: 15 minutes

COOKING TIME: 35 minutes

Serves 4–6

Salt of the Earth

FENNVILLE, MICHIGAN

FOUNDED IN 2009 BY STEVE DARPEL AND MARK SCHROCK, Salt of the Earth remains committed to using locally sourced foods. Set in a fully restored historic storefront in downtown Fennville, the restaurant sits just a stone's throw from many surrounding farms, ranches, orchards, wineries, breweries, and cider houses that provide ingredients for the menu.

"In 2009 in Western Michigan, working with farmers was not as trendy and marketable as it is now, and actually pretty unheard of," says chef Matthew Pietsch, who has made it his mission to nurture close relationships with nearby growers and producers. "The joke is that I spent more time in my car than in the kitchen, driving to all the nearby farms and farmers' markets the first year we opened."

Word of mouth led him to more and more farms, even ones raising Icelandic sheep and growing heirloom runner beans. Pietsch even has a "pig guy" as well as a farmer who raises chickens, turkeys, and grass-fed beef exclusively for the restaurant. Salt of the Earth also has an in-house bakery led by Pietsch and artisan baker Carla Wagner, who have forged partnerships with local, artisan-style mills and churn out fresh breads like the popular Sote Seedy, a soft sourdough-style bread baked in a wood-fired oven and encased in a crispy crust studded with gray sea salt and aromatic poppy, flax, fennel, sesame, and onion seeds. In addition to baking bread for the restaurant and takeout, Salt of the Earth even bakes bread for its sister restaurant, Principle, in Kalamazoo, as well as for gourmet stores in the area, including Farmhouse Deli.

CRANBERRY-NUT BREAD

CRANBERRIES GROW WELL IN MICHIGAN *because of its pockets of bogs and marshes. They are available fresh in the fall and often frozen at other times throughout the year. I typically use walnuts for this recipe, but if you can get your hands on some black walnuts, which grow in Michigan and are typically foraged, they'll bring an even richer and deeper nut flavor to the bread. I like to spread a generous swath of cream cheese or crème fraîche on a warm slice of this bread before devouring it with coffee or Cold-Brewed Coffee (page 43). The bread also freezes well.*

Adapted from a recipe in an old heritage cookbook from the Saugatuck-Douglas library, Cultivated Tastes from the Douglas Garden Club Cookbook (1990), this recipe swaps in cranberry juice for orange juice to add more tartness and calls for real butter instead of the (gasp) margarine that was once favored.

1. Preheat the oven to 350°F (180°C). Coat a 5- by 9-inch loaf pan with cooking spray.

2. Combine the flour, granulated sugar, baking soda, baking powder, and salt in a large bowl. Beat the eggs in a medium bowl. Stir in the milk, cooled butter, and orange zest. Add the wet ingredients to the dry ingredients and mix just until the dry ingredients are moistened. Stir in the cranberries and the walnuts.

3. Spread the batter into the prepared pan and bake for 50 to 55 minutes, until a wooden pick inserted in the center comes out clean. Transfer the pan to a wire rack to cool for 10 minutes. Unmold the bread onto the wire rack and cool completely.

4. For the glaze, if desired, whisk together the confectioners' sugar, cranberry juice, and orange zest in a bowl. If the glaze is too thick, add additional cranberry juice 1 teaspoon at a time. Spoon the glaze over the completely cooled bread.

FOR THE BREAD

- 2½ cups unbleached all-purpose flour
- 1 cup granulated sugar
- 1 teaspoon baking soda
- 1 teaspoon baking powder
- ½ teaspoon salt
- 2 eggs
- 1 cup whole milk
- ½ cup (1 stick) unsalted butter, melted and cooled
- 2 teaspoons grated orange zest (optional)
- 1¼ cups fresh or frozen cranberries (not thawed), coarsely chopped
- 1 cup coarsely chopped toasted walnuts or black walnuts

FOR THE GLAZE (OPTIONAL)

- 1 cup confectioners' sugar
- 2 tablespoons cranberry juice, plus more if needed
- ¾ teaspoon grated orange zest

PREP TIME: 20 minutes

BAKING TIME: 55 minutes

Makes 1 (9-inch) loaf

Bacon-Wrapped MEATLOAF

ONE HUNGRY DAY WHILE STAYING IN DOUGLAS, *my family and I loaded our basket at Christine Ferris's Farmhouse Deli with crunchy kale salad, hot pastrami sandwiches with Detroit-based Grobbel's meat on marble rye from DeBoers in Holland, an extra loaf of bread from Salt of the Earth (for, you know, toast or something; see page 216), jars of pickles and artisan jams, and of course, a couple pieces of decadent, bacon-wrapped meatloaf. I'm not sure if the meatloaf was just a special that day, because I don't always see it, but Ferris, a prolific and successful caterer, made hers shaped in half domes with two pieces of bacon crisscrossed over the top. Here, I've attempted something similar, but in a larger loaf and with extra bacon for extra richness to share with a larger group — or stomach.*

INGREDIENTS

- 1 tablespoon unsalted butter or olive oil
- 1 medium onion, chopped
- 3 garlic cloves, minced
- 1½ pounds ground beef round or meatloaf mix (pork, veal, and beef)
- 8 ounces hot or mild bulk breakfast sausage
- ¾ cup fresh multigrain or whole wheat breadcrumbs (process torn bread in a food processor)
- 2 eggs
- ⅓ cup smoky barbecue sauce
- ¾ teaspoon salt
- ¼ teaspoon freshly ground black pepper
- 8 bacon strips

1. Preheat the oven to 375°F (190°C). Line a large rimmed baking sheet with aluminum foil.

2. Melt the butter in a large skillet over medium heat. Add the onion and garlic and sauté until softened, about 6 minutes. Let cool for 5 minutes.

3. Meanwhile, combine the beef, sausage, breadcrumbs, eggs, barbecue sauce, salt, and pepper in a large bowl and mix well. Add the onion mixture and mix well. Transfer the meat mixture to the baking sheet and shape to form a 6- by 8-inch loaf.

4. Shape the bacon into a lattice by arranging 4 slices of the bacon on a large sheet of waxed paper with the edges touching. Peel back the odd number of slices all the way back down to within 1 inch from the end. Lay another slice of bacon crosswise over the even slices so they touch the bent-back slices. Replace the bent-back slices so they cover the crosswise slices.

PREP TIME: 30 minutes

BAKING TIME: 1 hour

Serves 6–8

Now, peel back the even numbered pieces all the way to the first crosswise slices. Lay another slice over the odd pieces so that it touches the bent-back even slices. Replace the even slices to their original position. Continue with this method until you have used all 8 slices. Use the waxed paper to turn over and drape the bacon blanket over the meatloaf. Remove the waxed paper. Tuck the ends of the bacon under the meatloaf.

5. Bake for 55 minutes to 1 hour, until the internal temperature reaches 165°F (74°C). Let stand for 5 minutes before slicing.

RUSTIC APPLE GALETTE

with Goat Cheese, Caramelized Onions, and Thyme

I CAME UP WITH THE IDEA FOR THIS SWEET AND SAVORY APPETIZER *after tasting creamy and tangy fresh chèvre from Evergreen Lane Farm (see page 223) and sweet-tart Michigan apples together. Baked in a tart with a flaky crust and some onions and thyme for savory notes, the galette hits on all your senses. If you can't get to Evergreen Lane, try other local fresh chèvre and apples.*

FOR THE PASTRY

- 1¼ cups unbleached all-purpose flour
- ½ teaspoon salt
- ½ cup (1 stick) unsalted butter, cut into pieces, cold
- 4–6 tablespoons ice water

FOR THE TOPPING

- 1½ tablespoons unsalted butter
- 1 cup very thinly sliced red onion
- 1½ tablespoons chopped fresh thyme leaves
- 2 large Empire or other tart red apples halved, cored, and cut into very thin slices (2 cups)
- 1 tablespoon fresh lemon juice
- 1 egg, beaten
- 3–4 ounces goat cheese

1. For the pastry, combine the flour and salt in a medium bowl. Add the butter and use a pastry blender or two knives to cut in the butter until it is the size of coarse crumbs. Drizzle 4 table-spoons of the ice water over the top and stir with a fork. Gently knead the mixture with your hands until the dough holds together. If it is dry, add more ice water, 1 tablespoon at a time, and knead until the dough holds together. Shape into an oval disk, wrap in plastic wrap, and refrigerate for at least 30 minutes.

2. Meanwhile, for the topping, melt the butter in a 10-inch deep skillet over medium heat. Separate the onion slices into rings and add to the skillet. Cook, stirring frequently, until the onions are golden brown and tender, about 25 minutes. Remove from the heat and let cool to room temperature. Stir in 1 tablespoon of the thyme. Toss the sliced apples with the lemon juice in a bowl.

Recipe continues on next page

PREP TIME: 30 minutes, plus
30 minutes to chill

BAKING TIME: 35 minutes

Serves 8–10

3. Preheat the oven to 375°F (190°C). Butter a rimmed baking sheet or line with parchment paper. On a lightly floured surface, roll the dough into a 14-inch circle about ⅛ inch thick. Transfer the dough to the prepared baking sheet. Spread the onion mixture in a 10-inch circle in the center of the dough. Arrange the apple slices in concentric circles over the onions.

4. Bring up the edges of the pastry, folding as you go and pressing it over the filling to partially cover it. Brush the egg over the edges of the pastry (discard any remaining egg). Bake for 35 minutes or until the pastry is golden brown. Transfer the baking sheet to a wire rack and crumble the goat cheese over the exposed filling. Sprinkle the remaining ½ tablespoon thyme over the goat cheese. Let stand for at least 15 minutes before serving warm or at room temperature.

Evergreen Lane
Artisan Cheese

FENNVILLE, MICHIGAN

CATHY HALINSKI AND HER HUSBAND, TOM, moved to quiet Fennville in 2000, leaving behind high-stress IT jobs to switch gears into farming. Little did Halinski realize that the 40-acre farm and apple orchard would become the place for an artisan cheese-making business that has earned her countless accolades.

It all started with a lost goat. "One summer when we were remodeling the farmhouse, we had a door open and a goat ran into the living room," she says. "I took her to other farms nearby, but no one claimed her." It was a sign. Eventually that goat turned into two, and two turned into a small herd. A lot of trial and error and several professional cheese-making classes in Montreal later, she opened her creamery in 2008.

At the peak of the cheese-making season in the summertime, Halinski milks 114 goats three or four times a week. The milk is pasteurized and mixed with a little starter and rennet and left to coagulate over a period of 12 to 18 hours. It's then used as fresh chèvre or shaped and aged for nuttier, more developed cheeses, such as the popular Pyramid Point, an earthy French ash–brushed goat cheese. The Poet's Tomme is a 60-day aged cheese that has been washed with Poet beer from New Holland Brewery. LaMancha Moo is a Camembert-style cheese perfect for spreading on crackers. Her cheeses are available for purchase at her farm store, at specialty stores in the area like Farmhouse Deli, and in Chicago.

SUMMER FRUIT BISCUIT BAKE

MARI TERCZAK, OWNER OF KISMET FARM AND BAKERY (*see page 226*), *developed the recipe for these dessert biscuits as a way to use up all the summer fruit she grows each year. Though she prefers pairing raspberries with peaches, any combination of sweet summer fruit will work.*

FOR THE BISCUITS

1	cup (2 sticks) unsalted butter, cubed
4½	cups all-purpose white flour
1	cup granulated sugar
1	tablespoon baking powder
1	teaspoon salt
1	cup whole milk or cream
2	large eggs
1	tablespoon pure vanilla extract
½	teaspoon grated lemon zest

FOR THE FRUIT FILLING

6	cups sliced strawberries or a combination of diced peeled peaches, blueberries, and/or raspberries
2	tablespoons granulated sugar
2	tablespoons cornstarch
1	tablespoon lemon juice
¾	teaspoon cinnamon

FOR THE LEMON GLAZE

2½	cups powdered sugar (preferably organic)
¼	cup fresh lemon juice
1	tablespoon unsalted butter, melted
½	teaspoon pure vanilla extract

1. For the biscuits, place the butter in the freezer and freeze for 4 hours. Combine the flour, sugar, baking powder and salt in a large bowl and refrigerate. Combine the milk and eggs in a medium bowl and thoroughly whisk together. Whisk in the vanilla and lemon zest and refrigerate.

2. Add one half of the flour mixture and 1 stick of the frozen cubed butter to a food processor fitted with a metal blade. Pulse until the mixture is the consistency of breadcrumbs, then place in a large bowl and refrigerate. Pulse the remaining flour and butter, then add it to the flour mixture in the refrigerator. Chill for about 15 minutes.

3. Gradually add the chilled milk and egg mixture to the butter and flour mixture, mixing just until the dry ingredients are moistened.

PREP TIME: 8 hours for freezing, plus 30 minutes

BAKING TIME: 30–40 minutes

Makes 24 biscuits

4. Line a cookie sheet with parchment paper. Spread the dough into a 12- by 9-inch rectangle on the lined cookie sheet. Using a large knife, cut the dough into 2-inch squares. There should be 24 biscuits. Leave the dough on the cookie sheet and freeze for at least 4 hours. Break apart the frozen biscuits and place in a zip top bag if not using that day. Biscuits can be frozen for up to 1 month.

5. Preheat the oven to 350°F (180°C).

6. For the fruit filling, combine the strawberries, sugar, cornstarch, lemon juice, and cinnamon in a medium bowl and mix well.

7. For the lemon glaze, place the powdered sugar in a medium bowl and gradually whisk in the lemon juice, melted butter, and vanilla. If the mixture is too thin, add more powdered sugar. If it's too thick, add a little more lemon juice.

8. Arrange 12 frozen biscuits on the bottom of a 12- by 9-inch baking dish. Top with the fruit filling, then add the remaining frozen biscuits. Bake for 35 to 40 minutes or until golden brown. If halving the recipe, arrange layers of 6 frozen biscuits each, with the fruit in the middle, in an 8-inch square baking dish and bake for 30 minutes. Let cool at least 10 minutes before transferring to serving dishes. Drizzle with the lemon glaze.

Kismet Farm and Bakery

FENNVILLE, MICHIGAN

NAMED AFTER A WORD with Turkish and Arabic roots that means "fate, destiny, or luck," Kismet Farm is the lifelong dream of Mari Terczak, a third-generation cook and, since 2004, a first-generation farmer. Driving on Blue Star Highway through Fennville, if you're not paying attention, it's easy to miss the small storefront set on 23 acres of 70-year-old pear and apple orchards, nut trees, and other wild abundance. Stop inside during the season, and you'll usually catch Terczak alternatingly greeting customers and pulling large trays of baked delights out of the massive French Gueulard-style wood-fired oven she designed herself.

Terczak opened the bakery part of the business, just steps away from her farm, in 2012, after years of restaurant work. Her love of holistic health and organic farming led her to also grow organic peaches, raspberries, heirloom tomatoes, and other vegetables. It's no surprise, then, that the flours and grains Terczak uses are GMO-free and organic when possible. This makes a huge difference; the breads are so fresh and moist that nearby restaurants and shopkeepers clamor for them.

The Original Seedy Salt, Terczak's signature loaf, uses a more than 50-year-old sourdough starter, a variety of aromatic seeds, and a sprinkling of French sea salt on the crust. It's nutritious thanks to its fermented process and delicious when eaten warm and slathered with artisan butter or homemade Herb Butter (page 19). Many also flock to Kismet Farm Bakery for the endless assortment of scones, biscuits, rich and chocolaty brownies, cinnamon buns, coffee cakes, and cookies. Lovers of savory baked goods appreciate the flaky, buttery OMG Biscuits stuffed with bacon and three cheeses, roasted poblano peppers, and other surprises.

Chapter 8

TRAVERSE CITY and THE PENINSULAS

DUBBED THE "CHERRY CAPITAL OF THE WORLD," Traverse City may be home to countless cherry trees, but it also has a continually growing crop of top chefs, restaurants, breweries, wineries, cider houses, and more. Strolling through the downtown streets, it's easy to stumble upon great food and drink.

A trip to Traverse City wouldn't be complete without a drive through Leelanau Peninsula with its quiet beach towns, like Suttons Bay and Northport, or through the rolling hills and wineries of Old Mission Peninsula set on the same 45th parallel north that accounts for some of the most beautiful wines from France, Italy, and Oregon. You'll see countless bumper stickers, T-shirts, mugs, and other paraphernalia in this area labeled M-22, the mark for that gorgeous stretch of road (part of the Lake Michigan Circle Tour) that follows the lake's shoreline on the Leelanau Peninsula.

In addition to the top restaurants, farms, and shops featured in the following pages, other great stops include Grand Traverse Pie Company for classic cherry pie, the Boathouse and the Cove Restaurants for waterfront dining and fresh seafood, Barb's Bakery for doughnuts, Jolly Pumpkin for craft beer, Tandem Ciders or Taproot for cider, and Trattoria Stella for Italian-inspired dishes made with homemade pasta and local ingredients.

CRISPY-SKINNED LAKE TROUT

with Creamed Local Spinach and Radishes

THE CRISPIEST FISH I HAVE EVER HAD IN MY LIFE *was at The Cooks' House in Traverse City (see page 232). Eric Patterson believes in the importance of letting the ingredients speak for themselves. For this simple recipe, he recommends buying the freshest lake trout possible — preferably caught that morning (he uses fresh trout from Carlson's Fisheries; see page 260). The freshest possible spinach is also important. Patterson uses cream and butter made from the milk collected from local cows that feasted on the area's sweet grasses.*

INGREDIENTS

2   lake trout fillets, with skin (6–7 ounces each)

1   teaspoon kosher salt, plus a pinch

1½   tablespoons sunflower oil or grapeseed oil

2   tablespoons unsalted butter

2   shallots, minced

8   cups (8 ounces) packed large-leaf spinach (not baby spinach)

¼   cup heavy cream

½   teaspoon freshly ground black pepper

4   small radishes, very thinly sliced

2   teaspoons extra-virgin olive oil

1   teaspoon fresh lemon juice or white wine vinegar

Microgreens, for garnish (optional)

1. Pat the trout skin with a paper towel to make sure it's dry. Cut several slits into the skin. Turn over and sprinkle ½ teaspoon of the salt over the fillets.

2. Heat the oil in a large skillet over medium-high heat. When the oil is hot, add the trout, skin side down, and cook until the fish begins to turn opaque, 6 to 8 minutes depending on the thickness of the fillets. Turn off the heat, turn the trout over, and cook for 30 seconds longer.

3. Meanwhile, melt the butter in a large skillet over medium heat. Add the shallots and sauté until soft and translucent, about 2 minutes. Add the spinach and cream and cook until the spinach has wilted and the sauce has thickened, turning often with tongs. Add another ½ teaspoon salt and the black pepper, mixing well. Transfer the spinach mixture to serving plates and top with the trout, crispy skin side up.

4. Toss the radish slices with the olive oil, lemon juice, and the remaining pinch of salt and sprinkle over the trout. Garnish with microgreens, if desired.

PREP TIME: 10 minutes

COOKING TIME: 10 minutes

Serves 2

The Cooks' House

TRAVERSE CITY, MICHIGAN

CHEF ERIC PATTERSON OPENED THE COOKS' HOUSE IN 2008 with Jennifer Blakeslee, whom he met while working at Andre's French Restaurant in Las Vegas. It was Blakeslee who suggested opening a restaurant in her childhood city of Traverse City, and Patterson who fell in love with the area at first sight when he came to move with his wife.

To this day, The Cooks' House has only a handful of tables and 28 seats. Reservations are like gold; service is like family; dining is like sitting in a four-star chef's home and having him cook for you. Literally, the restaurant is in an old house, with a wraparound porch, herb pots in the front, and all. These days, Patterson lets sous chef Adam McMarlin, a talented young chef who's worked around the country, run the kitchen. Visible from the tiny dining room, he can be seen working quietly and diligently.

Patterson, McMarlin, and the team use the most flavorful fish, lamb, pork, grass-fed beef, cheese, fruits, vegetables, butters, and breads from small-scale farmers, producers, foragers, and artisans just miles away. "I am becoming more and more convinced that one of the most important trends in the future will consist of doing as little as possible to food," Patterson wrote in the cookbook he co-wrote with Blakeslee, *Cooks' House: The Art and Soul of Local, Sustainable Cuisine* (2010). "The days of complex, overworked food will come to an end. The next generation of cooks will take a carrot and let the carrot tell its story. They will take a beautiful, grass-fed piece of beef and simply cook it properly. Perfectly grown peaches will be served as they are, with little adornment."

ROASTED GOLDEN BEET
SALAD *with Raita Sauce and Quail Eggs*

FRESH BEETS AND GREENS ARE KEY TO THIS RECIPE. *If in the area, visit the Sara Hardy farmers' market in downtown Traverse City. Oryana Natural Foods Market carries local quail eggs, but fresh chicken eggs from local farms also work well for this dish. Patterson prefers to skip peeling the beets, to preserve maximum flavor. The mint raita is a refreshing, cooling garnish that pairs well with the tang of the vegetables and the richness of the eggs.*

FOR THE BEETS

- 4 medium golden beets
- 2 garlic cloves, smashed
- 1 fresh thyme, rosemary, sage, or oregano sprig
- 2 tablespoons olive oil

FOR THE RAITA SAUCE

- 1 cup whole-milk yogurt
- ¼ cup fresh mint leaves, finely chopped
- 1–2 teaspoons ground cumin, as desired
- 1–2 teaspoons ground coriander, as desired
- ½ teaspoon sugar
- Pinch of salt

FOR THE SALAD

- 8 quail eggs, or 4 chicken eggs
- 2 tablespoons olive oil
- 1 tablespoon rice vinegar
- 4 cups packed arugula or mixed baby greens
- Sea salt and freshly ground black pepper
- Pea shoots or other microgreens, for garnish (optional)

1. For the beets, preheat the oven to 350°F (180°C). Trim off any exposed roots or stems and place the beets, garlic, and thyme sprig on one side of a rectangular piece of aluminum foil. Drizzle the olive oil over all and close the foil packet by folding the other half over the beets and sealing the edges all around by folding up the edges of the foil. Place the beet package on the middle or top rack of the oven and bake until tender enough to easily pierce with a knife, about 1 hour or longer, if necessary. Remove from the oven, carefully open the foil, and allow to cool to room temperature.

Recipe continues on next page

PREP TIME: 20 minutes

COOKING TIME: 1 hour

Serves 4

2. Meanwhile, for the raita sauce, whisk together the yogurt, mint, cumin, coriander, sugar, and salt in a bowl. Add cold water by the ¼ teaspoonful as needed to thin out the sauce so it has the consistency of a dressing that can be drizzled over the salads.

3. For the salad, place the eggs in a medium saucepan of cold water and bring to a rolling boil over high heat. Turn off the heat, cover, and let stand for 1 minute for quail eggs or 6 minutes for chicken eggs. Drain and rinse with cold water to cool. When cool enough to handle, peel the eggs. Halve the quail eggs, or quarter the chicken eggs.

4. Slice the beets into ½-inch-thick slices or wedges and arrange on chilled plates, fanning them out in the center or layering them in a rectangular fashion so they are slightly overlapping, depending on the shape of the plate. In a large bowl, whisk together the olive oil and vinegar. Add the arugula and lightly toss until coated. Spoon the arugula over the beets and top with sea salt and pepper to taste. Drizzle about 1 tablespoon or more of the raita sauce over each plate. Arrange the halved or quartered eggs around the salad. Garnish with pea shoots, if desired.

DEAD MAN'S SALMON ROULADES *with Wild Rice and*

Mushroom Stuffing and Zinfandel Reduction

THE ATTENTION-GRABBING NAME OF THIS DISH *hails from a storm that ravaged Lake Michigan near Traverse City in 1974, costing many sailors their lives. Eric Mansavage (owner of Farmhouse restaurants in Chicago and Evanston) served this dish at a special Traverse City–inspired dinner. Earthy, local mushrooms and the wild rice, harvested by Native Americans of the Ojibwe tribe who "knock" the rice from their watery beds using their paddles in canoes, together give the dish a nutty and deep umami flavor. A note about using the apple cores in the reduction: Their natural pectin helps thicken the sauce.*

FOR THE STUFFING

- 1¼ cups water
- ⅓ cup wild rice
- 2 tablespoons unsalted butter
- ⅓ cup minced shallots
- 8 ounces mushrooms, such as cremini and/or oyster, coarsely chopped
- 2 garlic cloves, minced
- 2 tablespoons heavy cream
- Salt and freshly ground black pepper

FOR THE SALMON ROULADES

- 2 long skinless salmon fillets (10–12 ounces each), pin bones removed
- Salt and freshly ground black pepper

FOR THE ZINFANDEL REDUCTION

- 2 cups Zinfandel
- 2 fresh rosemary sprigs
- 2 fresh thyme sprigs
- 1 or 2 apple cores
- 2 tablespoons butter

1. For the stuffing, bring the water to a boil in a medium saucepan over high heat. Stir in the rice, reduce the heat to low, cover, and simmer until the rice is tender, about 55 minutes.

Recipe continues on next page

PREP TIME:	20 minutes
COOKING TIME:	55 minutes
CHILLING TIME:	1 hour
BAKING TIME:	14 minutes

Serves 4

2. Meanwhile, melt the butter in a 10-inch skillet over medium heat. Add the shallots and sauté for 2 minutes. Add the mushrooms and garlic and sauté until the juices are released and then absorbed by the mushrooms, about 8 minutes. Add the cream and sauté until thickened, about 3 minutes longer. Drain the rice and stir in the mushroom mixture. Season to taste with salt and pepper.

3. For the salmon, place the 2 long salmon fillets on a work surface with the dark sides up. Season with salt and pepper. Spoon half of the stuffing over each of the fillets. Starting at the wider end, roll up the salmon. Wrap each in plastic wrap and refrigerate for 1 hour to firm up.

4. Preheat the oven to 375°F (190°C). For the Zinfandel reduction, pour the wine into a medium saucepan. Add the herb sprigs and apple core(s). Bring to a boil over high heat. Reduce the heat and simmer until reduced to ⅔ cup, about 20 minutes. Use a small strainer to discard the apple cores and herbs. Set aside.

5. Line a rimmed baking sheet with parchment paper. Unwrap the salmon and, using a very sharp knife, cut each roll in half crosswise, forming 4 roulades. Place the roulades on the baking sheet, cut side down. Bake for 12 to 14 minutes, until the fish is opaque and the stuffing is hot.

6. Just before the roulades are done, reheat the wine reduction and stir in the butter until melted. Place the roulades on warm serving plates and spoon the wine reduction around them.

Ruleau Bros. CSF

STEPHENSON, MICHIGAN

RULEAU BROS. IN STEPHENSON, MICHIGAN, introduced the Community-Supported Fish (CSF) program. Similar to Community-Supported Agriculture (CSA), but for fish instead of crops, the pre-purchased fish shares give members regular access to fresh-caught Door County whitefish and the ability to support local fisheries. The CSF program offers those who buy shares weekly or biweekly packages of whitefish fillets, smoked whitefish, and/or lake smelts delivered to local drop-off sites throughout the state.

The Ruleau family's history of commercial fishing on Lake Michigan dates back to 1826, when they first settled near Mackinac Island. The fishery now fishes in the waters of the adjacent Green Bay, alongside Door County on the other eastern side, and uses sustainable trap net or trawling methods to catch the Lake Michigan whitefish.

RUSTIC WHITEFISH
TARLETS *with Tarragon Beer Mustard Cream*

WHITEFISH COOKED IN AROMATICS *and blended with a buttery sauce creates the surprise filling in this essentially open-faced pasty of sorts. Ruleau Brothers in Stephenson is one supplier of whitefish.*

FOR THE PASTRY

- 3 cups unbleached all-purpose flour, plus more for rolling dough
- 1 cup (2 sticks) unsalted butter, cut into ½-inch slices
- ¼ teaspoon salt
- ¾ cup ice water

FOR THE COURT BOUILLON AND WHITEFISH

- 5 cups cold water
- ¾ cup red wine vinegar
- 1 small leek (white and pale green parts only), sliced
- 1 carrot, thinly sliced
- 1 celery stalk, thinly sliced
- 3 garlic cloves, peeled
- 2 bay leaves
- 1 fresh thyme sprig

- 1½ teaspoons white or black peppercorns
- 1 teaspoon sea salt
- 18–20 ounces Lake Michigan boneless, skinless whitefish fillets

FOR THE TARRAGON BEER MUSTARD CREAM

- ½ cup lager beer
- 2 tablespoons finely chopped shallot
- ¼ cup heavy cream
- ¼ teaspoon salt
- ⅛ teaspoon freshly ground white pepper
- 2 sticks (1 cup) unsalted butter, cut into tablespoon-size pieces, cold
- 1½ tablespoons chopped fresh tarragon, plus more for garnish (optional)
- 1½ tablespoons stone-ground mustard
- 1 egg, beaten

1. For the pastry, combine the flour, butter, and salt in a food processor. Process until the butter is finely minced with the flour. With the motor running, drizzle the water through the feed tube. Stop the motor when a ball begins to form. Wrap the dough in plastic and refrigerate for at least 40 minutes.

Recipe continues on next page

PREP TIME: 1 hour	
BAKING TIME: 25 minutes	
Serves 4	

Anne's CROUTE *au* FROMAGE

THIS IS ANNE HOYT'S GO-TO APPETIZER, *featuring her No. 1 cheese, raclette, and croute, French for "crust," or a piece of toasted bread on which savory snacks can be served. It pairs excellently with a local dry Gewürztraminer (from Peninsula Cellars, perhaps?) or Pinot Gris, or even a not-too-hoppy beer from one of the nearly 20 microbreweries in the area.*

INGREDIENTS

- 2 eggs, separated
- 1 cup whole milk
- 1 garlic clove, minced
- ⅛ teaspoon salt
- ⅛ teaspoon freshly ground black pepper
- ⅛ teaspoon ground nutmeg
- 8 ounces raclette cheese, grated
- ½ cup dry white wine (such as a dry Riesling or Pinot Gris)
- 1 (8-inch) French baguette, split in half lengthwise

1. Preheat the oven to 425°F (220°C). Butter or grease an 8-inch square baking dish.

2. Blend the egg yolks with the milk, garlic, salt, pepper, and nutmeg in a small bowl. Use a handheld beater to beat the egg whites in a medium bowl until stiff. Fold in the egg yolk mixture and the cheese.

3. Pour the wine into a pie plate and soak the bread in the wine on both sides. (Some wine will be left in the plate.) Place the bread in the bottom of the baking dish. Cover with the egg and cheese mixture, smoothing the top with a rubber spatula.

4. Bake for 12 to 15 minutes, until slightly puffed and golden on top. Cut into 8 squares and serve immediately.

PREP TIME: 20 minutes

BAKING TIME: 15 minutes

Serves 8

Leelanau Cheese Co.

SUTTONS BAY, MICHIGAN

ANNE AND JOHN HOYT'S CHEESE-MAKING TRAINING IN SWITZERLAND, plus Anne's French roots, make them the cheese power couple of Leelanau County. After many years making cheese abroad, they settled in northern Michigan, falling in love with the area that reminded them of the climate and culture in Europe. They opened Leelanau Cheese Co. in 1995.

The Hoyts' specialty is raclette, the semihard cow's milk cheese from the Swiss and French Alps that becomes ooey-gooey when melted. In its region of origin, the popular appetizer cheese gets heated on a raclette grill and enjoyed atop bread and potatoes or used for fondues and fancy grilled cheeses. You'll find Leelanau Cheese Co. products on countless restaurant, winery, and brewery menus throughout the Traverse City area, but you can also buy their cheese on-site at their small cheese-making operation in Suttons Bay, down the street from Black Star Farms.

In back of the shop, the Hoyts built an impressive temperature-controlled cheese cave out of the side of a hill. The cave, built with reinforced walls and beams, provides the naturally cool and low humidity environment that raclette and other aged cheeses crave. While the Hoyts' signature raclette and creamy, spreadable, French-style fromage blanc (like a less tangy chèvre) can be found at select local groceries in the area, their specialty cheeses — like aged raclette and a fromage blanc spiked with black truffles imported from Italy — can only be found at their store.

Traverse City WHISKEY SMASH

CHRIS FREDRICKSON AND MOTI GOLDRING, *founders of Traverse City Whiskey Co., set out to produce the smoothest, greatest whiskey possible. Their story dates as far back as the early twentieth century, when Frederickson's great-grandfather and accomplished brewmaster John Silhavy Sr. emigrated from Czechoslovakia and settled in Saginaw. His recipes for whiskey and gin form the basis for the distillery's spirits, which use corn, barley, and rye grown on the family's farm. A cousin of the Kentucky mint julep, this classic nineteenth-century cocktail centers around whiskey, and in this case, Traverse City's signature spirit.*

1. To make the simple syrup, combine the sugar and water in a small saucepan and heat over medium heat until dissolved, stirring occasionally. Pour into a glass or other container and refrigerate until cool. The syrup will keep in the refrigerator for up to 3 months.

2. For the drink, place the mint, lemon, and ½ ounce simple syrup in a mixing glass and muddle using a muddler or wooden spoon until fragrant, about 30 seconds. Add the water and whiskey, and stir. Transfer to a rocks glass filled with a few ice cubes. Garnish with mint leaves.

FOR THE SIMPLE SYRUP

- 1 cup sugar
- 1 cup water

FOR THE DRINK

- 2 or 3 fresh mint leaves, plus more for garnish
- 1 slice lemon
- 1 ounce water
- 2 ounces Traverse City Whiskey

  Ice cubes

PREP TIME: 10 minutes

Serves 1

Creamy CHERRY
CHICKEN SALAD

I OFTEN SEE CHERRY CHICKEN SALAD ON THE MENU *at different Traverse City restaurants and cafés. Sometimes I see the salad prepared with mayo for a creamy treat atop greens or bread, as in this variation. For fresh bread, look for naturally leavened, artisan-made bread, like that which comes from Pleasanton Bakery in Traverse City. I like their golden wheat, manna grain, and miche breads for these sandwiches.*

INGREDIENTS

- 1 pound boneless, skinless chicken breast halves
- ½ teaspoon salt, plus more as needed
- ⅓ cup mayonnaise
- 2 tablespoons grainy or Dijon mustard
- ¾ cup drained bottled pitted tart cherries or dried tart cherries
- 1 celery stalk, diced
- ½ cup coarsely chopped walnuts, toasted

  Freshly ground black pepper
- 4 large croissants, split, lightly toasted if desired
- 4 red or green leaf lettuce leaves

1. Arrange the chicken in a medium skillet. Add water to come halfway up the sides of the chicken. Sprinkle the salt over the chicken and bring to a simmer over high heat. Simmer gently for 5 minutes. Turn the chicken with tongs and continue to simmer until the internal temperature of the chicken reaches 160°F (71°C), 4 to 5 minutes longer. Drain and transfer to a carving board. Cool for 10 minutes.

2. Combine the mayonnaise and mustard in a medium bowl, mixing well. Stir in the cherries, celery, and walnuts.

3. Cut the cooled chicken into ½-inch pieces and add to the bowl. Toss well. Season to taste with salt and pepper. Refrigerate for at least 30 minutes or up to 1 day.

4. Serve the chicken salad in croissants lined with lettuce leaves.

PREP TIME: 20 minutes

COOKING TIME: 10 minutes

CHILLING TIME: 30 minutes–1 day

Serves 4

MONTMORENCY CHERRIES

Tart Montmorency cherries are what give Traverse City the nickname Cherry Capital of the World. While Door County, Wisconsin, led the nation's cherry production in the 1950s, Michigan has since surpassed Wisconsin, producing 75 percent of the more than 650 million pounds of tart cherries produced in the United States each year.

Said to have been brought to America by early settlers in the 1600s and later propagated by French colonists from Normandy, Montmorency cherries grow especially well in these northern climates with the help of the cool Lake Michigan breeze. Modern-day production began in the mid-1800s and has only grown since then.

All things cherry are celebrated at Traverse City's annual Cherry Festival, held in July. And cherries are found in countless dishes across northern Wisconsin. While many cherries are sold fresh during the summer season, countless buckets-full are pitted and then frozen, dried, or preserved with their juices in jars and containers for enjoyment year-round. It takes 8 pounds of fresh Montmorency cherries to make 1 pound of dried cherries. Sugar-infused cherries use a whopping 5 pounds of sugar for every 25 pounds of cherries, though many producers now preserve their cherries without any added sweeteners.

Mackinac Island PEANUT BRITTLE

IT'S EASY TO FIND MACKINAC FUDGE _all over the Traverse City area, and, of course, on Mackinac Island. At home, it can be difficult to re-create. Luckily, Mackinac peanut brittle is just as tasty but much easier to make yourself. This recipe was inspired by Murdick's Fudge on Mackinac Island._

INGREDIENTS

1	cup lightly salted roasted peanuts
½	cup sugar
2	tablespoons water
1	tablespoon honey
1	tablespoon butter
1	teaspoon vanilla extract

1. Line a baking sheet with parchment paper or aluminum foil. Combine the peanuts, sugar, water, and honey in a medium heavy-bottomed saucepan. Heat over medium-high heat, stirring occasionally, until the mixture comes to a gentle simmer.

2. Reduce the heat to maintain the gentle simmer and cook, stirring occasionally, until the mixture is a deep caramel color, 8 to 10 minutes, watching closely to prevent burning. Remove from the heat and add the butter and vanilla, stirring until the butter is fully incorporated (the mixture will sizzle).

3. Immediately pour the mixture onto the prepared baking sheet, and spread it out so there are no mounds of peanuts. Let cool completely. Break the peanut brittle into desired pieces and store in an airtight container.

PREP TIME: 10 minutes

COOKING TIME: 10 minutes

Serves 8

OLD MISSION WALDORF SALAD

LOCAL APPLES AND FARMERS' MARKET GREENS TRULY MAKE THIS DISH. *I created this recipe after enjoying a similar salad at Old Mission Tavern in Traverse City. To sweeten up the salad, "candy" the walnuts by sautéing them in about 1 tablespoon butter and ¼ teaspoon sugar until just coated. Quickly place the walnuts on a sheet tray or large plate, separating them from one another, and refrigerate until hardened. Crème fraîche in place of the traditional mayonnaise lightens up the dish and gives it a little extra tang.*

INGREDIENTS

- ¾ cup crème fraîche
- ¼ cup plain yogurt
- 1 tablespoon fresh lemon juice
- 3 medium red apples, cut into ½-inch chunks
- 1 celery stalk, thinly sliced
- ¾ cup dried tart cherries or drained bottled pitted tart cherries
- ½ cup walnut pieces, toasted

  Bibb or red leaf lettuce leaves, for serving

  Freshly ground black pepper (optional)

Combine the crème fraîche, yogurt, and lemon juice in a medium bowl, mixing well. Stir in the apples, celery, cherries, and walnuts. Cover and refrigerate for at least 30 minutes. Serve on lettuce leaves, and sprinkle with pepper, if desired.

PREP TIME: 20 minutes

CHILLING TIME: 30 minutes

Serves 6

PASTIES TWO WAYS

THE ENGLISH DESCENDANTS OF MICHIGAN'S UPPER PENINSULA GAVE US PASTIES,
the portable pot-pie-of-sorts encased in a flaky, buttery crust. Most traditional pasties come filled with chicken or beef; here are recipes for one of each, using local meat and seasonal vegetables. While some pasty purists gawk at the use of a gravy, others revel in it. The ale gravy here adds another flavor dimension and makes for fun dipping. The UP's answer to the sandwich can be baked and served warm or cooled and then frozen. Reheat in a 300°F (150°C) oven until warmed through, about 20 minutes.

1. For the pastry, combine the flour, butter, and salt in a food processor. Process until the butter is finely minced with the flour. With the motor running, drizzle the ice water through the feed tube. Stop the motor when a ball begins to form. Wrap the dough ball in plastic wrap and refrigerate for at least 40 minutes.

2. Meanwhile, for the chicken filling, combine the chicken, sweet potato, zucchini, rosemary, salt, and pepper in a large bowl, mixing well.

3. Preheat the oven to 375°F (190°C). Line a large rimmed baking sheet with parchment paper. Cut the dough into 6 even pieces, about 4¼ ounces each, and form into balls. Roll out each ball of dough on a well-floured work surface into an 8-inch circle. Evenly divide the filling (about 1 cup per pasty) on one half of each dough circle. Brush the edges with some of the beaten egg. Fold the dough over to cover the mixture and crimp the edges with your fingers, or use a fork to press the edges together. Place on the prepared baking sheet. Cut three small slits in the top of each pasty. Brush the pasties with the remaining egg.

4. Bake for about 45 minutes or until the crust is golden brown and flaky. Serve warm or at room temperature, with mustard if desired.

Recipe continues on next page

Chicken and Sweet Potato Pasties

FOR THE PASTRY

- 3 cups unbleached all-purpose flour, plus more for rolling dough
- 1 cup (2 sticks) unsalted butter, cut into ½-inch slices
- ¼ teaspoon salt
- ¾ cup ice water

FOR THE CHICKEN FILLING

- 12 ounces cooked chicken, cut into ¼-inch pieces (2 cups)
- 8 ounces sweet potato, cut into ¼-inch pieces (2 cups)
- 8 ounces yellow or green zucchini, cut into ¼-inch pieces (2 cups)
- 2 tablespoons chopped fresh rosemary or thyme leaves
- ¾ teaspoon salt
- ¾ teaspoon freshly ground black pepper

- 1 egg, beaten
  Dijon or spicy brown mustard, for serving (optional)

PREP TIME:	40 minutes
CHILLING TIME:	40 minutes
BAKING TIME:	45 minutes

Serves 6

Beef and Ale Pasties

FOR THE BEEF FILLING

12	ounces ground beef, 85% lean, preferably grass-fed
1	cup finely chopped sweet onion
⅓	cup chopped fresh parsley
2	garlic cloves, minced
1½	teaspoons salt
1½	teaspoons freshly ground black pepper
1	teaspoon dried thyme
1	teaspoon dried oregano
8	ounces carrots, cut into ½-inch pieces (2 cups)
1	cup fresh or frozen peas (not thawed)
1	egg, beaten
	Amber Ale Gravy, for serving (optional; recipe below)

1. Prepare the dough as directed for the Chicken and Sweet Potato Pasties.

2. For the beef filling, combine the beef, onion, parsley, garlic, salt, pepper, thyme, and oregano in a medium bowl, mixing well. Add the carrots and peas and mix well.

3. Roll and fill the pastry, brush with the egg, and bake as directed for the Chicken and Sweet Potato Pasties. Serve with ale gravy on the side, if desired.

PREP TIME: 40 minutes

CHILLING TIME: 40 minutes

BAKING TIME: 45 minutes

Serves 6

Amber Ale Gravy

INGREDIENTS

3	tablespoons butter
1	medium sweet onion, very thinly sliced
3	tablespoons unbleached all-purpose flour
1½	cups amber ale
1½	cups beef broth or stock
	Salt and freshly ground black pepper

Melt the butter in a medium skillet over medium heat. Separate the onion into rings and add to the pan. Sauté until tender and golden brown, about 8 minutes. Sprinkle the flour over the onions and cook for 1 minute, stirring frequently. Stir in the ale and simmer for 5 minutes, stirring occasionally. Stir in the broth and simmer for 8 to 10 minutes, to the desired thickness. Season to taste with salt and pepper. Serve warm.

PREP TIME: 3 minutes

COOK TIME: about 30 minutes

Makes about 4 cups gravy

STRAWBERRY SALAD

AT HER RESTAURANT, KATE VILTER USES FRESH STRAWBERRIES *from Bardenhagen Farms in Suttons Bay to make this tasty salad, but any sweet, seasonal local strawberries will do. She pairs the strawberries with lettuces from Sweeter Song Farm in Cedar, toasted walnuts, fresh mint from the garden, and goat cheese from Idyll Farms just up the road in Northport.*

1. For the dressing, place the parsley, chives, garlic, shallot, vinegar, mustard, and salt in a blender. Purée on high speed until smooth, 30 seconds to 1 minute. Remove the round disk from the top of the blender. With the blender on medium speed, slowly pour the oil through the top to emulsify. Chill until ready to serve. The dressing will keep in the refrigerator for up to 3 days.

2. For the salad, place half of the dressing in a large bowl. Add the lettuce and toss lightly to coat. Transfer to serving plates and top with the strawberries, walnuts, goat cheese, and mint. Serve with pepper and extra dressing on the side, if desired.

FOR THE DRESSING

- 5 fresh parsley sprigs, stems removed
- 4 fresh chives
- 1 garlic clove, peeled
- 1 shallot, peeled and halved
- ½ cup balsamic vinegar
- 2 teaspoons whole-grain mustard
- ¼ teaspoon sea salt
- 1 cup extra-virgin olive oil

FOR THE SALAD

- 6 ounces Sweeter Song butter lettuce, torn into bite-size pieces
- 2 cups sliced strawberries
- ½ cup coarsely chopped walnuts, toasted
- ½ cup crumbled Idyll Farms goat cheese or other goat cheese
- 8–10 large fresh mint leaves, torn

  Freshly ground black pepper (optional)

PREP TIME: 25 minutes

Serves 4

Grilled Carlson's
WHITEFISH *and* VEGETABLES

THIS SIMPLE BUT FLAVORFUL RECIPE *relies on nothing but fresh whitefish caught that morning and local, seasonal produce. If the Butterball potatoes are not in season, you may substitute Yukon gold potatoes. This recipe is an homage to Carlson's Fisheries (see page 260) just across the way from The Riverside Inn (see page 258), but of course any local whitefish will do.*

INGREDIENTS

4 medium or 8 small German Butterball potatoes (about 1 pound), cut into wedges

1 red bell pepper, julienned

1 medium white onion, julienned

2 tablespoons unsalted butter, cut into 4 pieces

Kosher salt and freshly ground black pepper

5 tablespoons olive oil

4 (8-ounce) whitefish fillets, with skin

1 teaspoon lemon pepper or freshly ground black pepper

½ teaspoon cayenne pepper

12 stalks asparagus

Chopped fresh rosemary, for garnish

4 lemon wedges, for garnish

1. Prepare a gas or charcoal grill for medium-high-heat grilling.

2. On a large square of heavy-duty aluminum foil, layer the potatoes, bell pepper, onion, and butter in the center of the foil. Season to taste with salt and pepper. Fold two sides up over the vegetables and fold the edges together. Fold over the edges of the two other sides tightly to form a pouch. Place the pouch on the top rack of the gas grill or on the grid of the charcoal grill. Cover and cook for 25 minutes or until the potatoes are almost tender.

3. Meanwhile, drizzle 1 tablespoon of the oil over the skin sides of the fish. Drizzle 3 tablespoons of the oil over the flesh sides of the fish. Season the fish with 2 teaspoons salt, the lemon pepper, and cayenne. Place the remaining 1 tablespoon oil in a shallow dish or pie plate. Add the asparagus, turning to coat with the oil. Season to taste with salt and pepper.

PREP TIME: 15 minutes

COOKING TIME: 35 minutes

Serves 4

4. After the foil pouch has cooked for 25 minutes, move the pouch to the edge of the grill and place the fish, skin side down, directly over the center of the grill. Place the asparagus spears around the fish. Cover the grill and cook for 5 minutes. Uncover and turn the asparagus with tongs until charred on all sides. When the fish is opaque in the center, 2 to 3 minutes longer, transfer to a large serving platter. Arrange the asparagus around the fish. Carefully open the foil pouch and arrange the vegetables around the fish. Drizzle the butter from the pouch over the vegetables. Serve garnished with chopped rosemary and lemon wedges.

The Riverside Inn

LELAND, MICHIGAN

WHEN ANTOINE MANSEAU FOUNDED THE TOWN OF LELAND in 1852, it was primarily a logging town. Jacob Schwarz, a German immigrant to Leelanau County, left logging to open the Riverside Inn in 1901, a respite for locals and visitors alike — many from Chicago, Cincinnati, and Detroit, who were looking to escape to a more rural, beachfront setting.

After changing hands a few times, The Riverside Inn was sold in 1997 to the current owners, mother-daughter team Barbara and Kate Vilter, who originally hail from Cincinnati but spent countless summers in Leland over the years. They transformed the restaurant into an acclaimed culinary destination and must-visit during any trip to Leelanau Peninsula. The Riverside Inn is also a major supporter of local Carlson's Fisheries (see page 260), Leelanau Cheese Co. (see page 243), and many other local farmers and food artisans. Their menu changes frequently to reflect the seasons.

WALLEYE FISH CAKES

with Lemon Aioli

WHILE WALLEYE IS NO LONGER FISHED IN LAKE MICHIGAN, *some fisheries and specialty markets (such as Carlson's Fisheries, page 260, and Burritt's Fish Market) often sell the fish caught from Canadian waters or Lake Huron. Jake's Country Meats (based in Cassopolis) sells walleye caught by Native Americans at Chicago's Green City Market. You can also substitute locally caught whitefish for the walleye in this recipe.*

1. For the aioli, combine the mayonnaise, lemon juice, lemon zest, garlic, and hot pepper sauce in a small bowl, mixing well. Transfer to a serving dish and refrigerate while making the fish cakes.

2. For the fish cakes, place the fish fillets in a medium skillet, add 1 tablespoon water, and bring to a simmer over medium heat. Cover the skillet and cook just until the fish is opaque, 3 to 4 minutes. Drain well and cool in the refrigerator for 10 minutes.

3. Meanwhile, tear the bread into pieces and process in a food processor or blender to coarse crumbs. Transfer the crumbs to a medium bowl (you should have about ¾ cup crumbs). Add the chives, mayonnaise, mustard, egg, hot pepper sauce, and salt, and mix well. Break the cooled fish into small pieces and add to the bowl. Mix very well. Shape the mixture into 4 round patties about ½ inch thick.

4. Melt the butter in a large skillet over medium-high heat. Stir in the oil and heat until very hot. Add the fish cakes in a single layer and cook until the bottoms are golden brown, about 4 minutes. Turn and cook until the second sides are golden brown, 4 to 5 minutes. Serve immediately with the aioli.

FOR THE AIOLI

- ½ cup mayonnaise
- 1 tablespoon fresh lemon juice
- 1 teaspoon grated lemon zest
- 1 garlic clove, crushed
- ¼ teaspoon hot pepper sauce

FOR THE FISH CAKES

- 1 pound skinless, boneless walleye fillets
- 1 slice whole-grain bread
- ¼ cup chopped fresh chives or scallions (optional)
- 2 tablespoons mayonnaise
- 2 teaspoons Dijon mustard
- 1 egg
- ¼ teaspoon hot pepper sauce
- ¼ teaspoon salt
- 2 tablespoons unsalted butter
- 1 tablespoon olive oil or canola oil

PREP TIME: 25 minutes

COOKING TIME: 10 minutes

Serves 4

Carlson's Fisheries
and Fishtown
LELAND, MICHIGAN

NELS CARLSON EMIGRATED FROM NORWAY to the Upper Peninsula of Michigan over a century ago to fish the waters off Lake Michigan. Since then, the torch of the family business has been passed to Will, Lester, Bill, and now fifth-generation Nels Carlson.

Carlson's Fisheries, co-owned by Nels Carlson and Joe Campo, not only supplies restaurants and residents with the day's fresh catch, namely whitefish, but it also offers smoked fish and other specialty fish creations like whitefish sausage and pâté. Carlson's Fisheries also helped develop Fishtown in the 1940s, the historic, photo-worthy boardwalk off the Leland River, with its weathered fish shanties, smokehouses, hanging docks, fish tugs, and charter boats.

Fishtown is the home of Carlson's Fisheries, as well as a number of charter-fishing businesses and two working smokehouses that will smoke your fresh catch for you. Carlson's and the Fishtown Preservation Society have done their part to maintain a healthy fishing environment in the area, working with the Michigan Fish Producers Association, the Department of Natural Resources, and Michigan Sea Grant.

RECIPES BY TYPE

STARTERS AND SNACKS

Compound Butters, 19

Belgian-Style Hand-Cut Fries, 47

Parmesan-Garlic Bread, 65

Swiss Cheese Fondue, 72

Peanut Butter Bites, 99

Cheddar, Cherry, and Pistachio Cheese Ball, 100

Soft Pretzels with Cheddar and Gouda Beer Sauce, 102

Beer-Battered Cheese Curds with Homemade Ranch Dip, 106

Green Garlic Custard, 115

Tempura Asparagus, 135

Turnip, Squash, and Scallion Vegetable Platter with Soppressata and Mint, 141

Harvest Ratatouille Crostini, 152

Pork Rillettes with Pickled Cherries, 171

Deviled Eggs Two Ways, 174

Smoked Whitefish Pâté with Tart Cherry Jam, 182

Mini Hoecakes with Great Lakes Golden Caviar, 186

Rustic Apple Galette with Goat Cheese, Caramelized Onions, and Thyme, 221

Anne's La Tarte Flambé, 241

Anne's Croute au Fromage, 242

SOUPS AND SALADS

Creamy Coleslaw, 15

Wedge Salad with Blue Cheese Dressing, Bacon, and Cherry Tomatoes, 34

Tangy Potato Salad, 86

Homemade Mayonnaise, 87

Wurst Soup with Homemade Herb-Parmesan Croutons, 88

Beer Cheese Soup, 89

Grilled Summer Corn and Veggie Salad with Goat Cheese and Tomato-Dill Vinaigrette, 125

Heirloom Tomato Salad with Balsamic Vinegar and Basil, 129

Green Zebra Green Salad, 148

Creamy Gazpacho, 151

Sweet Potato and Pineapple Salad, 161

Melon and Mint Salad, 194

Roasted Golden Beet Salad with Raita Sauce and Quail Eggs, 233

Creamy Cherry Chicken Salad, 246

Grilled Chicken Salad with Greens and Cherry Vinaigrette, 248

Old Mission Waldorf Salad, 252

Strawberry Salad, 255

VEGETABLE SIDE DISHES

Green Bean Casserole with Kale, 96

Asparagus Sauté with Green Garlic and Herbs, 113

Creamed Corn with Bacon, 123

Roast Acorn Squash with Toasted Pecans, 128

Enchiladas de Berrien Springs, 165

Beach House Cheesy Potatoes, 170

MEAT AND POULTRY

Northern Wisconsin Chicken and Rib Booyah, 26

Grilled Grass-Fed Waseda Farm Bacon Cheeseburgers, 50

Grilled Waseda Farms Rib Steak with Roasted Tomato, Jalapeño, and Cilantro Salsa and Grilled Asparagus, 53

Red Wine–Braised Brisket with Autumn Root Vegetables and Fresh Horseradish, 56

Leftover Brisket Chili, 58

Swedish Meatballs, 69

Standing Rib Roast with Yorkshire Pudding and Horseradish Cream Sauce, 70

Beer-Braised Bratwurst and Onions, 82

Homemade Sheboygan-Style Bratwurst, 84

Duck Breast with Cranberry-Port Sauce, 91

Beef Pot Roast with Seasonal Root Vegetables and Parsley Gremolata, 92

Chicken Shawarma Burritos, 130

HBFC Original Fried Chicken Sandwich, 138

Griddle-Style Double Cheeseburgers, 149

New Buffalo Bill's Wood-Smoked BBQ Ribs, 159

Simple Barbecue Sauce, 160

Spicy Fennel Sausage and Peppers with Garlicky Heirloom Tomato Sauce, 172

Brined Pork Chops with Caramelized Onions and Apples, 177

Korean Pork Bao Sandwich, 180

Red Curry Chicken Skewers with Apricot Chutney, 184

Herb-Grilled Farm Chicken with Lemon Confit and Greens, 209

Braised Pork Shoulder, 211

Fresh Pasta Bolognese, 214

Bacon-Wrapped Meatloaf, 218

Pulled Pork Sandwiches with Cherry Barbecue Sauce, 249

Pasties Two Ways, 253

FISH

Home-Style Fish Boil, 12

Panfried Perch with Tartar Sauce, 16

Whitefish with Basil Pesto and Arugula Salad, 30

Whitefish Tacos with Pickled Red Onions, Red-Hot Aioli, and Guacamole, 44

Homemade Dill-Cured Salmon with Lemon Crème Fraîche and Accoutrements, 59

Whitefish Chowder, 64

Smoked Trout Spread, 66

Crispy-Skinned Lake Trout with Creamed Local Spinach and Radishes, 230

Dead Man's Salmon Roulades with Wild Rice and Mushroom Stuffing and Zinfandel Reduction, 235

Rustic Whitefish Tartlets with Tarragon Beer Mustard Cream, 239

Grilled Carlson's Whitefish and Vegetables, 256

Walleye Fish Cakes with Lemon Aioli, 259

BREAKFAST AND BAKED GOODS

Bavarian Dark Rye Bread, 14

Buttery Dinner Rolls, 18

Wisconsin Cheddar Cheese Scones, 32

Cherry Streusel Muffins, 37

Door County Cherry French Toast, 39

Swedish Pancakes with Lingonberries, 67

Maple Granola with Nuts and Seeds, 73

Wisconsin Ham and Swiss Brunch Strata, 98

Abigail's Miso Sweet Corn Sunrise with Poached Eggs, 120

Sweet Corn Cornbread with Honey Butter, 127

Rolled Oat and Maple Syrup Scones, 142

Morning Glory Muffins, 145

Poached Eggs with Leaning Shed Summer Salsa, 168

Smoked Leek Sausage Frittata with Summer Squash and Goat Cheese, 176

Spiced Breakfast Sausage Patties, 185

Grandma's German Apple Pancake, 190

Heirloom Apple Butter, 191

Apple-Cinnamon Fritters, 192

Blueberry Sour Cream Coffee Cake, 193

Blackberry-Blueberry Jam, 198

Cranberry-Nut Bread, 217

SWEETS

Door County Cherry Pie, 21

Apple Cake, 24

Cherry-Poached Pears with Mascarpone Cream, 28

Wilson's Vanilla Sundaes with Seaquist Orchards Cherry Topping, 40

Cherry-Chocolate Oatmeal Cookies, 77

Wisconsin Quark Cheesecake, 109

Quark Soufflés, 111

Michigan Peach Crisp, 200

Strawberry-Rhubarb Hand Pies, 203

Strawberry Shortcakes, 205

Summer Fruit Biscuit Bake, 224

Mackinac Island Peanut Brittle, 250

DRINKS

Cold-Brewed Coffee, 43

Death's Door Caipiroska, 79

Boone Brandy Old-Fashioned, 112

Warm Winter Wassail, 197

Blueberry-Mint Soda, 199

Traverse City Whiskey Smash, 245

Acknowledgments

It's been a dream of mine for many years to capture such a strong part of my childhood, and that of so many others. The endless bites of warm cherry pie à la mode at the local supper club, the fried perch with tartar sauce, the warm baked goods I woke up to at bed-and-breakfasts, the hours upon hours of playing at the beach and the elaborate picnics we made to refuel — these are some of the strongest food memories I have, and they all took place in and around Lake Michigan.

Thanks, first, to the many farmers, fisheries, chefs, restaurant and inn owners, shopkeepers, cheese makers, and other food artisans who either provided recipes for the book or inspired so many others.

Thank you to the various city tourism departments in Wisconsin and Michigan, who assisted in connecting me with many of these sources, and for sponsoring press trips over the years that helped inspire this book in the first place.

Thank you to my agent, Jenni Ferrari-Adler, who believed in and helped present my idea for this book. Of course, thank you to Storey Publishing and my editors, Sarah Guare and Jennifer Travis, for your patience, diligence, and expertise in turning this manuscript into a beautiful book. Thanks, also, to photographers Johnny and Charlotte Autry, Teri Genovese, and David Nevala for capturing the beauty of the foods, scenes, and people of Lake Michigan.

An enormous thank you to my mom, a veteran recipe developer who helped edit and test many of the recipes in this book, working with me from start to finish. Ever since I was a child, when my mom was writing her own cookbooks and I would help her test and taste-test the recipes, we've been an inseparable pair in the kitchen. And thank you, Dad, for helping out with the very necessary taste-testing and important feedback.

Last but not least, another huge thank you to my loving husband, who has been yet another amazing taste-tester and number 1, rock-solid supporter throughout the writing of three books. Thank you, also, to my son Jonah, who even as a toddler tried some of the recipes, developing a special fondness for the cherry pie, soft pretzels, muffins, and jams in the book. He even ate and enjoyed the house-cured salmon. Thank you, too, to my daughter Liliana (Lily), who, while I was pregnant with her, helped with my appetite for all these delicious foods.

Thank you, everyone, for your help along the way in this huge labor of love.

RESOURCES

Farmers' Markets

Here I've included only markets near Lake Michigan destinations mentioned in this book.

ILLINOIS

Green City Market

Logan Square Farmers' Market

INDIANA

Michigan City Farmers' Market

MICHIGAN

Three Oaks Farmers' Market

St. Joseph Farmers' Market

Benton Harbor Farmers' Market

South Haven Farmers' Market

Saugatuck-Douglas Greenmarket

Holland Farmers' Market

Grand Haven Farmers' Market

Spring Lake Farm & Garden Market

Muskegon Farmers' Market

Sweetwater Local Foods Market

Sara Hardy Farmers' Market
Traverse City

Leelanau Farmers' Markets
Suttons Bay
Empire
Lake Leelanau
Glen Arbor
Leland
Northport
Cedar

WISCONSIN

Door County Farmers' Markets
Sturgeon Bay
Jacksonport
Fish Creek
Baileys Harbor
Sister Bay

Profiled and Contributing Businesses

ILLINOIS AND INDIANA

Abigail's American Bistro
www.abigails493.com
Highland Park, IL

Chicago's Green City Market
www.greencitymarket.org
Chicago, IL

Farmhouse
http://farmhousechicago.com/
Chicago, IL

Girl and the Goat
http://girlandthegoat.com/
Chicago, IL

Green Zebra
www.greenzebrachicago.com
Chicago, IL

Half Acre
www.halfacrebeer.com
Chicago, IL

Hewn Bakery
http://hewnbread.com
Evanston, IL

Honey Butter Fried Chicken
www.honeybutter.com
Chicago, IL

Iron Creek Farm
www.ironcreekfarm.com
LaPorte, IN

Little Goat Diner
http://littlegoatchicago.com
Chicago, IL

Local Foods
http://localfoods.com
Chicago, IL

North Pond Restaurant
http://northpondrestaurant.com
Chicago, IL

Prairie Grass Café
www.prairiegrasscafe.com
Northbrook, IL

MICHIGAN

Carlson's Fisheries
www.carlsonsfish.com
Leland, MI

The Cooks' House
www.cookshousetc.com
Traverse City, MI

Ellis Family Farms
www.ellisfamilyfarm.com
Benton Harbor, MI

Evergreen Lane Artisan Cheese
www.evergreenlanefarm.com
Fennville, MI

Flagship Specialty Foods and Fish Market
http://flagship-foods.com
Lakeside, MI

Free Run Cellars
www.drinkmichigan.com/
free-run-cellars
Berrien Springs, MI

Froehlich's Deli
www.shopfroehlichs.com
Three Oaks, MI

Kismet Farm and Bakery
www.kismetorganics.com
Fennville, MI

Leaning Shed Farm
http://leaningshed.com
Barrien Spring, MI

Leelanau Cheese Co.
www.leelanaucheese.com
Suttons Bay, MI

New Buffalo Bill's
http://newbuffalobills.com
New Buffalo, MI

The Riverside Inn
www.theriverside-inn.com
Leland, MI

Round Barn Winery
www.drinkmichigan.com/
round-barn
Baroda, MI

Ruleau Bros.
www.doorcountywhitefish.com
Stephenson, MI

Salt of the Earth
www.saltoftheearthfennville
 .com
Fennville, MI

Seedling Farm
www.seedlingfruit.com
South Haven, MI

Virtue Cider
www.virtuecider.com
Fennville, MI

WISCONSIN

The American Club
www.americanclubresort.com
Kohler, WI

Bleu Mont Dairy Co.
Blue Mounds, WI

Boone and Crockett
http://boonemilwaukee.com
Milwaukee, WI

Braise
www.braiselocalfood.com
Milwaukee, WI

Clock Shadow Creamery
www.clockshadowcreamery.com
Milwaukee, WI

Death's Door Spirits
www.deathsdoorspirits.com
Middleton, WI

Door County Coffee & Tea
www.doorcountycoffee.com
Sturgeon Bay, WI

Eagle Harbor Inn
www.eagleharborinn.com
Ephraim, WI

La Merenda
www.lamerenda125.com
Milwaukee, WI

Savory Spoon Cooking School
www.savoryspoon.com
Ellison Bay, WI

Seaquist Orchards
www.seaquistorchards.com
Sister Bay, WI

Sweetie Pies
www.doorcountypies.com
Fish Creek, WI

Sweet Mountain Farm
http://sweetmountainfarm.com
Washington Island, WI

Waseda Farms
www.wasedafarms.com
Baileys Harbor, WI

Wickman House
www.wickmanhouse.com
Ellison Bay, WI

Wilson's Ice Cream
http://wilsonsicecream.com
Ephraim, WI

METRIC CONVERSION CHARTS

Unless you have finely calibrated measuring equipment, conversions between US and metric measurements will be somewhat inexact. It's important to convert the measurements for all of the ingredients in a recipe to maintain the same proportions as the original.

Weight

TO CONVERT	TO	MULTIPLY
ounces	grams	ounces by 28.35
pounds	grams	pounds by 453.5
pounds	kilograms	pounds by 0.45

Volume

TO CONVERT	TO	MULTIPLY
teaspoons	milliliters	teaspoons by 4.93
tablespoons	milliliters	tablespoons by 14.79
fluid ounces	milliliters	fluid ounces by 29.57
cups	milliliters	cups by 236.59
cups	liters	cups by 0.24
pints	milliliters	pints by 473.18
pints	liters	pints by 0.473
quarts	milliliters	quarts by 946.36
quarts	liters	quarts by 0.946
gallons	liters	gallons by 3.785

INDEX

Page numbers in *italic* indicate photographs.

A

Abigail's American Bistro (Highland Park, Illinois), 122

Abigail's Miso Sweet Corn Sunrise with Poached Eggs, 120, *121*

Acorn Squash, Roasted with Toasted Pecans, 128

aioli
Walleye Fish Cakes with Lemon Aioli, 259
Whitefish Tacos with Pickled Red Onions, Red-Hot Aioli, and Guacamole, 44, *45*

Al Johnson's Swedish Restaurant (Sister Bay, Wisconsin), 68, *68*, 69

Alliance for the Great Lakes, 61

Amber Ale Gravy, 254

The American Club (Kohler, Wisconsin), 81, 89, 91, 94, *95*, 96

Anne's La Tarte Flambé, 241

antioxidants, 74

apple cider
Warm Winter Wassail, 197

Apple Holler (Kenosha, Wisconsin), 192

apple(s)
Apple Cake, 24
Apple-Cinnamon Fritters, 192
Brined Pork Chops with Caramelized Onions and Apples, 177
Grandma's German Apple Pancake, 190
Heirloom Apple Butter, 191
Old Mission Waldorf Salad, 252
Rustic Apple Galette with Goat Cheese, Caramelized Onions, and Thyme, *220*, 221
SweeTango, 38
Virtue Cider and, 213

Apricot Chutney, Red Curry Chicken Skewers with, 184

Arugula Salad, Whitefish with Basil Pesto and, 30

asparagus
Asparagus Sauté with Green Garlic and Herbs, 113, *113*
Grilled Carlson's Whitefish and Vegetables, 256, *257*
Grilled Waseda Farms Rib-Eye Steak with Roasted Tomato, Jalapeño, and Cilantro Salsa and Grilled Asparagus, *52*, 53
Tempura Asparagus, *134*, 135

avocado(s)
Whitefish Tacos with Pickled Red Onions, Red-Hot Aioli, and Guacamole, 44, *45*

B

B&E's Trees (Driftless Area, Wisconsin), 142

bacon
Anne's La Tarte Flambé, 241
Bacon-Wrapped Meatloaf, 218
Creamed Corn with Bacon, 123
Grilled Grass-Fed Waseda Farm Bacon Cheeseburgers, 50, *51*
Wedge Salad with Blue Cheese Dressing, Bacon, and Cherry Tomatoes, 34

barbecue sauces
Cherry Barbecue Sauce, 249
Simple Barbecue Sauce, 160

Barb's Bakery, 229

Bardenhagen Farms (Suttons Bay, Michigan), 255

Basil Pesto and Arugula Salad, Whitefish with, 30

Bavarian Dark Rye Bread, 14

Beach House Cheesy Potatoes, 170

beef
Bacon-Wrapped Meatloaf, 218
Beef Pot Roast with Seasonal Root Vegetables and Parsley Gremolata, 92
Griddle-Style Double Cheeseburgers, 149
Grilled Grass-Fed Waseda Farm Bacon Cheeseburgers, 50, *51*
Grilled Waseda Farms Rib-Eye Steak with Roasted Tomato, Jalapeño, and Cilantro Salsa and Grilled Asparagus, *52*, 53
Leftover Brisket Chili, 58
Meatballs, 69
Northern Wisconsin Chicken and Rib Booyah, 26
Pasties Two Ways, 254
Red Wine–Braised Brisket with Autumn Root Vegetables and Fresh Horseradish, 56
Standing Rib Roast with Yorkshire Pudding and Horseradish Cream Sauce, 70

beer
Amber Ale Gravy, 254
Beer-Battered Cheese Curds with Homemade Ranch Dip, 106, *107*
Beer-Braised Bratwurst and Onions, 82, *83*
Beer Cheese Soup, 89
Milwaukee and, 105
Pasties Two Ways, 254
Rustic Whitefish Tartlets with Tarragon Beer Mustard Cream, 239
Soft Pretzels with Cheddar and Gouda Beer Sauce, 102

bees, 74–75, *74–75*

Beet Salad, Roasted Golden with Raita Sauce and Quail Eggs, 233

Belgian-Style Hand-Cut Fries, 47, *48*

BelGioso (Brownsville, Wisconsin), 148

Berrien Springs, Enchiladas de, *164*, 165

beverages
    Blueberry-Mint Soda, 199
    Boone Brandy Old-Fashioned, 112
    Capital Brewery's Island Wheat Ale, 78
    Cold-Brewed Coffee, 43
    Death's Door Caipiroska, 78
    Door County Coffee & Tea and, 42
    Traverse City Whiskey Smash, *244*, 245
    Warm Winter Wassail, 197

Biscuit Bake, Summer Fruit, 224

Blackberry-Blueberry Jam, 198

Black Star Farms (Traverse City and Suttons Bay, Michigan), 241

Black Wolf Run at the American Club (Kohler, Wisconsin), 96

Blakeslee, Jennifer, 232, *232*

Bleu Mont Dairy (Blue Mounds, Wisconsin), 33

blueberry(ies)
    Blackberry-Blueberry Jam, 198
    Blueberry-Mint Soda, 199
    Blueberry Sour Cream Coffee Cake, 193
    Rolled Oat and Maple Syrup Scones, 142, *143*
    Summer Fruit Biscuit Bake, 224

blue cheese
    Blue Cheese and Herb Butter, 19
    Wedge Salad with Blue Cheese Dressing, Bacon, and Cherry Tomatoes, 34

Bolognese, Fresh Pasta, 214, *215*

Boone and Crockett (Milwaukee, Wisconsin), 112

Boone Brandy Old-Fashioned, 112

Booyah, Northern Wisconsin Chicken and Rib, 26

Braise (Milwaukee, Wisconsin), 84, 114, *114*, 115

Braised Pork Shoulder, 211

Brandy (Boone) Old-Fashioned, 112

bratwurst
    Beer-Braised Bratwurst and Onions, 82, *83*
    Homemade Sheboygan-Style Bratwurst, 84
    Wurst Soup with Homemade Herb-Parmesan Croutons, 88

breads
    Bavarian Dark Rye Bread, 14
    Buttery Dinner Rolls, 18
    Cranberry-Nut Bread, 217
    Hewn Bakery and, 146–147
    Kismet Bakery and, 226
    Parmesan-Garlic Bread, 65
    Pleasant Bakery and, 246
    Salt of the Earth and, 216

Brined Pork Chops with Caramelized Onions and Apples, 177

brisket
    Leftover Brisket Chili, 58
    Red Wine–Braised Brisket with Autumn Root Vegetables and Fresh Horseradish, 56

Bumbaris, George, 140

burbot, 62, *62*

burgers
    Griddle-Style Double Cheeseburgers, 149
    Grilled Grass-Fed Waseda Farm Bacon Cheeseburgers, 50, *51*

Burritos, Chicken Shawarma, 130, *132*

Burritt's Fish Market, 259

butterkäse cheese
    Beach House Cheesy Potatoes, 170

butters
    Compound Butters, 19
    Heirloom Apple Butter, 191

Buttery Dinner Rolls, 18

C

cabbage
    Creamy Coleslaw, 15

Caipiroska, Death's Door, 79

cakes
    Apple Cake, 24
    Blueberry Sour Cream Coffee Cake, 193
    Strawberry Shortcakes, 205
    Wisconsin Quark Cheesecake, 109

Campo, Joe, 260

cachaça, 79

Capital Brewery's Island Wheat Ale, 78

Carlson, Nels, 260

Carlson's Fisheries (Leland, Michigan), 230, 256, 258, 259, 260, *260–261*

carrot(s)
    Beef Pot Roast with Seasonal Root Vegetables and Parsley Gremolata, 92
    Morning Glory Muffins, 145
    Red Wine–Braised Brisket with Autumn Root Vegetables and Fresh Horseradish, 56

Casserole, Green Bean with Kale, 96

caviar
    Flagship Specialty Foods & Fish Market and, 187
    Mini Hoecakes with Great Lakes Golden Caviar, 186

Chambas, Matt, 47, 49, *49*, 50

Charlie's Smokehouse (Ellison Bay, Wisconsin), 49, 66

cheddar cheese
    Beach House Cheesy Potatoes, 170
    Beer Cheese Soup, 89
    Bleu Mont Dairy and, 33
    Cheddar, Cherry, and Pistachio Cheese Ball, 100, *101*
    Enchiladas de Berrien Springs, *164*, 165
    Soft Pretzels with Cheddar and Gouda Beer Sauce, 102
    Wisconsin Cheddar Cheese Scones, 32

cheese
  Anne's Croute au Fromage, 242
  Anne's La Tarte Flambé, 241
  Beach House Cheesy Potatoes,
    170
  Beer Cheese Soup, 89
  Bleu Mont Dairy and, 33
  Blue Cheese and Herb Butter, 19
  Cheddar, Cherry, and Pistachio
    Cheese Ball, 100, *101*
  Clock Shadow Creamery and,
    110, *110*
  Enchiladas de Berrien Springs,
    164, 165
  Evergreen Lane Farm and, 223
  Green Zebra Green Salad, 148
  Griddle-Style Double
    Cheeseburgers, 149
  Grilled Grass-Fed Waseda
    Farm Bacon Cheeseburgers,
    50, *51*
  Grilled Summer Corn and
    Veggie Salad with Goat
    Cheese and Tomato-Dill
    Vinaigrette, 125
  Leelanau Cheese Co. and, 243
  Melon and Mint Salad, 194, *195*
  Parmesan-Garlic Bread, 65
  Quark Soufflés, 111
  Rustic Apple Galette with
    Goat Cheese, Caramelized
    Onions, and Thyme, *220*, 221
  Schoolhouse Artisan Cheese
    and, 19, 31, 34, 50, 72
  Smoked Leek Sausage Frittata
    with Summer Squash and
    Goat Cheese, 176
  Soft Pretzels with Cheddar and
    Gouda Beer Sauce, 102
  Swiss Cheese Fondue, 72
  Wedge Salad with Blue Cheese
    Dressing, Bacon, and Cherry
    Tomatoes, 34
  Wisconsin and, 35
  Wisconsin Cheddar Cheese
    Scones, 32
  Wisconsin Ham and Swiss
    Brunch Strata, 98
  Wisconsin Quark Cheesecake,
    109

  Wurst Soup with Homemade
    Herb-Parmesan Croutons,
    88
Cheesecake, Wisconsin Quark,
    109
Cheese Curds, Beer-Battered
    with Homemade Ranch Dip,
    106, *107*
Cherry Festival (Traverse City,
    Michigan), 247
cherry(ies)
  Cheddar, Cherry, and Pistachio
    Cheese Ball, 100, *101*
  Cherry-Chocolate Oatmeal
    Cookies, *76*, 77
  Cherry Mitten cider, 213
  Cherry-Poached Pears with
    Mascarpone Cream, 28, *29*
  Cherry Streusel Muffins, *36*, 37
  Creamy Cherry Chicken Salad,
    246
  Door County Cherry Pie, 20, 21
  Door County French Toast, 39
  Grilled Chicken Salad
    with Greens and Cherry
    Vinaigrette, 248
  Old Mission Waldorf Salad, 252
  Pork Rillettes with Pickled
    Cherries, 171
  Pulled Pork Sandwiches with
    Cherry Barbecue Sauce, 249
  Smoked Whitefish Pâté with
    Tart Cherry Jam, 182
  Traverse City and peninsulas
    and, 229, 247, *247*
  Wilson's Vanilla Sundaes with
    Seaquist Orchards Cherry
    Topping, 40
Cherry Tomatoes, Wedge Salad
    with Blue Cheese Dressing,
    Bacon, and, 34
Chicago, Illinois
  Abigail's American Bistro and,
    122, *122*
  Half Acre Beer Company and,
    130, 133, *133*, 135
  Hewn Bakery and, 142, 145,
    146–147, *146-147*
  Local Foods market and, 136
  overview of, *116–117*, 119

  Prairie Grass Cafe and, 140,
    140, 141
Chicago, Illinois, recipes
  Abigail's Miso Sweet Corn
    Sunrise with Poached Eggs,
    120, *121*
  Chicken Shawarma Burritos,
    130
  Creamed Corn with Bacon, 123
  Green Zebra Green Salad, 148
  Griddle-Style Double
    Cheeseburgers, 149
  Grilled Summer Corn and
    Veggie Salad with Goat
    Cheese and Tomato-Dill
    Vinaigrette, 125
  HBFC Original Fried Chicken
    Sandwich, 138
  Heirloom Tomato Salad with
    Balsamic Vinegar and Basil,
    129
  Morning Glory Muffins, 145
  Roast Acorn Squash with
    Toasted Pecans, 128
  Rolled Oat and Maple Syrup
    Scones, 142, *143*
  Sweet Corn Cornbread with
    Honey Butter, 127
  Tempura Asparagus, *134*, 135
  Turnip, Squash, and Scallion
    Vegetable Platter with
    Soppressata and Mint, 141
chicken
  Chicken Shawarma Burritos,
    130, *132*
  Creamy Cherry Chicken Salad,
    246
  Grilled Chicken Salad
    with Greens and Cherry
    Vinaigrette, 248
  HBFC Original Fried Chicken
    Sandwich, 138
  Herb-Grilled Farm Chicken
    with Lemon Confit and
    Greens, *208*, 209
  Northern Wisconsin Chicken
    and Rib Booyah, 26
  Pasties Two Ways, 253
  Red Curry Chicken Skewers
    with Apricot Chutney, 184

chicken salads
  Creamy Cherry Chicken Salad,
    246
  Grilled Chicken Salad
    with Greens and Cherry
    Vinaigrette, 248
Chihuahua cheese
  Enchiladas de Berrien Springs,
    164, 165
chile pepper(s)
  Enchiladas de Berrien Springs,
    164, 165
  Poached Eggs with Leaning
    Shed Summer Salsa, 168
Chili, Leftover Brisket, 58
Chinook salmon, 62, 62
Chocolate-Cherry Oatmeal
  Cookies, 76, 77
Chowder, Whitefish, 64
chub, 62, 62
chuck, beef
  Beef Pot Roast with Seasonal
    Root Vegetables and Parsley
    Gremolata, 92
Chutney, Apricot, 184
cider
  Virtue Cider and, 212–213,
    212–213
  Warm Winter Wassail, 197
Cidre Nouveau, 213
Cikowski, Christine, 138
Circle Tour (Lake Michigan), 6,
    7, 229
Clario Farms (Algoma,
    Wisconsin), 214, 215
Clario pasta, 214
Clock Shadow Creamery
  (Milwaukee, Wisconsin),
    106, 109, 110, 110
CoachStop Farms (Zeeland,
    Michigan), 209, 211
cocktails. See also beverages
  Boone Brandy Old-Fashioned,
    112
  Death's Door Caipiroska, 78
coffee
  Cold-Brewed Coffee, 43
  Door County Coffee & Tea and,
    42

Coffee Cake, Blueberry Sour
  Cream, 193
coho salmon, 62, 62
Cold-Brewed Coffee, 43
Coleslaw, Creamy, 15
Collins, Rachel, 186, 187
Collins Caviar, 186, 187
Community-Supported Fish (CSF)
  program, 238
Compound Butters, 19
Confit (Lemon) and Greens,
  Herb-Grilled Farm Chicken
  with, 208, 209
The Cookery (Fish Creek,
  Wisconsin), 64
Cookies, Cherry Chocolate
  Oatmeal, 76, 77
The Cooks' House (Traverse City,
  Michigan), 230, 232, 232
corn
  Abigail's Miso Sweet Corn
    Sunrise with Poached Eggs,
    120, 121
  Creamed Corn with Bacon, 123
  Grilled Summer Corn and
    Veggie Salad with Goat
    Cheese and Tomato-Dill
    Vinaigrette, 124, 125
  Sweet Corn Cornbread with
    Honey Butter, 127
Cotija cheese
  Enchiladas de Berrien Springs,
    164, 165
Cove Restaurant (Leland,
  Michigan), 229
cranberry(ies)
  Cheddar, Cherry, and Pistachio
    Cheese Ball, 100, 101
  Cranberry-Nut Bread, 217
  Duck Breast with Cranberry-
    Port Sauce, 90, 91
Creamed Corn with Bacon, 123
Creamy Cherry Chicken Salad,
    246
Creamy Coleslaw, 15
Creamy Gazpacho, 151
Crème Fraîche (Lemon) and
  Accoutrements, Homemade
  Dill-Cured Salmon with, 59

Creswick Farms (Ravenna,
  Michigan), 211
Crispy-Skinned Lake Trout with
  Creamed Local Spinach and
  Radishes, 230, 231
Croissant, Susan, 23
Crostini, Harvest Ratatouille,
  152, 153
Croute au Fromage, Anne's, 242
Croutons (Homemade Herb-
  Parmesan), Wurst Soup
  with, 88
cucumber(s)
  Creamy Gazpacho, 151
Curds, Beer-Battered Cheese
  with Homemade Ranch Dip,
  106, 107
Curry (Red) Chicken Skewers
  with Apricot Chutney, 184
Custard, Green Garlic, 115

D

The Danish Mill (Washington
  Island, Wisconsin), 75
Darpel, Steve, 216
Dead Man's Salmon Roulades
  with Wild Rice and
  Mushroom Stuffing and
  Zinfandel Reduction, 235,
  237
Death's Door Caipiroska, 79
Death's Door Spirits (Middleton,
  Wisconsin), 78, 79
DeBoers (Holland, Michigan), 218
desserts
  Apple Cake, 24
  Cherry-Chocolate Oatmeal
    Cookies, 76, 77
  Cherry-Poached Pears with
    Mascarpone Cream, 28, 29
  Cranberry-Nut Bread, 217
  Door County Cherry Pie, 20, 21
  Mackinac Island Peanut Brittle,
    250, 251
  Michigan Peach Crisp, 200, 201
  Peanut Butter Bites, 99
  Quark Soufflés, 111
  Rolled Oat and Maple Syrup
    Scones, 142, 143

Strawberry-Rhubarb Hand
    Pies, *202*, 203
Strawberry Shortcakes, 205
Summer Fruit Biscuit Bake, 224
Wilson's Vanilla Sundaes with
    Seaquist Orchards Cherry
    Topping, 40
Wisconsin Quark Cheesecake,
    109
Deviled Eggs Two Ways, 174
Dill-Cured Salmon, Homemade
    with Lemon Crème Fraîche
    and Accoutrements, 59
Dinner Rolls, Buttery, 18
Domkpe, Sue, 74–75, *74*
Donny's at Glidden Lodge
    (Sturgeon Bay, Wisconsin), 16
Door County, Wisconsin
    Bleu Mont Dairy and, 33
    Death's Door Spirits and, 78, 79
    farmers' markets and, 25
    fish boils and, 13
    fish fries and, 17
    ice cream and, 40, 41
    Al Johnson's Swedish
        Restaurant and, 68, *68*, 69
    overview of, 11
    Savory Spoon Cooking School
        and, 31
    Seaquist Orchards and, *36*,
        37, 38
    Sweetie Pies and, *20*, *21*, 23
    Sweet Mountain Farm and, 74
    Waseda Farms and, 49, 50, 53,
        55, *55*, 56, 58
    Wickman House and, 47, 49, 50
Door County, Wisconsin, recipes
    Apple Cake, 24
    Bavarian Dark Rye Bread, 14
    Belgian-Style Hand-Cut Fries,
        47, *48*
    Buttery Dinner Rolls, 18
    Cherry-Chocolate Oatmeal
        Cookies, *76*, 77
    Cherry-Poached Pears with
        Mascarpone Cream, 28, *29*
    Cherry Streusel Muffins, *36*, 37
    Cold-Brewed Coffee, 43
    Compound Butters, 19
    Creamy Coleslaw, 15

Death's Door Caipiroska, 79
Door County Cherry French
    Toast, 39
Door County Cherry Pie, *20*, 21
Door County Coffee & Tea and,
    42
Grilled Grass-Fed Waseda
    Farm Bacon Cheeseburgers,
    50, *51*
Grilled Waseda Farms Rib-Eye
    Steak with Roasted Tomato,
    Jalapeño, and Cilantro Salsa
    and Grilled Asparagus, *52*, 53
Homemade Dill-Cured Salmon
    with Lemon Crème Fraîche
    and Accoutrements, 59
Home-Style Fish Boil, 12
Leftover Brisket Chili, 58
Maple Granola with Nuts and
    Seeds, 73
Northern Wisconsin Chicken
    and Rib Booyah, 26
Panfried Perch with Tartar
    Sauce, 16
Parmesan-Garlic Bread, 65
Red Wine–Braised Brisket with
    Autumn Root Vegetables
    and Fresh Horseradish, 56
Smoked Trout Spread, 66
Standing Rib Roast with
    Yorkshire Pudding and
    Horseradish Cream Sauce, 70
Swedish Meatballs, 69
Swedish Pancakes with
    Lingonberries, 67
Swiss Cheese Fondue, 72
Wedge Salad with Blue Cheese
    Dressing, Bacon, and Cherry
    Tomatoes, 34
Whitefish Chowder, 64
Whitefish Tacos with Pickled
    Red Onions, Red-Hot Aioli,
    and Guacamole, 44, *45*
Whitefish with Basil Pesto and
    Arugula Salad, 30
Wilson's Vanilla Sundaes with
    Seaquist Orchards Cherry
    Topping, 40
Wisconsin Cheddar Cheese
    Scones, 32

Door County Coffee & Tea
    (Sturgeon Bay, Wisconsin),
    42
Douglas, Michigan, overview of,
    154, 207
Douglas, Michigan, recipes
    Bacon-Wrapped Meatloaf, 218
drinks. *See* beverages
Duck Breast with Cranberry-Port
    Sauce, 90, 91
Dyrek, Dave and Denise, 167

E

Eat Wisconsin Fish, 61
Edelweiss Creamery (Monroe,
    Wisconsin), 98
eggplant
    Harvest Ratatouille Crostini,
    152, *153*
egg(s)
    Abigail's Miso Sweet Corn
        Sunrise with Poached Eggs,
        120, *121*
    Deviled Eggs Two Ways, 174
    Poached Eggs with Leaning
        Shed Summer Salsa, 168
Ellis Family Farms (Benton
    Harbor, Michigan), 190, 200
Ellison, Brian, 78
Enchiladas de Berrien Springs,
    164, 165
Evergreen Lane Farm (Fennville,
    Michigan), 221, 223, *223*

F

farmers' markets, 25, 211
Farmhouse Deli (Chicago), 218,
    223
Farmhouse restaurants (Chicago
    and Evanston, Illinois), 235,
    239
Fennville, Michigan
    Evergreen Lane Farm and, 221,
        223, *223*
    Kismet Farm and Bakery and,
        224, 226, 226–227
    overview of, *154*, 207

Fennville, Michigan, *continued*
Salt of the Earth and, 209, 214, 216, *216*, 218
Virtue Cider and, 212–213, *212–213*
Fennville, Michigan, recipes
Braised Pork Shoulder, 211
Fresh Pasta Bolognese, 214, *215*
Herb-Grilled Farm Chicken with Lemon Confit and Greens, *208*, 209
Rustic Apple Galette with Goat Cheese, Caramelized Onions, and Thyme, *220*, 221
Summer Fruit Biscuit Bake, 224
Ferris, Christine, 218
fish
Carlson's Fisheries and, 260
Crispy-Skinned Lake Trout with Creamed Local Spinach and Radishes, 230, *231*
Dead Man's Salmon Roulades with Wild Rice and Mushroom Stuffing and Zinfandel Reduction, 235, *237*
Grilled Carlson's Whitefish and Vegetables, 256, *257*
Homemade Dill-Cured Salmon with Lemon Crème Fraîche and Accoutrements, 59
Home-Style Fish Boil, 12
Panfried Perch with Tartar Sauce, 16
Ruleau Bros. CSF and, 238
Rustic Whitefish Tartlets with Tarragon Beer Mustard Cream, 239
Smoked Trout Spread, 66
Smoked Whitefish Pâté with Tart Cherry Jam, 182
types of in Lake Michigan, 62–63, *62–63*
Walleye Fish Cakes with Lemon Aioli, 259
Whitefish Chowder, 64
Whitefish Tacos with Pickled Red Onions, Red-Hot Aioli, and Guacamole, 44, *45*
Whitefish with Basil Pesto and Arugula Salad, 30

fish boils
Home-Style Fish Boil, 12
overview of, 13
fish fries
overview of, 17
fishing, in Lake Michigan, 61–63
Fishtown (Leland, Michigan), 260
Flagship Specialty Foods & Fish Market (Lakeside, Michigan), 186, 187, *187*
Fondue, Swiss Cheese, 72
Fredrickson, Chris, 245
Free Run Cellars (Berrien Springs, Michigan), 178–179, *178–179*, 180, *181*, 182, *183*, 184
French Toast, Door County, 39
Fresh Pasta Bolognese, 214, *215*
Freshwater Future, 61
Fried Chicken Sandwich, HBFC Original, 138
Fries, Belgian-Style Hand-Cut, 47, *48*
Frittata, Smoked Leek Sausage with Summer Squash and Goat Cheese, 176
Fritters, Apple-Cinnamon, 192
Froehlich's Deli (Three Oaks, Michigan), 174, 175, *175*
fromage blanc
Anne's La Tarte Flambé, 241
Fruit Biscuit Bake, Summer, 224

G

garlic
Asparagus Sauté with Green Garlic and Herbs, 113, *113*
Green Garlic Custard, 115
Parmesan-Garlic Bread, 65
Gazpacho, Creamy, 151
Gelder, René, 190
Girl & the Goat (Chicago, Illinois), 197
goat cheese
Grilled Summer Corn and Veggie Salad with Goat Cheese and Tomato-Dill Vinaigrette, 125

Rustic Apple Galette with Goat Cheese, Caramelized Onions, and Thyme, *220*, 221
Smoked Leek Sausage Frittata with Summer Squash and Goat Cheese, 176
goats on roof, 68, *68*
Goldring, Moti, 245
Go Traveling Culinary School (Milwaukee, Wisconsin), 114
Gouda Beer Sauce, Soft Pretzels with Cheddar and, 102
grains, heritage, 146–147
The Granary (Washington Island), 62
The Grand Café (Glen Arbor, Michigan), 249
Grandma's German Apple Pancake, 190
Grand Traverse Culinary Oils (Traverse City, Michigan), 241
Grand Traverse Pie Company (Traverse City, Michigan), 229
Granola, Maple with Nuts and Seeds, 73
gravlax, 59
Gravy, Amber Ale, 254
Green Bean Casserole with Kale, 96
Green Garlic Custard, 115
Greenwood Supper Club, 16
Green Zebra (Chicago, Illinois), 148
gremolata
Beef Pot Roast with Seasonal Root Vegetables and Parsley Gremolata, 92
Red Wine–Braised Brisket with Autumn Root Vegetables and Fresh Horseradish, 56
Griddle-Style Double Cheeseburgers, 149
Grilled Carlson's Whitefish and Vegetables, 256, *257*
Grilled Chicken Salad with Greens and Cherry Vinaigrette, 248
Grilled Grass-Fed Waseda Farm Bacon Cheeseburgers, 50, *51*

Grilled Summer Corn and Veggie
    Salad with Goat Cheese and
    Tomato-Dill Vinaigrette,
    124, 125
Gruyère cheese
    Swiss Cheese Fondue, 72
Guacamole, Whitefish Tacos with
    Pickled Red Onions, Red-Hot
    Aioli, and, 44, *45*

H

Half Acre Beer Company
    (Chicago, Illinois), 130, 133,
    133, 135
Halinski, Cathy and Tom, 223
Hall, Greg, 212–213
Ham and Swiss Brunch Strata,
    Wisconsin, 98
Harbor Country, Michigan
    Flagship Specialty Foods & Fish
        Market and, 186, 187, *187*
    Free Run Cellars and, 178–179,
        178–179, 180, *181*, 182, *183*, 184
    Froehlich's Deli and, 174, 175,
        175
    Leaning Shed Farm and, 129,
        165, 167, 168, 172
    New Buffalo Bill's and, 161, 162,
        162–163
    overview of, *154*, 157
    Round Barn Winery and, 178–
        179, *178–179*
Harbor Country, Michigan,
    recipes
    Beach House Cheesy Potatoes,
        170
    Brined Pork Chops with
        Caramelized Onions and
        Apples, 177
    Deviled Eggs Two Ways, 174
    Enchiladas de Berrien Springs,
        164, 165
    Korean Pork Bao Sandwich, 180
    Mini Hoecakes with Great
        Lakes Golden Caviar, 186
    New Buffalo Bill's Wood-
        Smoked BBQ Ribs, *158*, 159
    Poached Eggs with Leaning
        Shed Summer Salsa, 168

Pork Rillettes with Pickled
    Cherries, 171
Red Curry Chicken Skewers
    with Apricot Chutney, 184
Simple Barbecue Sauce, 160
Smoked Leek Sausage Frittata
    with Summer Squash and
    Goat Cheese, 176
Smoked Whitefish Pâté with
    Tart Cherry Jam, 182
Spiced Breakfast Sausage
    Patties, 185
Spicy Fennel Sausage and
    Peppers with Garlicky
    Heirloom Tomato Sauce,
    172, *173*
Sweet Potato and Pineapple
    Salad, 161
Hardy, Sara, 233
Harvest Ratatouille Crostini, 152,
    153
Havarti cheese
    Beach House Cheesy Potatoes,
        170
Hazzard, Anthony, 147
Hazzard Free Farm (Pecatonica,
    Illinois), 142, 147
HBFC Original Fried Chicken
    Sandwich, 138
Hearth & Vine Café, 241
Heirloom Apple Butter, 191
Heirloom Tomato Salad with
    Balsamic Vinegar and Basil,
    129
Herb Butter, 19
Herb-Grilled Farm Chicken with
    Lemon Confit and Greens,
    208, 209
Heston Supper Club (La Porte,
    Indiana), 149
Hewn Bakery (Evanston, Illinois),
    142, 145, 146–147, *146–147*
Hoecakes, Mini, with Great Lakes
    Golden Caviar, 186
Homemade Mayonnaise, 87
Homemade Sheboygan-Style
    Bratwurst, 84
Home-Style Fish Boil, 12
honey, 74–75, *75*
Honey Butter Fried Chicken, 138

Hook's Little Boy Blue cheese, 19
Horse and Plow Tavern (Kohler,
    Wisconsin), 89
horseradish
    Red Wine–Braised Brisket with
        Autumn Root Vegetables
        and Fresh Horseradish, 56
    Standing Rib Roast with
        Yorkshire Pudding and
        Horseradish Cream Sauce, 70
hovmästarsas, 59
Hoyt, Anne, 241, 242, 243
Hoyt, John, 243
hummus
    Chicken Shawarma Burritos,
        130, *132*

I

ice cream
    Wilson's Ice Cream and, 40,
        41, *41*
    Wilson's Vanilla Sundaes with
        Seaquist Orchards Cherry
        Topping, 40
Idyll Farms (Northport,
    Michigan), 255
Indiana (northwest)
    Iron Creek Farm and, 150, 151,
        152
    overview of, 116–117, 119
Indiana (northwest) recipes
    Creamy Gazpacho, 151
    Harvest Ratatouille Crostini,
        152, *153*
Iron Creek Farm (La Porte,
    Indiana), 150, 151, 152
Izard, Stephanie, 197

J

Jackie Shen's Café, 185
Jake's Country Meats
    (Cassopolis, Michigan), 177,
    259
Jalapeño, Roasted Tomato, and
    Cilantro Salsa and Grilled
    Asparagus, Grilled Waseda
    Farms Rib-Eye Steak with,
    52, 53

Jam, Blackberry-Blueberry, 198
Janie's Organic Farm (Danford, Illinois), 147
Jerusalem salad
  Chicken Shawarma Burritos, 130, *132*
Jervis, Don, 77
Johnson, Al, 68
Johnson, Rolf, Lars, and Annika, 68, *68*
Al Johnson's Swedish Restaurant (Sister Bay, Wisconsin), 68, *68*, 69
Jolly Pumpkin (Traverse City, Michigan), 229
Joly, Charles, 133

K

Kale, Green Bean Casserole with, 96
Kimura, Ryan, 136
King, Ellen, 142, 145, 146–147, *146*, *147*
Kismet Farm and Bakery (Fennville, Michigan), 224, 226, *226–227*
K. K. Fiske, 62
Klein, Peter, 196
Klug, Mick, 135
Kohler, John Michael, 94
Kohler, Walter J., 94
Kohler, Wisconsin. *See also* Sheboygan and Kohler, Wisconsin, recipes
  The American Club and, 81, 89, 91, 94, 96
  overview of, 81
Korean Pork Bao Sandwich, 180
Koyen, Ken, 62
Kulp, Josh, 138
Kurtis, Bill, 140

L

LaCasse, Nick, 130, 133, 135
Lake Michigan Circle Tour, 6, *7*, 229
lake trout, 63, *63*
LaMancha Moo cheese, 223

La Merenda (Milwaukee, Wisconsin), 111
Lapinette cider, 213
La Tarte Flambé, Anne's, 241
Lea, Corinne, 23
Lea, Dave and Renny, 23
Leaning Shed Farm (Berrien Springs, Michigan), 129, 165, 167, 168, 172
Leek Sausage (Smoked) Frittata with Summer Squash and Goat Cheese, 176
Leelanau Cheese Co. (Suttons Bay, Michigan), 241, 242, 243, *243*, 258
Leelanau Peninsula, Michigan, 229
Lehner, Willi, 33, 100
Levitt, Rob, 136
Lingonberries, Swedish Pancakes with, 67
Local Foods (Chicago, Illinois), 136, *136–137*
Lutsey, Andrew, 136
Lutsey, Matt, 53, 55, *55*, 58

M

Mackinac Island Peanut Brittle, 250, *251*
MacReady Artisan Bread Company (Egg Harbor, Wisconsin), 65
Magliaro, Gabriel, 133
Mansavage, Eric, 235, 239
Maple Leaf Farms (Milford, Indiana), 91
maple syrup
  Maple Granola with Nuts and Seeds, 73
  Rolled Oat and Maple Syrup Scones, 142, *143*
Mark, Tamera and Patrick, 150
Martin, Sarah, 40, 41
Mascarpone Cream, Cherry-Poached Pears with, 28, *29*
Mayonnaise, Homemade, 87
Mazurek, Cathy and Larry, 23
McClain, Shawn, 133, 148
McMarlin, Adam, 232
Meatballs, 69

Meatloaf, Bacon-Wrapped, 218
Melon and Mint Salad, 194, *195*
melons
  Melon and Mint Salad, 194, *195*
  Seedling Farm and, 196, *196*
La Merenda (Milwaukee, Wisconsin), 111
Michigan, *154–155*. *See also* Douglas; Fennville; Harbor Country; Saugatuck; Southwest Michigan
Michigan, Lake
  Circle Tour and, 6, 7, 229
  fishing in, 61–63
  overview of, 189
Michigan Brut cider, 213
Michigan Peach Crisp, 200, *201*
Mick Klug Farm (St. Joseph, Michigan), 135
Midwestern Bread Experiment, 147
The Mill (Sturgeon Bay), 16
milling of wheat, 146–147
Milwaukee, Wisconsin
  Braise and, 84, 114, 115
  Clock Shadow Creamery and, 106, 109, 110, *110*
  overview of, 105
  Restaurant-Supported Agriculture and, 114
Milwaukee, Wisconsin, recipes
  Asparagus Sauté with Green Garlic and Herbs, 113, *113*
  Beer-Battered Cheese Curds with Homemade Ranch Dip, 106, *107*
  Boone Brandy Old-Fashioned, 112
  Green Garlic Custard, 115
  Quark Soufflés, 111
  Wisconsin Quark Cheesecake, 109
Mini Hoecakes with Great Lakes Golden Caviar, 186
mint
  Blueberry-Mint Soda, 199
  Mint and Melon Salad, 194, *195*
Mirai corn, 127
Miso Sweet Corn Sunrise with Poached Eggs, Abigail's, 120, *121*
The Mitten cider, 213

Moersch, Matt and Christian, 178–179
Moersch, Richard, 178–179, 182
Montmorency cherries, 247, *247*
Morgan, Jack, 6
Morning Glory Muffins, 145
mozzarella cheese
   Melon and Mint Salad, 194, *195*
muffins
   Cherry Streusel Muffins, *36*, 37
   Morning Glory Muffins, 145
Mullins, Pat, 171, 172
Murdick's Fudge (Mackinac Island, Michigan), 250
Mushroom and Wild Rice Stuffing and Zinfandel Reduction, Dead Man's Salmon Roulades with, 235, *237*

N

Nedderson, Natalie and Nedd, *36*, 37
New Buffalo Bill's (New Buffalo, Michigan), 161, 162, *162–163*
New Buffalo Bill's Wood-Smoked BBQ Ribs, *158*, 159
Nordic Creamery (Westby, Wisconsin), 19
Northern Wisconsin Chicken and Rib Booyah, 26
North Pond Restaurant (Chicago, Illinois), 129

O

oats
   Cherry-Chocolate Oatmeal Cookies, *76*, 77
   Maple Granola with Nuts and Seeds, 73
   Rolled Oat and Maple Syrup Scones, 142, *143*
Old Mission Peninsula, Michigan, 229
Old Mission Waldorf Salad, 252
Olson, Krista, 77
onion(s)
   Beer-Braised Bratwurst and Onions, 82, *83*

Brined Pork Chops with Caramelized Onions and Apples, 177
Green Bean Casserole with Kale, 96
Rustic Apple Galette with Goat Cheese, Caramelized Onions, and Thyme, 220, 221
Original Seedy Salt loaf, 226
Oryana Natural Foods Market, 233

P

pancakes
   Grandma's German Apple Pancake, 190
   Swedish Pancakes with Lingonberries, 67
Parmesan cheese
   Parmesan-Garlic Bread, 65
   Wurst Soup with Homemade Herb-Parmesan Croutons, 88
parsnip(s)
   Beef Pot Roast with Seasonal Root Vegetables and Parsley Gremolata, 92
   Red Wine–Braised Brisket with Autumn Root Vegetables and Fresh Horseradish, 56
Pasta Bolognese, Fresh, 214, *215*
Pasties Two Ways, 253
Patellie's Pizza (Three Oaks, Michigan), 171, 172
Patterson, Eric, 230, 232
Paulsen, Michael, 120, 122, *122*
peach(es)
   Michigan Peach Crisp, 200, *201*
   Summer Fruit Biscuit Bake, 224
peanut(s)
   Mackinac Island Peanut Brittle, 250, *251*
   Peanut Butter Bites, 99
pear(s)
   Cherry-Poached Pears with Mascarpone Cream, 28, *29*
   Morning Glory Muffins, 145
Pecans, Roast Acorn Squash with Toasted, 128
pepper(s)
   Creamy Gazpacho, 151

Harvest Ratatouille Crostini, 152, *153*
Poached Eggs with Leaning Shed Summer Salsa, 168
perch
   overview of, 63, *63*
   Panfried Perch with Tartar Sauce, 16
Percheron cider, 213
Pesto (Basil) and Arugula Salad, Whitefish with, 30
pies (meat)
   Pasties Two Ways, 253
pies (sweet)
   Door County Cherry Pie, *20*, 21
   Strawberry-Rhubarb Hand Pies, *202*, 203
Pietsch, Matthew, 209, 211, 214, 216
Pineapple and Sweet Potato Salad, 161
Pistachio, Cherry, and Cheddar Cheese Ball, 100, *101*
Pleasant Bakery (Traverse City, Michigan), 246
Poached Eggs with Leaning Shed Summer Salsa, 168
Poet's Tomme cheese, 223
pork
   Braised Pork Shoulder, 211
   Brined Pork Chops with Caramelized Onions and Apples, 177
   Homemade Sheboygan-Style Bratwurst, 84
   Korean Pork Bao Sandwich, 180
   New Buffalo Bill's Wood-Smoked BBQ Ribs, *158*, 159
   Pork Rillettes with Pickled Cherries, 171
   Pulled Pork Sandwiches with Cherry Barbecue Sauce, 249
   Spiced Breakfast Sausage Patties, 185
potato(es)
   Beach House Cheesy Potatoes, 170
   Belgian-Style Hand-Cut Fries, 47, *48*
   Grilled Carlson's Whitefish and Vegetables, 256, *257*

potato(es), *continued*
 Red Wine–Braised Brisket with
 Autumn Root Vegetables
 and Fresh Horseradish, 56
 Tangy Potato Salad, 86
Pot Roast (Beef) with Seasonal
 Root Vegetables and Parsley
 Gremolata, 92
Prairie Grass Cafe (Northbrook,
 Illinois), 140, *140*, 141
Pretzels (Soft) with Cheddar and
 Gouda Beer Sauce, 102
Principle (Kalamazoo, Michigan),
 216
pub cheese
 Griddle-Style Double
 Cheeseburgers, 149
 Pulled Pork Sandwiches with
 Cherry Barbecue Sauce, 249
Pyramid Point cheese, 223

Q
Quail Eggs with Raita Sauce,
 Roasted Golden Beet Salad
 and, 233
quark cheese
 Quark Soufflés, 111
 Wisconsin Quark Cheesecake,
 109

R
raclette cheese
 Anne's Croute au Fromage, 242
 Anne's La Tarte Flambé, 241
 Leelanau Cheese Co. and, 243
Radishes, Crispy-Skinned Lake
 Trout with Creamed Local
 Spinach and, 230, *231*
rainbow smelt, 63, *63*
Raita Sauce and Quail Eggs,
 Roasted Golden Beet Salad
 with, 233
Ranch Dip, Homemade, Beer-
 Battered Cheese Curds with,
 106, *107*
Rand, Dave, 136
raspberry(ies)
 Summer Fruit Biscuit Bake, 224

Ratatouille Crostini, Harvest,
 152, *153*
Redamak's (New Buffalo,
 Michigan), 149
Red Curry Chicken Skewers with
 Apricot Chutney, 184
Red Streak cider, 213
Red Wine–Braised Brisket with
 Autumn Root Vegetables
 and Fresh Horseradish, 56
Renards (Sturgeon Bay,
 Wisconsin), 106
Restaurant-Supported
 Agriculture (RSA), 114
Revord, John, 112
Reynolds, Bill, 161, 162, *162*, *163*
Rhubarb-Strawberry Hand Pies,
 202, 203
Rib and Chicken Booyah,
 Northern Wisconsin, 26
Rib Roast, Standing, with
 Yorkshire Pudding and
 Horseradish Cream Sauce, 70
Ribs, New Buffalo Bill's Wood-
 Smoked BBQ, *158*, 159
Rib Steak (Grilled Waseda Farms)
 with Roasted Tomato,
 Jalapeño, and Cilantro Salsa
 and Grilled Asparagus, *52*,
 53
Rice (Wild) and Mushroom
 Stuffing and Zinfandel
 Reduction, Dead Man's
 Salmon Roulades with, 235,
 237
ricotta salata cheese
 Green Zebra Green Salad, 148
Riverside Inn (Leland, Michigan),
 255, 256, 258, *258*
Roast Acorn Squash with Toasted
 Pecans, 128
Roasted Shallot, Honey, and
 Black Pepper Butter, 19
Roelli, Chris, 50
Rolled Oat and Maple Syrup
 Scones, 142, *143*
Rolls, Buttery Dinner, 18
Roth Wisconsin, 98
Round Barn Winery (Baroda,
 Michigan), 178–179, *178–179*

RSA. *See* Restaurant-Supported
 Agriculture
Ruleau Bros. CSF (Stephenson,
 Michigan), 238, 239
Rustic Apple Galette with Goat
 Cheese, Caramelized Onions,
 and Thyme, *220*, 221
Rustic Whitefish Tartlets with
 Tarragon Beer Mustard
 Cream, 239
Rye Bread, Bavarian Dark, 14

S
salads
 Creamy Cherry Chicken Salad,
 246
 Creamy Coleslaw, 15
 Green Zebra Green Salad, 148
 Grilled Chicken Salad
 with Greens and Cherry
 Vinaigrette, 248
 Grilled Summer Corn and
 Veggie Salad with Goat
 Cheese and Tomato-Dill
 Vinaigrette, *124*, 125
 Heirloom Tomato Salad with
 Balsamic Vinegar and Basil,
 129
 Melon and Mint Salad, 194, *195*
 Old Mission Waldorf Salad, 252
 Roasted Golden Beet Salad
 with Raita Sauce and Quail
 Eggs, 233
 Strawberry Salad, 255
 Sweet Potato and Pineapple
 Salad, 161
 Tangy Potato Salad, 86
 Wedge Salad with Blue Cheese
 Dressing, Bacon, and Cherry
 Tomatoes, 34
salami
 Turnip, Squash, and Scallion
 Vegetable Platter with
 Soppressata and Mint, 141
salmon
 Dead Man's Salmon Roulades
 with Wild Rice and Mushroom
 Stuffing and Zinfandel
 Reduction, 235, *237*

Homemade Dill-Cured Salmon with Lemon Crème Fraîche and Accoutrements, 59
overview of, 62, *62*

salsa
Grilled Waseda Farms Rib-Eye Steak with Roasted Tomato, Jalapeño, and Cilantro Salsa and Grilled Asparagus, *52*, 53
Poached Eggs with Leaning Shed Summer Salsa, 168

Salt of the Earth (Fennville, Michigan), 209, 211, 214, 216, *216*, 218
Sandroni, Peter, 111

sandwiches
HBFC Original Fried Chicken Sandwich, 138
Korean Pork Bao Sandwich, 180
Panfried Perch with Tartar Sauce, 16
Pulled Pork Sandwiches with Cherry Barbecue Sauce, 249

sauces
Amber Ale Gravy, 254
Cherry Barbecue Sauce, 249
Homemade Mayonnaise, 87
Simple Barbecue Sauce, 160

Saugatuck, Michigan, overview of, *154*, 207
Saugatuck, Michigan, recipes
Cranberry-Nut Bread, 217
Saugatuck Farmers' Market, 211

sausage
Beer-Braised Bratwurst and Onions, 82, *83*
Homemade Sheboygan-Style Bratwurst, 84
Smoked Leek Sausage Frittata with Summer Squash and Goat Cheese, 176
Spiced Breakfast Sausage Patties, 185
Spicy Fennel Sausage and Peppers with Garlicky Heirloom Tomato Sauce, 172, *173*
Wurst Soup with Homemade Herb-Parmesan Croutons, 88

Savory Spoon Cooking School, 31

Schartner's (Door County, Wisconsin), 16
Schmakel, Stephen, 212–213
Schoolhouse Artisan Cheese (Egg Harbor and Ellison Bay, Wisconsin), 19, 31, 34, 50, 72
Schrock, Mark, 216
Schwartz Fish Company (Sturgeon Bay, Wisconsin), 66
Schwarz, Jacob, 258

scones
Rolled Oat and Maple Syrup Scones, 142, *143*
Wisconsin Cheddar Cheese Scones, 32

sea lamprey, 63, *63*
Seaquist Orchards (Sister Bay, Wisconsin), *36*, 37, 38
Seedling Farm (South Haven, Michigan), 193, 196, *196*, 197
Shawarma Chicken Burritos, 130, *132*
Sheboygan and Kohler, Wisconsin, overview of, 81
Sheboygan and Kohler, Wisconsin, recipes
Beef Pot Roast with Seasonal Root Vegetables and Parsley Gremolata, 92
Beer-Braised Bratwurst and Onions, 82, *83*
Beer Cheese Soup, 89
Cheddar, Cherry, and Pistachio Cheese Ball, 100, *101*
Duck Breast with Cranberry-Port Sauce, 90, *91*
Green Bean Casserole with Kale, 96
Homemade Mayonnaise, 87
Homemade Sheboygan-Style Bratwurst, 84
Peanut Butter Bites, 99
Soft Pretzels with Cheddar and Gouda Beer Sauce, 102
Tangy Potato Salad, 86
Wisconsin Ham and Swiss Brunch Strata, 98
Wurst Soup with Homemade Herb-Parmesan Croutons, 88
Sherman, Bruce, 129

Shortcakes, Strawberry, 205
Silhavy, John Sr., 245
Simple Barbecue Sauce, 160
Sister Bay Bowl, 16
Sky Brook Cheese, 50
Slagel Family Farms, 177

slaw, crunchy
HBFC Original Fried Chicken Sandwich, 138

smelt, 63, *63*
Smitala, Paul, 96
Smoked Leek Sausage Frittata with Summer Squash and Goat Cheese, 176
Smoked Trout Spread, 66
Smoked Whitefish Pâté with Tart Cherry Jam, 182
Soda, Blueberry-Mint, 199
Soft Pretzels with Cheddar and Gouda Beer Sauce, 102
Soppressata and Mint, Turnip, Squash, and Scallion Vegetable Platter with, 141
Sote Seedy bread, 216
Soufflés, Quark, 111

soups
Beer Cheese Soup, 89
Creamy Gazpacho, 151
Whitefish Chowder, 64
Wurst Soup with Homemade Herb-Parmesan Croutons, 88

sour cream
Meatballs, 69
Sour Cream Blueberry Coffee Cake, 193

southwest Michigan
Ellis Family Farms and, 190, 200
overview of, *154*, 189
Seedling Farm and, 193, 196, *196*, 197

southwest Michigan recipes
Apple-Cinnamon Fritters, 192
Blackberry-Blueberry Jam, 198
Blueberry-Mint Soda, 199
Blueberry Sour Cream Coffee Cake, 193
Grandma's German Apple Pancake, 190
Heirloom Apple Butter, 191
Melon and Mint Salad, 194, *195*

southwest Michigan recipes, *continued*
    Michigan Peach Crisp, 200, *201*
    Strawberry-Rhubarb Hand Pies, *202, 203*
    Strawberry Shortcakes, 205
    Warm Winter Wassail, 197
Spiced Breakfast Sausage Patties, 185
Spicy Fennel Sausage and Peppers with Garlicky Heirloom Tomato Sauce, 172, *173*
Spinach (Creamed Local) and Radishes, Crispy-Skinned Lake Trout with, 230, *231*
Spread, Smoked Trout, 66
squash
    Roast Acorn Squash with Toasted Pecans, 128
    Smoked Leek Sausage Frittata with Summer Squash and Goat Cheese, 176
    Turnip, Squash, and Scallion Vegetable Platter with Soppressata and Mint, 141
Standing Rib Roast with Yorkshire Pudding and Horseradish Cream Sauce, 70
Steak, Grilled Waseda Farms Rib with Roasted Tomato, Jalapeño, and Cilantro Salsa and Grilled Asparagus, *52, 53*
Stegner, Sarah, 140, 141
stews
    Northern Wisconsin Chicken and Rib Booyah, 26
Strata, Wisconsin Ham and Swiss Brunch, 98
strawberry(ies)
    Strawberry-Rhubarb Hand Pies, *202, 203*
    Strawberry Salad, 255
    Strawberry Shortcakes, 205
    Summer Fruit Biscuit Bake, 224
Streusel Muffins, Cherry, *36, 37*
Suchy, Helen, 24
Summer Fruit Biscuit Bake, 224
Summer Squash and Goat Cheese, Smoked Leek Sausage Frittata with, 176

Sundaes (Wilson's Vanilla) with Seaquist Orchards Cherry Topping, 40
Swanson, Dave, 84, 114, 115
Swedish Pancakes with Lingonberries, 67
SweeTango apples, 38
Sweet Corn Cornbread with Honey Butter, 127
Sweeter Song Farm (Cedar, Michigan), 255
Sweetie Pies (Fish Creek, Wisconsin), 20, 21, 23, *23*
Sweet Mountain Farm (Washington Island, Wisconsin), 74–75, *74–75*
sweet potato(es)
    Pasties Two Ways, 253
    Sweet Potato and Pineapple Salad, 161
Swiss cheese
    Swiss Cheese Fondue, 72
    Wisconsin Ham and Swiss Brunch Strata, 98
syrup, storage of, 39

T

tabbouleh
    Chicken Shawarma Burritos, 130, *132*
Tacos (Whitefish) with Pickled Red Onions, Red-Hot Aioli, and Guacamole, 44, *45*
Tandem Ciders, 229
Tangy Potato Salad, 86
Taproot, 229
Tartar Sauce, Panfried Perch with, 16
Tarte Flambé, Anne's, 241
tea, 42
Tempura Asparagus, *134*, 135
Terczak, Mari, 224, 226
Thomas, Janice, 28, 30, 31, *31*
Thomas, Michael, 31
Thompson, Claire, 214, *215*
Thornburg, Ryan, 178–179, 180, 182, 184
Thorton, Cole, 241
Three Sisters Garden (Kankakee, Illinois), 128

tomato(es)
    Creamy Gazpacho, 151
    Enchiladas de Berrien Springs, *164*, 165
    Fresh Pasta Bolognese, 214, *215*
    Grilled Summer Corn and Veggie Salad with Goat Cheese and Tomato-Dill Vinaigrette, *124*, 125
    Grilled Waseda Farms Rib-Eye Steak with Roasted Tomato, Jalapeño, and Cilantro Salsa and Grilled Asparagus, *52, 53*
    Harvest Ratatouille Crostini, 152, *153*
    Heirloom Tomato Salad with Balsamic Vinegar and Basil, 129
    Leftover Brisket Chili, 58
    Poached Eggs with Leaning Shed Summer Salsa, 168
    Spicy Fennel Sausage and Peppers with Garlicky Heirloom Tomato Sauce, 172, *173*
    tips for preserving, 126
    Wedge Salad with Blue Cheese Dressing, Bacon, and Cherry Tomatoes, 34
Town Hall Bakery (Jacksonport, Wisconsin), 77
Trattoria Stefano (Sheboygan, Wisconsin), 81
Trattoria Stella (Traverse City, Michigan), 229
Traverse City and peninsulas, Michigan
    Carlson's Fisheries and, 230, 256, 258, 259, 260, *260–261*
    The Cooks' House and, 230, 232, *232*
    Leelanau Cheese Co. and, 241, 242, 243, *243*, 258
    Montmorency cherries and, 247
    overview of, *155*, 229
    Ruleau Bros. CSF and, 238, 239
Traverse City and peninsulas, Michigan, recipes
    Anne's Croute au Fromage, 242
    Anne's La Tarte Flambé, 241

Creamy Cherry Chicken Salad, 246

Crispy-Skinned Lake Trout with Creamed Local Spinach and Radishes, 230, *231*

Dead Man's Salmon Roulades with Wild Rice and Mushroom Stuffing and Zinfandel Reduction, 235, *237*

Grilled Carlson's Whitefish and Vegetables, 256, *257*

Grilled Chicken Salad with Greens and Cherry Vinaigrette, 248

Mackinac Island Peanut Brittle, 250, *251*

Old Mission Waldorf Salad, 252

Pasties Two Ways, 253

Pulled Pork Sandwiches with Cherry Barbecue Sauce, 249

Roasted Golden Beet Salad with Raita Sauce and Quail Eggs, 233

Rustic Whitefish Tartlets with Tarragon Beer Mustard Cream, 239

Strawberry Salad, 255

Traverse City Whiskey Smash, *244*, 245

Walleye Fish Cakes with Lemon Aioli, 259

Traverse City Whiskey Company, 245

Traverse City Whiskey Smash, *244*, 245

Trotter, Charlie, 133

trout
Crispy-Skinned Lake Trout with Creamed Local Spinach and Radishes, 230, *231*
Home-Style Fish Boil, 12
overview of, 63, *63*
Smoked Trout Spread, 66

turnip(s)
Beef Pot Roast with Seasonal Root Vegetables and Parsley Gremolata, 92
Turnip, Squash, and Scallion Vegetable Platter with Soppressata and Mint, 141

V

veal
Homemade Sheboygan-Style Bratwurst, 84

Vilter, Barbara, 258

Vilter, Kate, 255, 256, 258

Virtue Cider (Fennville, Michigan), 212–213, *212–213*

vodka
Death's Door Caipiroska, 78

W

Wagner, Carla, 216

Waldorf Salad, Old Mission, 252

walleye, 63, *63*

Walleye Fish Cakes with Lemon Aioli, 259

walnut(s)
Cranberry-Nut Bread, 217
Old Mission Waldorf Salad, 252

Warm Winter Wassail, 197

Waseda Farms (Baileys Harbor, Wisconsin), 49, 50, 53, 55, *55*, 56, 58

Washburne Culinary Institute (Chicago, Illinois), 161, 162

Wassail, Warm Winter, 197

Werp Farms (Buckley, Michigan), 148

wheat
Capital Brewery's Island Wheat Ale, 78
milling of, 146–147

Whiskey Smash, Traverse City, *244*, 245

whitefish
Carlson's Fisheries and, 260
Grilled Carlson's Whitefish and Vegetables, 256, *257*
Lake Michigan and, 61
Ruleau Bros. CSF and, 238
Rustic Whitefish Tartlets with Tarragon Beer Mustard Cream, 239
Smoked Whitefish Pâté with Tart Cherry Jam, 182
Whitefish Chowder, 64

Whitefish Tacos with Pickled Red Onions, Red-Hot Aioli, and Guacamole, 44, *45*

Whitefish with Basil Pesto and Arugula Salad, 30

White Gull Inn (Fish Creek, Wisconsin), 39

Wickman House (Ellison Bay, Wisconsin), 47, *48*, 49, *49*, 50

Wild Rice and Mushroom Stuffing and Zinfandel Reduction, Dead Man's Salmon Roulades with, 235, *237*

Wilken, Harold, 147

Wills, Bob, 110, *110*

Wilson's Ice Cream (Ephraim, Wisconsin), 40, 41, *41*

Wilson's Vanilla Sundaes with Seaquist Orchards Cherry Topping, 40

wineries, 178–179, *178–179*

Wisconsin. *See also* Door County; Milwaukee; Sheboygan and Kohler
cheese and, 35
fishing and, 61–63

Wisconsin Cheddar Cheese Scones, 32

Wisconsin Ham and Swiss Brunch Strata, 98

Wood-Smoked BBQ Ribs, New Buffalo Bill's, *158*, 159

Wurst Soup with Homemade Herb-Parmesan Croutons, 88

Y

yellow perch, 63, *63*

Yorkshire Pudding and Horseradish Cream Sauce, Standing Rib Roast with, 70

Z

zucchini
Turnip, Squash, and Scallion Vegetable Platter with Soppressata and Mint, 141

FILL UP ON FRESH FLAVORS WITH MORE BOOKS FROM STOREY

by Olwen Woodier

Apple pie is just the beginning. Discover the versatility of this iconic fruit with 125 delicious recipes for any meal, including apple frittata, pork chops with apple cream sauce, apple pizza, apple butter, and more.

by Rachael Narins

Make your skillet sizzle! These 40 recipes show off the versatility of this affordable and timeless cooking method, from cast-iron classics like cornbread, pan pizza, and the perfect grilled cheese sandwich to future favorites like Korean fried chicken, skillet catfish, and s'mores.

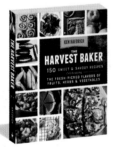

by Ken Haedrich

Put a fresh spin on baking with these 150 delicious recipes using fruits, veggies, and herbs in unexpected ways. With savory quiches, pot pies, pizzas, muffins, and hearty yeast breads plus sweet cakes, pies, and cookies, there's something for every taste.

by Erin James & CIDERCRAFT Magazine

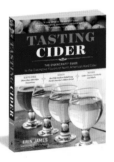

Drink in the deliciously diverse flavors of today's hard cider. Tasting guidelines highlight 100 selections — including single varietal, dessert, hopped, and barrel-aged — while 30 food recipes offer pairing suggestions and 30 cocktail recipes show off creative cider-based combinations.

Join the conversation. Share your experience with this book, learn more about Storey Publishing's authors, and read original essays and book excerpts at storey.com. Look for our books wherever quality books are sold or call 800-441-5700.